Has My French Love Affair Been Crushed?

By

Nigel Wilson

DEDICATION

I'd like to dedicate this book to my parents, Haydn and Betty, who initially took Simon, Hugh, and me to France on several highly enjoyable and memorable holidays.

There is a saying that travel expands the mind and enriches the spirit, so thanks, Mum and Dad. My life has certainly been deeply enriched.

Included in my dedications are my brothers Simon and Hugh and their respective families.

I also dedicate this book to my two daughters Lucy and Gemma and to my two stepdaughters Vicky and Jo. My four fantastic daughters and their families.

I dedicate this too to their children (our grandchildren) both existing and future.

Thanks to all our friends who are mentioned in this book, without whom our experiences wouldn't have been half as much fun.

And mention must be made too of our dog Freddie, who absolutely adores being with us at our house in France, and would we feel, prefer to live there than in the UK.

Finally, my dedication to my wonderful wife Patricia, for her inspiration, encouragement, support, and love.

And last but not least, none of these stories and experiences would have happened had it not been for the beautiful country that is France and its engaging people and their customs.

Je vous remercie.

Some names, locations and identifying details have been changed to protect the privacy of individuals mentioned in the book

FOREWORD

Over the past fifty-five years, I've had a love affair with France. Well, most of the time I'm in love, occasionally I fall out of love. There are reasons...

When I first went to there in 1966, it felt very different to England where I grew up. That was a huge attraction. Most of all, I wanted to be able to communicate with French people. When I was able to start learning the French language at school, I jumped in with both feet. It became my favourite subject. I continued to study the subject at A level, and also in further education, when I chose it to be one of my options for my HND in Business Studies.

The more I spoke the language the easier and more fun it became. I was very happy to be corrected; I just soaked it all up.

And that to me is the essence of visiting a country on a regular basis (notwithstanding actually living there). You really have to learn and speak the local language. Otherwise, it's difficult to fully immerse yourself in life there.

In 2004, my wife Patricia and I decided to buy a house in France. Buying a house there was a dream come true. In the past sixteen years since, we've had a wonderful time, and fully appreciated the freedom to be able to take off and go there at the drop of a hat. Sadly, Brexit has made this unnecessarily difficult.

There have been times I've fallen out of love with France. Certain attitudes and behaviours have gone beyond being simply frustrating, and on many occasions, my patience – which is generally reasonable – has been stretched.

But this loss of affection has only been temporary. As in all long and deep love affairs, the reasons why you fell in love spring back to the surface, and the situation reverts back to normal.

I think that most of all; I love the country for what it is. I adore the landscape and scenery; it truly is one of the most beautiful countries I've ever visited, with a wonderful contrast of mountains, valleys, hills, rivers, lakes, and coastlines, as well as some magnificent towns and cities.

I'm a big fan of French food and wine. My dad always said their wine is the smoothest in the world. Unfortunately, there is a perceived national conceit that their cuisine has been and continues to be the best in the world. That's certainly not true. I've eaten superbly in many other countries, and I've suffered many poor-quality meals at restaurants in France. There are also times when I tire of eating three, four, or even five-course meals; sometimes I just long for a plateful of simple, good food. But I don't want to be disingenuous. I love the way the indigenous population view food and drink, fully encompassing the joys and conviviality as they sit down to eat together. As we discovered in the village of Châteauneuf-du-Pape, food doesn't need to be grand to accompany fine wine. Simple food can also be savoured.

Over the years, I've realised how differently the French see life, certainly in comparison to the British. Life in their country is generally less frenetic, particularly away from urban areas. People are willing to come together more and will always greet each other with courtesy and sufficient time to exchange a few pleasantries – or more! Technology and digital life are generally less ubiquitous than in the UK; this can be frustrating sometimes, but conversely acts as a positive reminder that there is more to life than constantly being in touch electronically on devices.

I love the changes in the seasons, which are much more marked than in the UK. Summers are inevitably hot, and winters are genuinely cold. In between, there is real beauty in late spring and early autumn especially.

In conclusion, I wouldn't keep returning several times each year if I didn't have a deep love for the country and its people. And I guess this is a good life lesson: it's tolerance – being able to work through and get over the negatives so that you can really bask in and enjoy the positives.

Whatever happens, even Brexit, I hope my love affair with France and the French will continue for many, many more years.

THE 1960s

Our First Visit to France

1966

The summer of 1966 was memorable for various reasons. First, England won the World Cup on 30 July. I was ten years old, a complete football nut, and I remember seeing several games on our small black-and-white TV.

The other key event during that summer was my first trip abroad – to France.

In early August, after our meal one evening, my father announced that we'd be going on holiday to France. This came totally out of the blue and was a wonderful surprise. My father had been to France shortly after the Second World War, in the late 1940s, with a friend of his. They went to Nice, and my dad had spoken fondly of this experience.

The plan was that we would camp. We hadn't got a tent, but some friends of my parents, Pat and Gordon, had a frame tent, which slept four people, but at a push would accommodate a family of five with three small children.

On the Friday before we left, we all went to their house in Luton. They lived on the same road we had some years beforehand. I knew them as Auntie Pat and Uncle Gordon (although they weren't related to us; at that time, adults who were family friends were always called Auntie and Uncle), and they had two sons, Tony and Johnny, who were similar ages to my middle brother Simon and me.

I don't remember much about the evening, other than Dad and Uncle Gordon put the tent up and took it down several times. I found out later that Gordon was quite particular and wanted to make sure my parents knew how to correctly erect and take down the tent.

A few days later, my mother started to coordinate the packing of our clothes, and all the stuff we'd need for camping: bedding, cooking and kitchen items, games, books, etc. My parents packed up the car on the Monday evening – my dad was a great one for leaving things to the last minute, although in fairness he ran his own business, and worked long hours.

We left very early on the Tuesday morning – around 5 a.m. I seem to remember – and drove from our house in Aspley Guise, Bedfordshire to Dover. This entailed driving down the M1 to London, going through London, and taking the M2 to Dover. The crossing was around 9.30 a.m. with Townsend Ferries. I remember the time as once we were aboard, we all went to the restaurant and ordered breakfast – a full English each. However, once the ship had left the harbour, the moving waves caused my mum, brothers, and I to feel seasick. We went up to the deck for fresh air, while my dad stayed in the restaurant, and devoured his way through his and some of our combined breakfasts. He used to say it was the most expensive breakfast he'd ever had!

We arrived at Calais and started the French leg of the journey. Dad was quite keen to visit Bordeaux and the surrounding area. He'd heard the Arcachon basin had its own micro-climate, which was especially warm and sunny. In those days, there were few French autoroutes, and they were very expensive to travel on, unlike the motorways in the UK which were toll free.

We started our drive, in our Ford Corsair (the colour was sea foam blue, which was effectively a very pale green), initially towards Abbeville and Rouen. France felt very different from England, less traffic, long straight roads, and almost no other British cars.

We pulled off the roadside into a track – it wasn't a proper lay-by but enabled us to stop for a picnic. Mum had prepared the food at home, and we sat on the familiar picnic rugs which were brought out each summer. During our meal, we found a large snail sitting in the grass. Dad said they were common in France and explained the French actually ate them. We were disgusted. We decided to keep this snail, which Dad called Alphonse.

We finished our picnic, Mum and Dad packed the things into the car, and Dad shut the boot, which was a slam-shut boot lid without a button to open. He got into the car and asked Mum for the keys. She said she didn't have them.

'You must have,' said Dad. 'I gave them to you so you could open the boot.'

'Well, I haven't got them,' replied Mum.

'Then they must be in the boot,' exclaimed Dad.

'You must have left them there.' Mum looked through her handbag, then got us all out of the car so they could check the seats.

By this time, it was getting tense. Mum was becoming flustered, and Dad was getting more and more annoyed.

'What on earth are we going to do?' he said. 'That's it. You must have shut the keys in the boot when you packed the picnic things. For God's sake, we're only a few hours from England, and this happens. I need a cigarette.'

He put his hand in his pocket to pull out his lighter and guess what he found… the car keys! Panic over. Dad smoked his cigarette, Mum visibly relaxed, and we restarted the journey.

We stopped off in Rouen late afternoon for a break and had a short wander around. We then carried on and stopped off at Dreux for the night. We found a traditional hotel, and after taking the luggage up to our rooms, we went downstairs to the restaurant. This was getting exciting. We'd never eaten French food, and the menu was incomprehensible to us, as it was all written in French.

Dad managed to translate most of it, and then ordered our food from the waitress, using his schoolboy French, which actually worked pretty well. The waitress understood him, and there were smiles and laughter, which was Dad's way of getting through to people. The food arrived. I can't remember what I ate, but it was good. There appeared to be some sort of celebration going on in the restaurant, with lots of noise and singing, hands being clapped in time to booming music. Although we didn't know the words, we joined in the clapping. The atmosphere was electric – very different from the more formal restaurants we'd eaten at in the UK. It was warm and friendly.

AT BREAKFAST THE next morning, I spoke in French for the first time, when Dad asked me to go to the bar and say, 'Encore de café pour Maman et Papa s'il vous plaît.'

The waitress beamed, and I remember how good it felt talking in another language.

Our journey continued through Tours, Poitiers, and eventually to Angoulême where we stopped for the night. The weather was hot and sunny, which meant we had the car windows open pretty much all the time. The car was full, and in the back seat we had our pillows, books, and games. But at least the car keys didn't go missing again!

We were fascinated by the French toilets. Virtually every public toilet we encountered housed the hole in the ground, which was totally new to us. As Dad used to sing, 'Is the water potable? Are the toilets squattable?'

We found a motel outside Angoulême, which I found fascinating. Instead of going upstairs, we parked the car outside our room, or rather rooms – one for Mum and Dad, and one next door for us boys. That night we ate outside, underneath a huge pergola which was covered in foliage. Mum said it reminded her of India, where she lived for the first fourteen years of her life. Her grandparents were out there at the time of the British Raj. Mum's parents met each other in India, and her father was a doctor in the Indian army. Anyway, Mum said that in India, snakes would hide in the trees and bushes, and that she almost expected a snake to come down from above us, which I found quite alarming, even though she assured me there weren't snakes in France.

After breakfast the next morning, we continued our journey via the outskirts of Bordeaux before heading to Arcachon. We found the campsite which Dad had previously earmarked from his camping guide (written by Alan Rogers, who at the time was the 'guru' of camping in France). My brothers and I stayed in the car while Mum and Dad went into the reception to enquire about a camping pitch. I remember that the campsite was incredibly busy and noisy, and I guessed (correctly) that Dad wouldn't like it.

Our parents returned to the car after about twenty minutes and said we'd give it a try for one night. We drove to the emplacement and unpacked the tent and all our necessities for the night. Dad seemed to know what he was doing and was giving us all orders – 'grab that corner,' 'pick up that cord,' 'hold those poles.' Eventually, after about an hour, the tent was up, and we moved our stuff inside.

The campsite was a short walk to the beach. Simon, Hugh, and I clamoured to go there, and after a while, Mum and Dad relented. It was exciting to see the sea, but it wasn't a great beach. The sea was far away, so we couldn't go in on our own, despite the fact that all three of us could swim. It was also very crowded. I knew Dad wouldn't like this place, and sure enough, that evening he announced that we'd move on the next day, to a place further up the coast near Royan. Uncle Gordon and Auntie Pat had been to a campsite at Saint

Palais Sur Mer, and Mum and Dad thought it was worth giving it a go.

We packed up the following morning, drove around Bordeaux again, to the site at St Palais. However, neither Mum nor Dad was particularly impressed. My father was quite a particular man and would take his time to make his decisions carefully. This was very much his style, for example, when deciding on a restaurant. If in the UK, we went out for a meal, he would invariably walk around an entire town, checking out all the eating establishments, before deciding which one he felt would be best. On that basis, I felt we'd be in for a long day.

We then drove to Saint-George-de-Didonne which was the other side of Royan, but again the campsite was deemed unsuitable. By this time, it was early evening, and we still hadn't found anywhere. Eventually, Dad suggested we park up in Royan, find a good restaurant, and then spend the night sleeping in the car. This sounded a great adventure.

We found a great, modern, fish restaurant in Royan, where, recommended by my mother, I ate lemon sole for the first time. Absolutely delicious. Our waiter was actually an English guy. He was in his early 20s and had to come to France to improve his French and learn his trade in French restaurants. I remember my parents being quite impressed with him. Given that Dad was a restaurateur who had owned a hotel and a couple of small restaurants in Woburn, I could see why he admired this young waiter, who seemed bright and ambitious.

After we'd eaten, we went back to the car. Dad parked in a public car park, and eventually we all fell asleep. It was uncomfortable, but we were all tired and full of good food. At around 7 a.m. the next morning, the car moved. Dad had woken up early and decided to get on with the day. He switched on the engine and drove towards the seafront. I remember my mum waking up in a shock, wondering what on earth was going on. Dad was full of the joys of spring (or summer), and quickly found a café, where we piled out of the car for coffee and croissants.

Rather than drive around Bordeaux again, Dad suggested we took the ferry across the Gironde, and drive on to the peninsula, which sticks out from Bordeaux. There are a couple of lakes there, and the thinking was there might be some decent campsites. After leaving the ferry, we came into the first small town, Soulac-sûr-Mer, and saw a campsite signposted – Camping Palace. Mum and Dad thought this was worth a punt, and we drove in around 10.30 a.m. They went into the reception, and ten minutes later came out with big smiles on their faces. It seemed we'd struck gold.

They were impressed with the people at the reception, who included the owners, who spoke some English. One of the owners had been stationed during the war at a village called Batford in Hertfordshire, which is where a relative of Mum's lived and she knew the town well, and they quickly swapped stories. It was a life lesson that's always since stuck with me: find common ground with the person you're talking to, and everything then seems so much easier.

We were taken to a pitch where we put up the tent and got on with the day.

The campsite was a ten-minute drive from the beach, which was sandy and fairly quiet. Perfection to Dad who wanted to curl up on the sand with a book, without noise or intrusion. The sea wasn't too far away, which meant Mum could see us, so we were allowed to paddle or swim near to the shore. The weather was generally good, and we had a lot of fun.

The campsite also had a decent children's play area, with swings, slide, and various climbing frames. The first time we went there was quite a revelation. All the other kids were French –with very few other English families on the site. They wandered across, and tried talking to us, which was hopeless as none of us spoke French. Suddenly, one of the boys said Banks, Wilson, Cohen, Moore, Bobby Charlton, Geoff Hurst, Peters. He could almost recite the England World Cup winning team as well as I could. What an icebreaker! I knew a few of the French players – Simon, Gondet, Bonnel. Suddenly we had conversation, albeit very limited. One of the boys produced a football, and we had a game, mostly passing and juggling the ball.

It taught me an important lesson. If you're ever with someone and you don't speak each other's language, then the international language is football. It's a great leveller!

The rest of the holiday seemed to pass quite quickly. The weather was good; we enjoyed the camping; the beach was fabulous, and as kids, we had a fair amount of freedom on the campsite. It was also wonderful having our parents joining us to swim, play badminton, and our regular games of cards.

On the journey back to the UK, Dad was keen to stop over at Tours, which he'd heard was a beautiful town. We found a campsite by the River Loire. We put up the tent, got changed, and discovered the tent had filled with mosquitos. My parents sprayed the tent thoroughly with insecticide, and then we left to go out to dinner to, what I remember as being, quite a posh restaurant. By the time we returned, there wasn't a mosquito in sight. Goodness knows what chemicals we ingested, but back in the 1960s it really wasn't a concern.

The following day, Dad was keen to take Mum clothes shopping. He thought the French had much more style and wanted Mum to take advantage of this. I remember going into several shops where Mum tried on countless dresses before choosing a beautiful navy one, which was certainly stylish and quite different to the styles in the UK. As we went into more shops, Dad suggested a coat, and Mum eventually saw something she really liked. My brothers and I began to get bored and had pangs of hunger. Then Dad said, 'And what about shoes?' Oh no! More shopping! Fortunately, Mum saw some shoes quite quickly, and then we went for some lunch. We found a classy restaurant, and I now realise that we were actually very lucky, in that having a father who was a restaurateur, we ate in some lovely restaurants, and were encouraged to try lots of new dishes. As Mum and Dad used to say, 'If you don't try, you'll never know.'

Eventually, we drove back to Calais and caught the ferry. This time, fortunately, the sea was much calmer.

We arrived home full of stories about our first French experiences.

OUR SECOND FRENCH FAMILY HOLIDAY

1968

We enjoyed our holiday at Camping Palace so much that two years later we decided to go back again. Once again, we borrowed the same tent from our friends, but this time, we found we'd outgrown the tent. My brothers and I had got bigger, and we also brought more stuff with us.

We had a good holiday again, which was made even more enjoyable because in the tent next to ours was a stunning sixteen-year-old French girl on holiday with her parents. Given I was only twelve, she clearly wasn't interested in me, although she did talk to my mother. I so much wanted to join the conversation, but with typical adolescent awkwardness I hid instead behind my Football Monthly magazine.

The weather that year wasn't quite so good, so Dad decided to move down to Spain. We spent a night at Hendaye, near the Spanish border. I remember Dad had to fill a form when checking into a hotel, and I saw he'd written Company Director as his profession. I queried this afterwards – I always said he was a hotelier. Dad patiently explained to me the structure of his business and his role as Partner/Director. My first lesson in business.

We drove to San Sebastian and stopped for lunch. This was my first experience of a Spanish lunch, which seemed to last forever – at least three hours. The food was wonderful. The weather was breaking, and we found a campsite nearby on what seemed to be the edge of a small mountain. We put the tent up, brewed a kettle for some tea, and suddenly a storm appeared. I thought the tent was going to blow away. At first it was exciting. However, later that night, the storm reared its head again. Rain penetrated the tent, and we spent a less than comfortable night. In the morning, Mum and Dad decided that was enough for camping that year. We packed up, drove into San Sebastian, and found a hotel.

At that time, I was getting into music, and wanted a guitar. The problem was I'd run out of holiday money. I saw one in a shop, which I really wanted. Mum and Dad were scrupulously fair with all three of their sons, and I could see this was going to be potentially awkward. I didn't over egg the situation, and overnight they must have thought it over, as the next day, we went to the shop, where I was bought the guitar, and Simon and Hugh were also given extra holiday money.

We stopped at a campsite in southern Brittany on the way back, and for the first time that holiday, I spoke in French. I'd been learning the language for a year at school, and I'd really taken to it. It was a question of finding the opportunity and having the confidence to make the most of it. I discovered the more I spoke, the more relaxed I felt. And the people I spoke to showed genuine appreciation and understanding, which gave me huge confidence.

THE 1970S

MY FRENCH EXCHANGE IN PARIS

1970

In 1970, I was fourteen and in the Fourth Form at school. My favourite subject was French, and when an opportunity came up to go on an exchange, I jumped at it. At that time, exchanges to France were organised through an organisation called the AIJ (Amitiés Internationales des Jeunes), to which my school subscribed. They organised it so that an English student spent three weeks with a French student and their family during the Easter holidays and reciprocated by having the same student back staying with them during the summer holidays in the UK.

The application was sent to the AIJ, who would assess your details, and try to match you up with someone similar and vice versa.

Around February 1970, I received a letter informing me I was paired with a boy called André who lived in Paris. We were encouraged to write to each other, which we duly did, albeit in a basic way, i.e. *I have two brothers and a dog.*

Four other boys from my school were also going at the same time, so the Head of Modern Languages at our school drove us to Victoria Station in London where we were met by a representative from the AIJ. We all boarded a train to Dover and caught the ferry across the Channel.

When we arrived in Calais, we caught the train to Gare du Nord in Paris, where an indomitable French lady from the AIJ organised us into queues. We were given a number each and matched with our corresponding family. It was like a conveyor belt, so numéro 160 (or whatever it was) Smith/Dupont, numéro 161 Wilson/Piaget… We were literally thrust together, and then rushed out of the way to keep the queue moving.

André's mother met me as he was still at the boarding school where he was a weekly boarder who only returned on Saturdays. As it was Friday, his mum and one of his brothers came to meet me. She had a green Mini, and she drove back to their apartment in the prosperous suburb of Paris 17.

That evening I met André's father, his four sisters, and his two brothers. Upon arrival, we sat down to dinner, which was served by their cook. André's father – who was very formal both in dress and manner (he was a successful businessman) – offered me wine, which he then watered down. I was trying to work out the various family members and noticed a girl who didn't say much. I later discovered she was English, and she was also on an exchange with one of André's sisters. After dinner, we went to watch TV – *L'Homme à la Valise* or *Man in a Suitcase* as I knew it in England.

The following morning after breakfast, Patrice, who at seventeen was the eldest child, suggested we went for a bike ride. We cycled into Paris, where he showed me the Eiffel Tower. We then cycled up the Champs-Élysées and past the Arc de Triomphe across Le Place de la République. I remember thinking my parents would be just a little nervous if they knew what I was doing.

When we got back, André was at home. He was quite cool – certainly for a fourteen old – in both demeanour and dress. That afternoon we visited the cinema to see a François Truffaut film L'Enfant Sauvage. When we got back, his father grilled me about the film, asking me what I thought, what was my favourite bit, etc. As we ate, I suddenly started to feel homesick, and my eyes filled with tears. I carried on eating but felt very subdued.

The following morning – Sunday – was all about church. André's father asked me, 'Catholique où Anglican?'

I replied, 'Anglican.'

After breakfast, the English girl, Vivienne, and I were dropped off at a massive Anglican church while the family went off to a Catholic church. Vivienne was two years older than me, and she clearly thought I was just a young boy who wasn't worthy of conversation. As we stood next to each other in the pew, I felt so very far away from my family, and I sobbed my way through the hymns and prayers.

We were collected from the church and went off for lunch at André's Parisian grandparents' house. They were very sweet, and I cheered up. André and I visited La Musée des Marines afterwards – his mother was insistent that I experienced as much culture as possible.

The following day was exciting. We were going to their country house, which was about an hour away, near to Soissons. André's mother drove the girls there. All the boys, along with bicycles, caught the train. We arrived at the railway station, and then cycled about twenty km to the village where their house was. It was a typically cold and windy March day, and I was seriously out of breath by the time we arrived.

We were greeted by his mum and sisters, his aunt and her children who were staying there. There must have been about fourteen of us in the house. I have memories of breakfast, which was a self-serve buffet, and which André's mother and his aunt supervised, both wearing overcoats over their nighties.

André's mother was a great organiser. She was very formal with her children and addressed them all as 'vous'.

Unless it was raining, she insisted we all played outside. The family had a record player, and André repeatedly played his one LP, which was 'Willy and the Poor Boys' by Creedence Clearwater Revival.

André's other grandparents had a farm about five km away, which we regularly visited. It was a picture-book setting – cream-coloured buildings with red roof tiles. They had a large herd of cattle and a bull, which were housed in various cow sheds. One of André's favourite activities was to go to where the bull was tethered and whack its testicles with a stick. The bull would snort and cry out and pull hard on its chain. I was always worried it would break free and inflict terrible violence upon us. Fortunately, that never happened.

One of the farmworkers had a ferret. We often accompanied him; he'd pull the ferret out of his pocket and stuff it down a rabbit hole, presumably with the aim of reducing the rabbit population. However, the ferret would inevitably appear on its own out of another rabbit hole nearby. The farmworker would groan and say 'merde' and shove the poor ferret down another hole. I never once saw it come out with a rabbit!

Easter Sunday was a big day. André's father had arrived on Good Friday (when we had the most enormous salmon for lunch). The adults and girls drove to the farm, and us boys cycled over for lunch, which was promptly served at midday. The starter was scrambled egg on melba toast. Scrambled egg was one of my favourite dishes. It seemed to be available in unlimited quantities and tasted absolutely delicious. After my third serving, André's grandmother reminded me there was more to come. We had huge portions of roast lamb, cheese, and dessert. Cycling back was a challenge on what was an extremely full stomach!

The rest of the week passed by with trips to the farm to see the bull. The weather was sunny, but freezing. One evening, André's mother took him and his cousins to see some other relatives. There wasn't enough room in the cars, so Vivienne and I stayed behind with his younger sisters. Later that evening, while we were watching TV, we were joined by their American au pair – Jill – who was there to look after the little girls. André's aunt also had an American au pair, and they joined us in the living room. I'd never spoken to these American girls, who were aged around nineteen, but they were friendly and outgoing, and we had a great evening together, speaking English for what was the first time for me in almost two weeks. I discovered that André's family was very wealthy. Jill mentioned she was fascinated by the fact they had a cook in Paris, who would spend almost all day preparing the soup for the evening meal, which was then devoured in thirty seconds by the father upon his return from work!

We went to Reims one day and visited the wine caves at Mumm, along with a tasting session, which was good fun. On the Saturday, we returned to Paris, as André had to be back at school for the Saturday evening.

To be totally honest, I wasn't terribly keen on André. He could be both aloof and patronising. Once he'd disappeared back to school, I felt more comfortable talking to his mother and his two brothers, with whom I got on well. The final week in Paris rushed by. We met his aunt again, to go around the Louvre and then the Palace at Versailles. His aunt and her family were even more wealthy and lived on Avenue Foch in Paris 16. I spent a day with his younger brother Freddy when I attended school with him. There was an awkward moment when the maths teacher questioned why I hadn't brought my homework and shouted at me. Fortunately, Freddy quickly explained, but it was a bit scary! That evening, I accompanied Freddy to his fencing classes. We went right across Paris, changing the Metro several times. I strongly remember the ever-present smell of garlic on peoples' breath in the crowded carriages, as well as the signs saying 'Défense de fumer et de cracher' – *no smoking or spitting.*

On the final day, André's mum took me shopping to buy presents for my family. We went to Le Printemps, and she reminded me that I'd bought for everyone, including myself, but not yet for my father. She took me to an expensive stationer and encouraged me to buy my dad a Waterman pen.

Suddenly, the three weeks were over. On the Friday morning she took me to Gare du Nord, deposited me in the queue, and waved au revoir. I met my schoolmates, and we made the long journey back to Bedford via Calais, Dover, and London.

IT WAS A very formative time in my life. I experienced homesickness for the first time, which I conquered with some pride. I spoke French almost continuously for three weeks, which I increasingly adored. I also became more independent and streetwise. I ate some unusual food, and in vast quantities, which I loved. The only thing I loathed was endives, which I didn't eat for thirty years until my wife Patricia reintroduced me to them. I remember the Camembert, the petit-suisses, and especially the gouttés which was the staple snack for kids returning home after school – French baguettes stuffed with chunks of chocolate.

Above all, I benefited hugely from learning about life with another family in another country. Experiences I will never, ever forget.

Finally, I should add, André came over to us as planned in July. He was even more obnoxious and self-obsessed. He was homesick, a fussy eater, and generally disinterested in wherever we went or whatever we did.

My mum thought he had beautiful clothes – designer labels such as Lacoste – although he wouldn't let her wash anything. He must have brought loads of socks and underwear – or wore the same ones every day!

A European Holiday

1971

In 1971, we went for a three-week family holiday to Italy. This time we borrowed a larger tent and trailer from Keith, a family friend. We crossed the Channel on a Thoresen ferry, which was a fascinating experience due to the unusual food. The restaurant menu consisted of a smorgasbord, which was essentially a buffet, but quite magnificent, with hot and cold meats, fish, and a choice of desserts and cheeses. Dad was quite horrified to see people filling their plates sky high with everything piled together and instructed us to go up several times, taking each course separately. For example, choose the fish to start with, then go up again for some meat, then once more for desserts, and only if we were still hungry to finish with some cheese.

We drove through France and Switzerland, arriving in Italy almost four days later. On the way down, we stopped at Montreux, Switzerland, and the following night camped at a site in Monza in Italy. Mum mentioned she was kept awake all night by the sounds of cars racing at the Monza track, although the rest of us slept soundly.

The following morning, which was a Sunday, was hot and sticky. We packed up the tent, with Dad doing the lion's share of the work. He was becoming hotter and hotter, sweating profusely, and becoming more and more irritable. He eventually got the tent and equipment into the trailer, and then placed the canvas cover on top, which was secured by rope attached to hooks on the side of the trailer. Dad pulled the rope, and a hook flew off. He cursed, which made Simon laugh.

Dad glowered at us, pulled the rope tighter, and another hook came away. Mum couldn't look, but I'm sure her shoulders were shaking with laughter. Another pull of the rope, and two more hooks came off. We just burst out laughing. Dad, however, didn't see the joke, and we stepped away until he lit up a cigarette once the top had finally been fitted. My father was generally very even-tempered and kept a strong sense of perspective. But when he blew...!

We continued our journey through Italy and finally got to the campsite later that afternoon. We'd booked an emplacement at a site near to Lido di Jesolo, called Camping NSU. It had originally been set up for employees from the NSU car company and factory in Germany and had since grown. Although the site was in Italy, it was largely owned and managed by Germans. So it was quite an experience to camp on a site where everything was run and managed extremely efficiently, with strict rules on noise and parking, and where the toilet and washing facilities were probably the cleanest I've ever come across on a campsite.

The campers consisted mostly of Italians, Germans, and some British. There was a loudspeaker system throughout the site, which not only was used to broadcast the day's events but also to remind people to keep the noise down during the siesta period (12 p.m. to 3 p.m.), as well as reminding them of certain camp rules if it was felt they were being ignored.

This was the summer of the 'clacker balls' – two solid plastic balls on a string with a ring that fitted on a finger. The object was to raise the hand up and down so that the balls would bounce off each other and make a clacking noise. It was hugely popular among kids who would spend ages 'clacking' the balls against each other. The noise was distinctive and loud, and it certainly kept the camp broadcasters busy enforcing the rules of silence both during the siesta period and after nine at night.

Although I'd briefly visited Germany in 1968 to stay with relatives who were stationed in the British Army at Dortmund, this was the first time I'd come into contact with so many Germans. They left a lasting impression on me. They appeared prosperous, well-dressed, and courteous. There was a touch of arrogance among some of them, which I put down to the fact that many of them spoke good English, whereas the Brits barely spoke a word of German. They looked fit and healthy, they drove beautiful cars, and even their tents and camping equipment smacked of quality.

As I was fifteen, I was allowed an occasional beer, and I clearly remember drinking my first German beer at the camp bar – Löwenbräu München.

We went to Venice for the day, where we ate our first ever pizza. This was very new – pizzas were yet to catch on in the UK. Ours was freshly made as we watched. I bought a pair of Bermuda style swimming shorts – I thought I was so cool. Meanwhile, Simon pestered my parents to buy him some plastic sandals. Mum thought they were cheap and nasty, and point-blank refused. But Simon persisted and persisted and eventually got his way.

My holiday that year was memorable for a couple of things: first, I was badly sunburnt. Second, I met a beautiful German girl!

I was freckly and pale skinned, and as much as I wanted to tan, it was going to be a challenge. The campsite was on the beach, and we spent a lot of time in the sea, mostly throwing and catching balls.

After two days, my shoulders became very pink and sore. Mum suggested I wore a T-shirt in the sea, and although I was reluctant to do this – no one else did – I could see, and feel, the sense. A day or two later, I started to peel. I remember swimming and one of my brothers screaming with laughter as a large swathe of my skin trailed behind me.

Some days later, when staying at a Pension in Austria, I went to change for dinner, and when I removed my T-shirt, the floor in our room looked as if it had been snowing, with thousands of skin flakes landing on the carpet.

One morning when we were at the campsite, playing in the sea, two German girls asked if they could join us. One looked about twelve. She was short-haired and came from Essen. The other was thirteen, although she looked sixteen. She was slim, blonde-haired, and very pretty. Her name was Ilona (Illy) and she came from Bavaria. I completely fell for her in the way that fifteen-year-old boys do – outwardly confident and showing off a bit, while inwardly shy and uncertain. Simon, Hugh, and I spent a few days playing in the sea with the girls, laughing and talking. Both girls spoke English, and I could speak some German, so communication was quite easy.

Eventually, I plucked up the courage to ask Illy if she would play table-tennis with me one evening. She had to ask her parents. Their tent was quite near to ours. I remember going to collect her and her father giving me a stern look. We walked off to the table-tennis tables, and started to play, only to find my two brothers standing outside five minutes later, watching our every move.

I told them to clear off, which eventually they did. After the game, we bought ice creams, and walked along the beach front. I'd been plucking up courage to take her hand, when she looked at me squarely and said, 'I think I'd better to go back now. My parents are expecting me.' Aah – lost opportunity! She was going back to Germany the next day, so we exchanged addresses, and we wrote to each other regularly for the next two years, until we became distracted with other things in our lives as we grew older. I wonder what she's doing now. Maybe she's now an Oma (grandma).

During our time in Italy, we drove to Trieste one evening, which was on the border with Yugoslavia. We drove back to Camping NSU through a massive thunderstorm and torrential rain. That evening, my brothers teased me mercilessly about Illy and how I was in love. Mum rather sweetly – but to my huge embarrassment – asked if I'd kissed her. Dad, bless him, realised how I was feeling, and said, 'Leave the poor boy alone.' And thankfully, the subject was changed.

Dad decided to take a leisurely drive home, spending a week travelling through Austria and Germany. We drove through the

Gross Glockner pass on the way to Austria, where the summer scenery was breathtakingly beautiful. Having spent the night near Innsbruck, we then drove into Germany and ended up in Munich, where we stayed overnight and had an early breakfast the following morning at the Bahnhof (railway station).

We travelled through Germany, gradually moving in a westerly direction, and ended up at a campsite on the Neckar near to Heidelberg. The weather had changed to rain and fresher temperatures. On the Friday, we woke up to pouring rain, so decided to go to Heidelberg for the day. I was really taken with Heidelberg, a major university city with some very attractive architecture and interesting shops.

We continued our journey home through Belgium and found a fantastic friterie near the coast and had some of the best chips I'd ever eaten. We drove down to Calais and caught the Thoresen boat back to Dover. This time, much to Dad's chagrin, instead of the smorgasbord, us boys wanted burgers and chips. Oh well – that's kids. Some things never change!

Discovering Dordogne

1973

Our next family holiday abroad was in 1973. We broke up from school on the Saturday. I'd rowed at Bedford Regatta (for the last time, which made it quite special) and then went to a disco that evening, before we all left home on the Sunday evening to begin our summer holiday. This time we had a caravan which my parents had bought earlier that year, so there was more space all round, not only in the car but also, the caravan had an awning, so there was plenty of room.

Our destination was Spain, which was a three-day journey. We had a different car this time. For years, Dad had wanted a Mercedes, and he bought a second-hand model the year before. It was a beautiful car, and this was the first holiday towing the caravan.

We had a leisurely journey down and stopped somewhere in mid-France. During the night, I had one of my nightmares; I occasionally suffered with claustrophobia, and woke up in the awning, not knowing where on earth I was. I decided in the heat of the moment to drag my bedding outside the awning. It was a warm night, and I slept contentedly until I could hear voices at around 8 a.m. and saw people walking past me on their way to the toilets. I got a few funny looks!

Our journey continued into Spain and headed towards Barcelona. Some friends of my parents had recommended a site – Camping Marius – which was slightly inland before Barcelona. The site was quite pleasant, but full of flies. They were everywhere. And my father absolutely hated flies. After a few days, we talked about moving on. The next day, another Englishman walked past and started talking with Dad, who explained the flies were driving him mad. During the conversation, a fly flew into Dad's mouth, at which point he said, 'Bugger! That's it. Come on, Betty. We're going.' And so we did.

Dad thought it would be better to camp nearer to the coast, where there were likely to be fewer insects. He looked at the camping guide and saw a site at Cambrils – Camping Albatross. This entailed driving through Barcelona, which wasn't a problem, until the car broke down. Basically, it overheated. Although Dad didn't know at the time, the Mercedes didn't have an oil cooler. However, towing a caravan in hot weather raised the temperature of the oil, and the engine ceased to function. The car broke down in the city centre. We unhooked the caravan and pushed it on to the pavement, and Dad drove the car into an underground car park.

While the engine cooled, he looked in the Mercedes handbook and found a dealer nearby. We all walked there, hoping someone there would speak English. But they didn't! I tried talking to them in French, but that didn't work. I tried German and suddenly elicited a response. Of course – a dealer for a German carmaker had to speak German. The trouble was it was all technical German. I didn't know the difference between an exhaust system and a cooling system in English let alone German. So we had a few challenges. But gradually, with patience and persistence, I managed to make the guy understand what had happened. He sent a mechanic to the car park, but by this time the oil temperature had lowered, so the car started OK. However, Dad decided it needed looking at, and he agreed to return to the garage the following day.

We drove to the campsite and installed the caravan on the beach. It wasn't the most attractive of campsites, but it had the sea, and most importantly, there were no flies!

The weather had somewhat deteriorated the following day. Mum and Dad drove into Barcelona to the dealer, and we stayed at the site. Hugh could swim for Europe he loved swimming so much, so he was happy to be anywhere near the sea. Simon wanted to explore the campsite, and I was happy to stay at the caravan and read. I also had a serious girlfriend at the time, Nikita, who Mum and Dad had said could come on holiday with us, but her school wouldn't let her take the last week of term off, so I spent several hours during the holiday writing letters to her.

Mum and Dad returned to the campsite but without the car. The dealer needed to keep it for another day for further tests. So they caught a bus back, which I thought was pretty enterprising of them, especially as they didn't speak Spanish. But Dad, being an entrepreneur, was happy to try things out and take a few risks, and getting a bus through a strange city to another town was a challenge he couldn't refuse. Mum, as always, steadfastly supported him.

We spent a couple more days at Camping Albatross; the car was duly fixed, and we decided to visit a restaurant on the last night for a paella. We ordered the food and waited… and waited… and waited. We'd called the waiter across a few times, but he was quite stressed and petulant, and kept saying, 'Is coming soon.' After almost an hour and a half, we decided to go. At which point the waiter ran over and remonstrated with us. He said we had to pay, and of course we refused. In the end, he asked for our passports and said he was calling the police. At which point my mother stood up, looked him squarely in the eye, and said, 'My good man, if you think for one moment you can have our passports or any payment whatsoever, then you are very much mistaken. So please step out of our way otherwise I will call the police.'

The waiter was so dumbstruck at this 'power lady' (visualise Margaret Thatcher hand-bagging her way out!) that he stepped aside, and we left. Fortunately, we found somewhere else fairly quickly.

On the journey back through France, we stopped at a wonderful site in the Dordogne – Camping Les Granges at Grolejac. There was a great swimming pool, walks in the woods, and plenty of space to play badminton outside our caravan. On that holiday I took my guitar (not the one I got in Spain – I'd upgraded by then). I used to play quite a bit at various pubs and at school, and drove my parents mad constantly tuning up, and part-playing songs over and over to get them right. I also remember visiting a splendid restaurant for lunch near to Périgueux, where I understood why the Dordogne was so renowned for the quality of its food.

Something triggered inside me; I really felt that the Dordogne was the heart of France I'd been hoping for. The scenery was stunning – forests and rivers. The villages were beautiful and enticing. As previously mentioned, the range and choice of food was astounding. Very different to anything we had in the UK, it all felt very much what I was looking for – very French! I loved the French coast, but the Dordogne really began to cement my growing love for the country.

For our final night in France, we stopped at a site in Normandy. It was quite late, and before bed we went to the toilets. At that time, I used to smoke cigarettes, not a lot, but Dad, while definitely not encouraging me, realised that as a smoker himself, it would be hypocritical to prevent me from doing so. I saw a couple of lads outside the toilets having a furtive fag and asked one of them for a light. To our mutual shock and surprise, it was a boy from our school – a year younger than me and a year older than Simon. We were so amazed to see each other I just said, 'Cheers, mate,' and walked off, only to walk back and ask him what he was doing there. He was with a friend's parents, who were less tolerant of smoking. It's a small world. Another one of life's lessons, in that regardless of where you might be in the world, there's a chance of meeting someone you already know.

Amazing though this coincidence might seem!

HITCH-HIKING IN FRANCE

1974

I left school in July 1974 after doing my A levels. I was actually quite sad to leave. It was the end of an era. I'd liked school a lot and had some great friends. I then spent six weeks working at Dad's hotel in Woburn as a waiter, where I lived in with the rest of the staff. I'd been offered a place at Manchester Polytechnic to pursue Business Studies, and I was keen to earn as much money as possible before moving up there.

I also wanted a holiday. Mum and Dad had planned a two-week holiday in France with Simon and Hugh. They asked if I wanted to join them. I was quite keen. I also had a close friend from school – Stephen. We'd played guitar together for the past two years. We quite fancied hitching around France, so Mum and Dad offered us the chance to travel down with them, stay for a bit, and then hitch our way around and back to England.

We drove down to southern Brittany and stayed at a campsite near the coast. Stephen was an easy-going chap and got on well with my family. He'd also taken an A level in French, so spoke the language. We all spent an enjoyable few days together. On the Monday morning, Stephen and I decided to make a move. I'd met a

French girl the previous summer, who came over to stay with an English family we knew. We went out together a few times and had kept in touch by letter. I knew she'd found a boyfriend in France, but that didn't matter. I called Isabelle a couple of days earlier. She wasn't in, but I spoke to her mother, who knew about me, and she insisted we called in to see them.

Mum and Dad dropped us off just outside Nantes. Neither Stephen nor I had a clue how long we might wait. But we had a small Union Jack which we held. Amazingly enough, after about an hour, a car stopped. It belonged to a guy in the British Army. He was on holiday with his wife and two small children and was driving back to West Germany where he was stationed. He'd spotted our flag and was happy to help. He put our rucksacks into the caravan he was towing, and Stephen and I squeezed into the back of his car with his kids.

The chap and his wife were quite young and friendly. We drove along the Loire, through Angers and Tours, and stopped at a campsite outside Orléans for the night. They weren't keen on Stephen and I smoking in their car, so it amused them to see us filling our lungs with cigarette smoke at every opportunity when we stopped for a break.

Isabelle and her family lived in a little town called Sens, which is about 90 miles south-west of Paris. The following morning, we were dropped off on the outskirts, and Stephen suggested we go for some lunch. We found a restaurant – a Routiers – and promptly ordered some food. We had the starter, and then the waitress brought a huge bowl of salad to the table. We were hungry, so we ate the lot, plus two baskets of bread. The waitress returned and looked astonished. She then came back with plates of hot chicken, plus bowls of vegetables and potatoes. We realised that the lettuce was a palate cleanser – we were only supposed to have a small amount, so that it could be shared with other diners! We carried on through desserts and cheese and finally paid the bill before making our way towards Isabelle's house.

Her father answered the door and explained she wasn't in but was with 'a friend'. He made a call, then said he'd take us there. We arrived at a block of flats, told to knock at a particular number, and Isabelle would be there. A young guy who looked like a hippy opened the door. He had long dark hair, a straggly beard, and was smoking a joint. He invited us in, and there we found Isabelle, who looked both pleased and awkward. We had coffee, listened to music, and had some conversation while Isabelle and her boyfriend cuddled up. A few hours later, the phone rang, and shortly afterwards a car pulled up outside. It was Isabelle's parents. They took us to a bar and then back home for dinner.

Her father was a real Anglophile, which is how he knew our family friends where Isabelle had stayed the previous year. Both her parents were charming. They refused to let us put up our tent in their garden, and instead showed us to a spare room with twin beds.

The following morning, Isabelle's father asked Stephen and me when we had to be back in England. We explained we wanted to get back over the weekend. He promptly insisted we stay for a few days, and he would take us to the main road to Paris on the Friday afternoon. There were to be no 'buts' or excuses.

Her mother was a splendid cook. We ate like lords: breakfast, 4-course lunch, and 5-course dinner in the evening. It got to the point that by Thursday lunchtime, I literally couldn't eat. Stephen insisted it would be perceived as rude, so I managed to push some food around my plate, but I was clearly in the overload zone.

It was apparent Isabelle's parents didn't approve of her boyfriend and cleverly used our presence there as an excuse to keep her away from him. I remember some wonderful conversations around the dinner table. Other friends were invited to join us, the food and wine were plentiful, and we talked about everything from Europe, war, history, philosophy, culture, and sport. Thank goodness Stephen and I both spoke half-decent French.

Friday afternoon came, and Isabelle's dad dropped us off. It was raining, but he assured us we wouldn't wait long. Sure enough, after about twenty minutes, a minibus pulled up. It contained about six other people, all about our age, though they didn't seem to know each other. There was a French guy driving, with his girlfriend in the front. They didn't say much, but they seemed to spend a lot of time picking up hitchhikers to and from Paris.

We drove along a motorway at breakneck speed in pouring rain. It felt a hazardous journey. Nobody spoke much. The driver dropped us all off in central Paris on the south bank and drove away. Neither Stephen nor I had a clue where to go, but he'd heard the Montmartre would be a good place to go. We managed to find a cheap, grotty hotel where we shared a room. We went out for something to eat, and afterwards, Stephen suggested going to a club. We were unsure what it would cost but thought it worth a go. We found a place that looked interesting and walked in.

We were shown to a table. The place was half empty, and there was nothing happening on stage. A waitress came to the table and asked if we'd like to order champagne. We asked how much, and when she told us the price, we said we'd just have a beer. She explained all the drinks were the same extortionate price, so we said we'd have nothing. After a couple of moments, a burly guy approached us. He asked in French what we'd like to drink. We both replied, 'rien'. *Nothing.* At which point he grabbed us and virtually threw us out. We probably got away lightly!

The following morning, Stephen and I decided to spend the remainder of our dwindling funds on a beer outside a café on the Champs-Élysées.

We'd thought about hitching to Calais but came to the conclusion it was going to be difficult. We managed to scrape enough cash to catch a train to Calais and arrived there around nine that evening. We caught a ferry to Dover and started to hitch-hike out of Dover at around two in the morning.

After an hour or so, a lorry stopped. There was a driver and his mate who was around our age. They not only took us to London, but the young guy offered to put us up for the night on the lounge floor at his flat in Herne Hill.

It was pretty chaotic, with people coming and going all night. We eventually fell asleep around five and left at about 9 a.m. for the final leg of our journey back to Bedfordshire.

WORKING ON A FRENCH CAMPSITE

Summer of 1975

At the campsite in Normandy, I mentioned during our holiday in 1973, my parents noticed there were tents there which belonged to an English holiday company. Apparently, this was a company who had pre-erected tents on about thirty sites throughout Europe, mostly France, but also Switzerland, Germany, and Italy. At each site where they had a presence, they employed couriers who were there as customer representatives, meeting and greeting the holidaymakers, and maintaining the tents, etc.

I didn't think much more about this until the spring of 1975. I was then a student at Manchester Polytechnic studying Business Studies. I wanted a holiday job through the summer, but I definitely didn't fancy working in a factory or doing bar work, which most of my friends did. The type of job and experience was more important than the money. Mum reminded me of the holiday company in France, and I became quite interested. She spoke to a friend, who mentioned they used to post an advertisement in the classified pages of The Times. I had a look and sure enough I saw an ad. I wrote a letter of application, and I received a reply inviting me to an interview.

I think my language skills were of interest to them. I studied French and German at A level, and I was continuing to study French with my Business Studies course.

The interview was at their head office just north of London on a Friday afternoon. This suited me well, as I could include a trip home for the weekend. I caught the train from Manchester, along with my girlfriend at the time. Dad collected us from our local railway station at Bletchley and drove us to the company's office for the interview.

I walked up the stairs to a rather poky office, to be invited into a small office where there were three men. It was quite an intense interview. They were all leaning towards me, and I noticed their chairs were higher than mine, which gave them the advantage of looking down at me. During the interview, one of the guys pulled out a Polaroid camera, and suddenly pointed it in front of my face and took a photograph. I was pretty relaxed, although it was quite an unusual thing to do. They then spent about five minutes interviewing me in French. They asked what I was good at and how I related to people. They then discussed dates and my availability. Essentially, they wanted couriers for the second half of the season, from July to September, about ten weeks.

They closed the interview and said they'd be in touch. Two weeks later, I received a letter with a formal offer. The pay was pretty poor – about 150 French francs a week, which amounted to about £14 per week. However, all transport costs would be covered, plus some petty cash for expenses.

I was asked to confirm my acceptance, and subsequently received another letter asking me to report to the head office on a date in July (all I can remember is that it was a Tuesday). At this stage, I still had no idea exactly where I would be going, simply that I'd be told when I reported to their office.

Although the pay was poor, what really appealed to me was that I'd be getting a ten-week holiday, hopefully somewhere in the sun in France, which would give me an opportunity to really develop my speaking skills. The campsites where the company's tents were located were spread around France – Normandy, Brittany, the Alps, Dordogne, the south coast, and the south-west coast near the Pyrenees. I was hoping for somewhere south. I had a girlfriend, Marie, who was a student at Manchester Polytechnic, and lived in the same hall of residence as I did. She was less than impressed that I'd be away all summer. But she lived near Blackpool, and I knew I wouldn't see much of her even if I remained in the UK.

I remember Mum being concerned I might get sunburnt. As I mentioned earlier, my track-record with the sun wasn't good. Mum had heard there were some tablets you could buy which contained carotene and helped to prime the skin. I remember taking a course of these, wondering if my skin would turn orange, but fortunately not!

On the allotted day, I said goodbye to Mum and my brothers, and Dad drove me to the company's head office, along with my suitcase and guitar. I went up to the boardroom, where there were about twenty other couriers. We were all given an envelope containing an advice slip to collect traveller's cheques, which were our wages for the summer. After a quick trip to the local bank and queueing up to collect the traveller's cheques, we returned to the office and met the company's owner. We all then trooped out to a local restaurant for lunch. Then it was back to the office, where one of the staff handed each one of us a large envelope. This contained details of where our destination, some cash for travel expenses (which I seem to remember was about £30), plus a manual detailing the responsibilities for a courier.

We were then bundled into a transit van, and taken to the local station, and told to get on with it. The plan was to make our way to our designated campsite. It was up to us to decide how, with the only proviso that each of us had to be there within forty-eight hours.

The campsite where I'd be working was at Argélès in the south-west of France. There were two sites there, one on the beach called Camping Le Soleil, and the other was at the foothills of the Pyrenees about five miles away from the other one, called Camping Le Bois Fleuri.

On the train to London, I got chatting with a guy who'd been a courier the year before in Brittany. His name was Adrian, and he was travelling down to the other site at Argélès – Camping Soleil, with another chap called Bob who was from Norfolk. They suggested we travelled together which seemed a good idea. Adrian also had his guitar with him, and he approved I'd taken mine, as he explained he'd organised camp singalongs the previous year.

We arrived at Euston Station, caught the Tube to Victoria, and discovered there was a train to Dover around 11 p.m., which would take us directly to the docks to catch a ferry which would depart at around 3.00 a.m.

Once we got to Victoria, we did what lads do, which was to go to the pub, have a few beers, and something to eat. When we got back to the station, I rang my parents from a public call box. I told them where I was going and how I would get there. As we were saying goodbye, the phone cut off as I'd run out of money. I ruminated afterwards that this would probably be the last time I'd speak to them for a couple of months, which felt a bit strange.

We got down to Dover, caught the ferry, tried to sleep – unsuccessfully, and arrived in Calais just before 6.00 a.m. We made our way to the station and caught the next train to Paris. From the Gard du Nord, we made our way to whichever station we needed to catch the train going south. I think the train went on to Barcelona, but it stopped at the main stations en route, as well as all the holiday resorts on the south coast.

We found a carriage and promptly fell asleep. I remember Adrian saying in a loud voice, 'Would you like a beer, Nigel?' This woke me up to see a ticket inspector in front of me. The lads had a good laugh at my expense!

The journey continued. We drank water and beer and ate fruit cake, which was the standard food fare on French trains. I read the manual, which was very comprehensive, detailing all the 'do's and don'ts' as well as how to mend chairs (called Samtis), tent zips, etc. I vividly remember reading the phrase 'Samtis are absolute bastards to fix'. No hope for me then. I was not a practical person.

Our train finally arrived at Argélès at around 7.45 p.m. It had been a long journey. Adrian, Bob, and I said cheerio, and we caught taxis to our respective campsites. I distinctly recall arriving at the entrance to Le Bois Fleuri at ten past eight. I walked into the reception and introduced myself. A rather glamorous looking woman greeted me. 'Ah, le nouveau responsable,' she cried. (Responsable is what the French called the couriers). She shook my hand and pointed me in the direction of the couriers' tents at the top of the site, near the entrance.

I wandered down and again introduced myself. There were a couple of guys and a couple of girls. They'd just finished dinner. The area looked a real mess – crockery, clothes, camping equipment all over the place. One of the guys seemed quite friendly, and his girlfriend was reasonably pleasant. She said that she'd have offered me some food, but it had all gone. Great! I was starving. They offered me a glass of wine, and said they were going out to the camp bar for drinks later, and that I might find some food there. The two of them occupied one tent, and the other two (who were friends from Wales who'd come over to see them) were staying in one of the unoccupied customer tents. I was shown a tent next door, which mostly contained camping equipment, including a dozen or so large gas bottles.

I chucked my stuff in, and shortly afterwards, we all went off to the bar. There wasn't any food, but for the price of an entrance ticket, there was unlimited wine available. We all got stuck in. This was fateful. After an hour or so, I realised the alcohol was going straight to my head, especially on an empty stomach. Half an hour later, I decided to call it a day. I was knackered and quite drunk. I staggered to the toilets, and promptly threw up, and with some difficulty, found my way back to the tent.

I was up early the next morning, around 8 a.m., but there was no sign of life. I was actually pleased. I felt pretty rough. I went for a shower, came back, boiled the kettle to make a coffee, and lit up a fag. I sat outside the tent, and it wasn't until about 10 a.m. that the others got up.

Over breakfast, they explained there was another courier coming to the site to work with me. He had his own car. His name was Jacob, and he'd been a courier at a different site the year before. I came to realise that the guy who I thought was a friend – the Welsh guy – was actually a courier working alongside the friendly guy – Martin. The Welsh guy was a miserable git, and his girlfriend was even worse. I was pleased to learn they would be leaving the following day, along with Martin and his girlfriend.

I was introduced to the general routines and administration, all of which seemed quite straightforward. Later that day, Jacob arrived. He was a student at Oxford University, and frightfully well-spoken. From first appearances, he seemed OK.

I was later introduced to another English guy called Geoff. He'd been a courier at the campsite the previous year, along with another guy called Chris, whose nickname was Scum. Geoff had secured a job at the campsite as Day Watchman. Basically, his job was to monitor all cars entering the campsite to check they had the campsite sticker on their windscreen. This would identify them as a bona fide resident. If there wasn't a sticker, Geoff had to challenge them. He was from the Midlands, tall and lanky, and spoke very loudly. He was sun-tanned, and his French was pretty much fluent. He was a true extrovert. Chris, on the other hand, just bummed around. He didn't have a job, so he had no money, and he just scrounged – everything, from cigarettes to drinks, food, old newspapers, money, etc. He was slightly eccentric and upper-class in manner.

Later that day, I met the campsite owner, Monsieur JP. He was in his late 60s early 70s and quite laid back. His wife ran the little supermarket, usually operating the till. The glamorous looking lady I met was the 'camp hostess'. She was a Parisienne in her late 40s. I've forgotten her real name, but Geoff and Scum called her Wazzle. She was having a semi-clandestine affair with M'sieur JP. I say semi – it wasn't obvious, but after watching him disappear across to her caravan several times a day, often adjusting his trousers on his way out, it was quite apparent they had some physical chemistry going on. Wazzle was very coquettish, and would change her clothes, normally smart dresses, five times a day.

Martin and co all departed the next day. They left behind one hell of a mess. They didn't wash crockery or saucepans unless absolutely necessary. The whole area around the tent was like a bomb site – un bordel, as the French would say. Jacob and I decided we needed to embark upon a serious clean-up, which took us most of the day. We seemed to have very little in common, and Jacob didn't have much of a sense of humour, but we worked together OK.

And so the summer season began – at least for us. The weather was generally magnificent, hot, sunny, and dry. The air was also dry, which made life much easier, especially when cleaning out tents or schlepping stuff around the campsite. The holiday company supplied each campsite with a moped – mobylette. As Jacob had his own car – a Morris 1000 van – I had almost exclusive use of the moped, which was great.

We bought food from the camp shop. Jacob was a reasonable cook – better than me, and we rubbed along OK together.

The following weekend, we were invited by Adrian and Bob at Soleil to visit them. As we were about to leave on the Saturday afternoon, Geoff and Scum decided they'd like to join us, so we all went off in Jacob's van. There were no seats in the back, so we just sat on the floor. No seat belts either. And obviously no air conditioning. It was absolutely stifling in the back of the van.

We all travelled down to the beach site and started drinking and chatting with our fellow couriers there. Each site had an appointments diary, showing which customers would be arriving on which day, the size of their party, etc. Geoff and Scum pored over the diary, to see if they recognised anyone from the previous year, when lo-and-behold, they discovered that a family who had camped at the Pyrenees site the previous year were actually due to turn up that afternoon for a fortnight's holiday at the beach camp.

The family had clearly made an impression as Geoff and Scum reminisced about these people, and both of them came to the conclusion that it would be good to 'have a laugh' at the family's expense.

They persuaded the couriers at the beach camp to change the name in the diary to something quite different and tick them off as having arrived. The plan was that when the family in question arrived, there would be no record of their holiday reservation, and that as the camp was full, they would have to go elsewhere.

Not the sort of thing you want when you've had a long, hot journey through France to your holiday destination. We waited for the sparks to fly.

There was no clear indication what time the family would arrive but given as it was then past 5.00 p.m., and that most people arrived by 6.00 p.m., Geoff and Scum decided to make themselves scarce. They took it in turns to keep a look out on the road entering the site by hiding up a tree.

After less than an hour, Geoff shot back to the couriers' tent to say that the family had arrived and that they would be making their way to the couriers' tent within a few minutes.

The family duly turned up and introduced themselves to check in. The couriers queried their name, and consulted their diary, before announcing they had no customer of that name who was due to arrive that day, or even during the next few weeks.

'There must be some sort of mistake,' said the customer.

'We've been holidaying with your company for four consecutive years. And we've never had a problem before,' added his wife.

'Look,' said one of the couriers. 'Here's our booking diary, and you can see that we have no reservation in your name. Are you sure you've come to right campsite?'

'Of course, I'm bloody sure,' exclaimed the husband in annoyance. 'We stayed at the other site in the Pyrenees last year, and after visiting this site for a day, we decided to come here this year. There's been a cock-up at your end.'

'Sorry, Sir,' said the courier, who was managing with difficulty to keep a straight face. The other courier had discreetly eased himself away, as he was finding it hard to hold it together.

'We'd certainly like to accommodate you and your family, but the campsite is fully booked, and all our tents are occupied.'

'That's no good,' retorted the customer who was now visibly sweating. 'We don't have our own tent, so we can't just do our own thing.'

'Well, Sir, these are our colleagues from the Pyrenees site. Perhaps they could accommodate you.'

Ooh, you bugger, I thought. *You're sharing this with me now and putting me on the spot.*

'Er...no. No. We're fully booked, too. Sorry, but can't help you.'

'This is outrageous!' The client was getting angry now. 'We've driven for almost two days, through considerable heat. The children are tired, we're tired, and frankly this isn't good enough. You're going to have to sort this out.'

He started to stomp about. The other courier returned looking worried, and both couriers were clearly thinking, *How do we get out of this*? There was no sign of Geoff, and Scum had disappeared.

'Well, what are you going to do?' demanded the wife, who was becoming equally stressed.

'Erm… not sure. Bear with us a moment.' The couriers looked around anxiously, hoping Geoff or Scum would come to their rescue.

I glanced across to the lookout point and saw Geoff bent double in laughter. I was on the point of walking across to him, to get him back and end the 'game', when suddenly the husband muttered an expletive.

'I think we're the butt of a practical joke, aren't we?'

'What do you mean, dear?' whined his wife.

'Hang on a minute. I've just seen a face I recognise.'

Scum – true to his name – had been on the scrounge for a cigarette. He'd walked back to the tent, and all too late, saw the family. He stood behind a tree, which was far too thin to hide him, and had a mild coughing fit. The husband had looked across and spotted him. Game up!

'Isn't that one of the couriers from last year standing over there trying to hide from us? I forget his name, but the other guy called him Scumbag or something. Oy, come here a second.'

Scum nonchalantly walked over to us, smiled broadly, and said, 'Hi,' except that instead of a bold greeting, it came out more like a whisper (rather like Whispering Bob Harris from *The Old Grey*

Whistle Test). He coughed and wheezed again. 'Fancy seeing you here!'

'You rotten so and so.' The husband smiled. 'It's no surprise to find you at the bottom of this. You really had us worried. Do you know this chap?' He turned to the couriers. They were still faintly embarrassed, probably wishing they weren't caught up in this.

'God! I remember you,' said the wife. 'You were always on the scrounge for a free meal, tea bags, anything. I remember the night you and that other guy came round to our tent, and almost ate and drank us out of house and home.'

'Amazing,' commented the husband drily. 'I suppose the other chap's got a proper job back in England, but you…' His words tailed off as we saw Geoff approaching us with a huge grin on his face.

'Oh, I don't believe it. Right, guys, you owe us one. All of you. I suggest you show us to our tent, and then half an hour later bring round a couple of bottles of wine.'

'We couldn't resist this,' said Geoff. 'We remembered your sense of humour.'

'Which has been clearly stretched now,' added the wife.

'But thanks for being good sports,' said Scum.

'Yeah, thanks' said the couriers. 'Sorry about this, but we were, well, persuaded…'

'Ha ha. You chaps be careful. Don't get caught up with these blokes. They'll certainly lead you astray,' advised the husband, who by now was also grinning broadly at the joke.

Hmm, I thought later that evening. *That was a good laugh.* Funny how people can change their mood so quickly, and how relieved they become when it's all over.

Little did I know then how great an impact this 'wind up' would have throughout my life!

WE CONTINUED TO have fun with Geoff and Scum, which to me was a huge relief, as Jacob's sense of humour was clearly lacking. As time went on, I was sure Geoff was going slightly mad, probably because he sat outside all day in the hot sun. To break up his day, every afternoon at around four, he and Scum would bring out a small table, boil a kettle, and make afternoon tea. How very British. They introduced me to Earl Grey tea, which they would often mix with another blend.

One morning, one of the workmen on the campsite brought out a hose, which he used to water down the gravel track leading down to the campsite. Otherwise, dust would keep flying up, especially if cars drove too fast, and this was pretty unpleasant for everyone nearby.

After the guy had finished, Geoff grabbed the hose and proceeded to shower himself. Scum walked up to him, and Geoff squirted him with the hose. This led to a massive water fight. I joined in, and even Jacob got involved. We started filling buckets with water and hurled them over each other. We were getting absolutely soaked, and after I'd thrown another full bucket of water over Scum, he suddenly shouted out. He used to keep his passport in the back pocket of his cut-off jean shorts.

He pulled out his passport and shouted, 'My recipes!'

Scum was apparently quite a keen cook, and he used to scribble down recipes for dishes he liked. The only thing he ever carried was his passport, so that's where he wrote his recipes.

We all collapsed with laughter. So, in response, Scum grabbed the hose. We shot off to the perceived shelter of our tents, but that wasn't good enough. Scum followed us, hose in hand, and proceeded to spray water all around the inside of our tents – sleeping bags, clothes, just everywhere. The mess was unbelievable!

The campsite had a swimming pool, which was a new addition that year. It was a beautiful, large, outdoor pool, and was policed by a swimming pool attendant, who just loved himself. He'd sit in a highchair at one end of the pool, wearing his trademark minuscule 'budgie smuggler' swimming trunks, and a pair of aviator-style sunglasses. He was in his early 40s, mostly bald, with a slight pot belly. All he had going for him was his suntan.

He'd spend all day glaring at everyone and shouting at kids who'd do anything to annoy him, such as running round the pool, jumping in and 'bombing' other swimmers, or asking for help or advice or pretty much anything. He was incredibly arrogant and unfriendly. His speciality was leering at females between the ages of 15 and 50. He lived in a small tent near the pool. Because he was such a miserable git, no one bothered to talk to him, so he became a sad, lonely Billy no-mates.

One evening, he wandered up the campsite with the pretext of going out. But really, he was desperate for company. Our tents, as previously mentioned, were at the top of the site, near to the entrance, and there was always a lot of activity there – Jacob, me, various clients of ours, other campers coming up for a chat, and of course Geoff and Scum were frequent visitors. The pool attendant stopped as we were finishing our evening meal, started to talk, and then grabbed a spare seat and sat down. He really was an arrogant bastard – full of himself, preening himself as any women walked past, and so full of how good France was in comparison to anywhere else, especially Angleterre.

We were becoming increasingly bored with him and tired of his presence. We'd been discussing alcoholic drinks, and he kept making the point that all Les Anglais made was le beer et le Scotch Whisky. I noticed Geoff looking into the tent, and suddenly he said, 'Voilà,' and went to pick up a small bottle. He returned with a bottle of Lea & Perrins Worcestershire Sauce.

He instructed us all to drain our wine glasses and proceeded to pour a few drops into all our glasses, apart from the pool attendant, whose glass he filled with about a centimetre of the liquid. Geoff explained that this was a peculiarly English digestif, which was expensive and very special, which is why we all only had a tiny measure while our guest had enough for a large mouthful. He went on to say that the customary way of drinking this was to down it in one. We raised our glasses, said 'santé' and watched.

The pool attendant – who we nicknamed Mr Macho – poured the contents of the glass into his mouth and swallowed. We waited. He began to cough. He tried to speak but couldn't. His eyes bulged and watered. He put his hands around his throat and tried to spit. He searched for water or anything to drink, but there was nothing else on the table.

'Ça va?' enquired Scum. 'Vous voulez encore?' *More?*

The guy could barely shake his head. At which point we couldn't hold back. We were in hysterics. Seeing such a bumptious, unpleasant individual fall for the joke, and really suffer, was too much. He leapt up and ran down the campsite, looking for a water tap. Needless to say, he didn't come back. And never again did he bother us with his presence.

The following evening, we went for a late swim before the pool shut. The guy tried to ignore us, but we made a point of ridiculing him, shouting in French whether our English sauce was too strong for him.

'C'est trop fort pour vous hein?'

I WAS SETTLING down to life as a courier. Life was pretty easy and relaxed. The weather was consistently hot and sunny, I was eating well, and the wine was cheap and flowing. We used to buy our wine from the local Cave Co-operative, which was incredibly cheap.

The work was pretty easy. I wasn't the most fastidious cleaner, but I'd make sure the tents were ready for incoming customers –

floors were swept, furniture was clean, the cookers were wiped, and the equipment was working.

The part of the job I really enjoyed was the interaction with customers. Most of whom were friendly, but even if they weren't initially, they'd relax and warm up after a few days. My parents and my education had instilled in me a strong sense of confidence, and I was happy and comfortable talking to people from all walks of life. My experience as a courier definitely honed my people skills, and I soon learnt how to read people, and which buttons to press to either engage or disengage them. I'd always look for common ground and found geography was key, so if people came from Bedfordshire or the south-east in general, that was always a good starting point. I was also attracted to northerners, especially anyone from Greater Manchester or Lancashire.

I found customers would often invite me to their tents for a drink, or even an evening meal, which was great. Given Jacob was quite a loner, this worked for both of us. I discovered that charm and authenticity were key to building and developing relationships.

I came across some unusual experiences. Three families came together. They all had children and seemed close friends. I was talking with a couple of the husbands one day, and they asked if there was a decent bar in Argélès where we could go for an early evening beer.

The three men and I drove into town and found a bar. We talked, getting to know each other. They were all decent, middle-class type people, probably in their mid/late 30s. As we talked, I discovered one of the guys was divorced. The only way he could bring his kids away on holiday was to come with a 'housekeeper' to help look after his children. Apparently, he'd advertised in England, and the lady he came out with wasn't his wife. He explained the deal with her was that there was to be no relationship, but that she'd simply help with the housekeeping. He went on to say she was looking for a bit of holiday romance (but not with him) and he was desperate for a discreet holiday fling.

I'd got to know a French girl who was on holiday with her parents, and he actually said to me that if I could fix things up for him with this French girl (who was about 18), he would reciprocate and introduce me to his 'housekeeper', who was an unattractive lady in her late 30s. I wasn't tempted, and common sense fortunately prevailed. I could see this would be fraught with difficulties.

There was another situation where two other families had come away together. I noticed that quite often when they went out, one of the women would turn back. I learnt she was suffering from the sun. The other husband appeared keen to go back and collect her later on, and the two of them would indulge in a bit of ex-marital nooky. I only discovered this when I walked past her tent one afternoon, to see if she needed any medication, etc., and the other chap turned up. He seemed a bit shocked to see me, and I could tell it was time for me to disappear. As their fortnight's holiday continued, I saw the pattern being repeated. How the other two weren't suspicious I just don't know, unless of course they also had a thing going on together.

Part of our job was to entertain our customers, so along with the couriers at Camping Soleil, we organised 'sangria evenings' on the beach. The first one was a great success. Adrian and I took our guitars, we had a massive group singalong, and all the kids joined in.

On the back of this success, we organised another sangria evening a few weeks later. But the vibe was very different. It was later on in the summer, and the kids were mostly teenagers. They weren't so keen on a beach event, so the majority of people who came were the parents. Some serious drinking went on! Couples rediscovered their love and became overly amorous. There were also a few who became a little too amorous with people they hadn't come with. Slightly awkward. The final straw came when one guy, who'd been drinking heavily, kept wandering up and down the beach, kicking the sand, and occasionally digging with his hands. It turned out he'd lost his car keys!

Talking of cars reminds me of another couple of stories. Towards the end of the summer, a family turned up in a large Mercedes convertible. The guy got out and immediately asked if any mail had arrived for him. I was a little taken aback. I'd not been asked this question before. He was clearly a high-powered businessman and was expecting his secretary to forward any important documents to him for approval. Given this was 1975, long before any technology, it was an unusual request.

The couple had two daughters aged seventeen and eighteen, and they seemed keen to palm them off with suitable chaps. When they discovered I was only a student at Manchester Poly, whereas Jacob was at Oxford University, I clearly didn't stand a chance in their eyes. The parents practically ignored me for their entire stay, only talking to Jacob. After all, he was probably 'someone like us.' It made me smile. And no mail ever turned up for the husband.

We had another couple of funny episodes. A Frenchman turned up one afternoon, hot and sweaty, on his bike. He said he was a cyclist and had cycled all the way down from his home at Brest, Brittany. His name was François, and he was late 30s, balding, pot-bellied, not unlike the swimming pool attendant. He decided to pitch his little tent close to ours, and later that evening, proceeded to tell us he was a chef. The following day, he announced he'd cook for the four of us – Geoff, Scum, Jacob, and me.

He commiserated we'd been brought up on a diet of English cooking. He would therefore create something special. Two days later, he said he'd go shopping, but didn't return with much. Later that day, he went to the camp supermarket and returned with a bag full of shopping. He sent us away while he cooked his extravaganza. When we got back, he was even more hot and sweaty than usual while he served out his creation, which was... cassoulet... made from cans of cassoulet he'd bought in the camp shop. As young Englishmen, we couldn't resist taking the mick. François became deeply offended. He replied we obviously didn't appreciate good food. He sulked so much we barely saw him again until he departed several days later.

A couple of weeks later, a French family arrived, and also pitched their tent near to ours. They didn't say a lot. They didn't need to. The father was a 'ronfleur' – a snorer. Apart from having a lunchtime siesta, he'd also go to bed quite early – to us anyway – around 10 p.m. and would start to snore. This guy was prolific. I mean, you could hear him several metres away.

We put up with it for a couple of nights, hoping our laughter would awaken him. But nothing worked. Not even a toy trumpet, which one of the guys had found, and which he played right outside the guy's tent. Eventually, one night Scum had had enough. He decided to go for a pee, right up against this chap's tent next to where he was sleeping. We howled hysterically. Suddenly we heard some conversation.

'Qu'est-ce que c'est? Il pleut?' They thought it was raining, which made us laugh even more.

Scum was desperate to find a job. He'd already been working as a 'plongeur' (washer up) in a restaurant in Argélès but got the sack after he was seen taking the remains of food left on plates into a bag for his later consumption. He was dismissed instantly, with the owner explaining this food was for the dog.

Scum looked further afield. He spoke both French and Spanish fluently and somehow saw a job advertised for a magazine who wanted a translator. He hitched a lift to Perpignan where he was interviewed. The role was to translate American porn mags into Spanish. Although Scum's Spanish was good, it wasn't that far-reaching, especially as he needed to find colloquial synonyms for a wide variety of sexual words and phrases. He decided to approach

Mad Albert, who was the dustman and general odd-job man at the campsite.

Albert – so-called 'mad' as when he spoke, no one could really understand him – was a Catalan who spoke Spanish. Scum joined him for breakfast one morning, which in Mad Albert's case consisted of bread, Roquefort cheese, and red wine. Albert agreed to help Scum, but apart from a small fee, he particularly wanted a copy of the porn magazine to keep for himself. I believe he and Scum worked on a couple of issues, but payment wasn't forthcoming, and eventually Scum decided to go back to England and look for work there.

As a consequence of Scum leaving, Geoff joined us less often in the evenings. He was quite close to Scum and missed him. Meanwhile, I became bored with Jacob's company during the evenings when I wasn't visiting our customers, and I visited Geoff regularly. His tent was at the bottom of the campsite. He had an area all to himself, quite far from anyone else. He had an old Mini traveller there, which had broken down the year before. This was the reason Geoff came back to the campsite – to repair and collect his car. Then he was offered the job of Day Watchman and had stayed ever since.

Geoff was a fair cook – very adventurous and quite bizarre in his blend of ingredients. But I grew to really like him. He was highly intelligent, with great people skills, totally non-conformist, and very witty. We had many, many conversations together, drinking copious amounts of wine, which stretched into the early hours. As neither of us had to get up early, we'd quite often still be chatting at 3 a.m. Geoff had a small record player, which had a tinny sound, and which was powered by an old car battery. We spent hours listening to his collection of Grateful Dead LPs.

Geoff knew lots of people, including a chap he called Mr Energy, who was a Frenchman who spent most of the summer at the site with his two children, a boy and a girl aged 10 and 12. He was so-called as he was always on the go, full of conversation, and… you guessed it, energy. One evening he invited us for dinner at his caravan. Mr Energy cooked, and we drank wine and talked. Geoff had pre-warned me that Mr Energy would dominate the conversation (which he did), shout at his kids (which he did), and become increasingly drunk, at which point we'd need to discreetly and quietly leave. I saw Mr Energy the following day and thanked him for dinner. He looked at me in amazement. He clearly had absolutely no recollection of the evening.

Towards the latter part of the season, during a quiet Saturday afternoon, a chap walked into the camp entrance. It was a school friend of mine, Simon. He was a year younger than me, but was a very clever guy, and had taken his A levels a year early. He was taking a year out before going up to Cambridge. Simon absolutely epitomised the phrase 'laid back'. He didn't appear to study, yet his French (and German) were faultless. He did everything slowly – he spoke slowly, and both ate and walked at the same pace. He had a very wry sense of humour and got on well with Geoff too. He stayed for a few days, and then said he had to leave, and walked out of the campsite, rucksack on his back. I never saw him again.

The season was drawing to a close. There were gaps on the campsite as holidaymakers packed up their tents. We now had fewer customers, so we had a number of our own tents, which were empty. One day Jacob returned from Argélès with two girls in his van. He'd seen them hitching a lift coming out of Argélès and stopped. As we had several empty tents, he said they could stay for a few nights.

One of the girls – tall and red-haired – had a guitar, and the two of them were travelling around France together. She would play her guitar at bars and restaurants, which earned enough money for them to live basically. The other girl was very quiet, almost morose. We chatted on the Friday afternoon and evening, and on the Saturday, they asked if I wanted to accompany them to Argélès, where the guitarist would look for places to play. She would ask the owner for permission, and start to play, mostly soft rock or folk. She was a talented musician, and surprisingly earned more than I thought.

When we got back to the tent, she became flirty. She'd told me earlier that evening she'd just split up from her husband; they'd got married at an early age, and the marriage only lasted a year; they weren't yet divorced. I quite liked her, but she was coming on strong, wanting to get together in the UK, and I had visions of being pursued by an angry ex-husband. Instinct told me not to get involved. She was on the rebound, looking for a new relationship, and so the two of them left early the following morning.

IN EARLY SEPTEMBER, the rain suddenly appeared. It poured constantly for three days. There hadn't been any rain since May, so it was very welcome, although it had a detrimental effect on the campers, many of whom discovered leaks in their tents. It also brought out the rats. They would scurry around the gas bottles in the main body of the tent outside my sleeping compartment.

After a couple of days, there was a break for a few hours in the early evening, and Geoff, me, Jacob, and a friend of his who'd come out from the UK, decided to go to the local open-air cinema at Argélès, to see the rock opera Tommy. When we arrived, the cinema was about half full, but when the rain reappeared after twenty minutes, almost everyone left, leaving a small nucleus of crazy people, including us four English guys.

We got absolutely soaked through, but the temperature was still warm, and we stayed to watch the entire film. Afterwards, we drove into Argélès and went for a beer. One of the guys took off his T-shirt and wrung it out, leaving a large puddle of water on the floor. The bar owner promptly asked us to leave, which was a slight overreaction. We went back to the campsite to find one of our customers outside our tent.

In the light of his torch, he explained he'd got a problem with the rain in his tent. We 'reassured' him that so had everyone else and didn't take him too seriously apart from giving him an extra lamp. He came back in the early hours and said the problem was worse. We got up, went to his tent, only to find that half of it was submerged under a couple of feet of water. Poor guy – and his family. We managed to move all of them, and their belongings, to an empty tent where they could spend the night. They were all so grateful – typically stoical Brits.

The following day, I walked around the campsite. It was fascinating to see how the different nationalities were coping with the intense rainfall we'd had. The Brits largely got on with it and made the best of it. The Germans had dug out small trenches, thus diverting the water away from their emplacements. One guy very cleverly channelled the water from his space directly down to a French family's pitch! The Dutch just didn't seem to care, carrying on eating, drinking, and talking as usual. The French moaned and groaned, packed up and departed. And the Italians – there were a couple of families there – well, they just packed up and went, leaving their tents behind!

It was early September, and Jacob and I started to pack up. This was a mammoth exercise. We had to empty each of the thirty tents of all the equipment, clean it all, and then take it to a barn on the campsite where it was all kept. We then had to take down each tent (they were huge – each one sleeping six people), making sure it was thoroughly cleaned, and then packed into a long oblong bag. This was immensely difficult, as it was an incredibly tight fit. The heat was still intense – probably around 25 degrees – and we sweated buckets.

Although the official finishing date was September thirtieth, I'd originally explained to the 'powers that be' at the UK head office that I would need to leave on or around the twentieth, as the next term at

Manchester started at the end of the September. I'd also told Jacob this, which I think he ignored. He probably didn't believe me.

The démènage continued slowly, and by the start of my final week, there were still about a dozen tents to take down. Jacob suddenly realised I wasn't joking and that I would be leaving at the end of the week. He contacted the company, who promised to dispatch some help.

I'd decided to leave on the Friday morning, aiming to get back home by Sunday evening, which would give me a full week before returning to Manchester. Jacob's friend was also going back, and he offered to give me a lift. He had one cassette in his car – *Physical Graffiti* by Led Zeppelin. We played it countless times, and although it's a great album, it was many months before I could hear it again.

We drove up through France, eating snacks, and spending the Friday night in the car. On the Saturday afternoon, he dropped me off at Avranches, which is about seventy-five miles south of Cherbourg. He was going on to Roscoff to catch a ferry to Plymouth, and I thought it would be easier to travel via Cherbourg to Southampton rather than Dover to Calais.

We had an enormous lunch at a restaurant just outside Avranches. He left me at the roadside so I could hitch a lift. It took ages to get a lift. I started hitching at about 4 p.m. and was still there at seven. A miserable Frenchman gave me a lift about halfway up, and fortunately a friendly young French guy saw me in the darkness at the side of the road and took me all the way to the dockside. The next ferry was in the morning, so I spent the night sleeping on a bench in the waiting room.

I queued up around 7 a.m. to get on to the boat. The weather was dull and raining, but I managed to get on the boat, and ended up at a table in the bar next to a couple of girls. The boat left Cherbourg, and then the wind picked up, and the crossing became rough, really rough. It was a five-hour journey, and it was not pleasant. One of the girls started looking green and went up on deck (with practically everyone else). It was a bit like watching an episode of Monty Python. People with stronger stomachs went up to the bar, ordered food, then went red, white, and green. There was vomit all over the floor.

Amazingly, I felt OK. It was almost twenty-four hours since I'd last eaten, and there was probably nothing in my stomach to throw up. The remaining girl also hadn't eaten, so she was OK too. After a couple of hours, I walked up to the bar, taking care not to slide on the puke-covered floor, and ordered a couple of beers. People looked at me as if I was mad (or a hero).

We started to approach Southampton. I'd got on well with the girl at my table. She and her friend were going to catch the train to London. She lived at Kensington and offered to put me up for the night. It was tempting, but I wanted to save my money by hitching. Also, I was keen to see my family again.

I exited the boat and started to thumb a lift. Once more, I waited for ages. Eventually, a guy stopped. I asked him where he was going. His reply amazed me. He basically said not to ask him where he was going, but to tell him where I was going. So, I said London, to which he said that he wasn't going there. I remarked that this was a pointless conversation and went to shut his passenger door when he told me to get in. I asked him why, if he wasn't going to London. He responded by saying he was going that way and could take me ten miles up the road. It was raining, and I couldn't be bothered to argue. So I got into his car and spent the next twenty minutes being told how to correctly hitch a lift.

He dropped me off at a main roundabout. I stood for almost an hour in the drizzle, when a van suddenly stopped. There were two guys driving to London. They literally slung me and my luggage in the back and drove off. They were actually friendly guys. I think the state of me appealed to their better nature, and they took me all the way to Euston Station.

I reverse charged a call to my parents and told them I'd be at Bletchley station in an hour. I climbed on to the train, and about 9 p.m., arrived at my destination. I got off the train, made my way down the stairs to the station exit, and walked to my dad's car . My brother Simon had actually gone on to the platform to greet me, but didn't spot me. As I ambled towards the waiting cars, my mother turned to my dad in their car and said, 'Don't you see some sights at railway stations. Look at that bedraggled scruffy chap with a beard, long hair, and hat carrying his bedroll and a guitar.'

That chap was me. No wonder my brother didn't recognise me!

In summary, I found my working holiday in France was a real turning point in my life. I discovered how it felt to be independent – away from family and educational institutions which had, up until then, been such a formative part of my life.

I learnt a lot about myself – not immediately, but upon reflection.

I noticed how to properly engage with people, how to build and influence relationships, and most importantly, how to use and trust my intuition – my gut feeling.

These were all great lessons, which have played an instrumental part throughout my life.

I also developed my sense of humour, particularly in playing the odd joke or prank on people. Humour is a great tool when used appropriately.

Above all, I recognised the importance of being authentic. As my dad used to tell me, *you can fool other people, but you can't fool yourself.* When you look in the mirror, that's you who you're looking at. Be true to yourself.

RETURN TO ARGÉLÈS AND THE LOVELY LANGUEDOC

1976

After my experience working as a courier, I'd managed to encourage my parents to visit the area. They suggested a holiday at the campsite where I worked. However, I felt Le Camping Soleil would be better. It was on the beach, and had more facilities, including a decent disco.

I had a different girlfriend that year. Jan had studied a degree in French at Manchester Poly. We were pretty keen on each other. So, much to my delight, Mum and Dad suggested that Jan came with us. There would be room in the car, as my brother Simon was working at a hotel in Jersey – L'Horizon at St Brelades Bay – all that summer.

My brother Hugh was sixteen, having just taken his O Levels that year. I don't know whether the thought of his brother bringing his girlfriend would make any difference to him, but hey!

We drove down towards Argélès, towing our caravan. I remember Dad not feeling well on the journey down. He'd picked up a virus, so we took our time driving the long journey south.

Earlier that summer, I'd written to the reception at Camping Soleil to book a spot. I hadn't heard back but thought that was pretty much par for the course in France. After almost three days of driving, we arrived at Le Soleil around 6 p.m. I walked into the reception and introduced myself. However, there was no receipt or confirmation of my booking. The campsite was full. There was nothing that could be done. I was furious and embarrassed.

Dad was pretty relaxed and suggested we try Camping Le Bois Fleuri where I'd worked the year before. We drove into the site entrance and walked into the reception. The camp hostess, Wazzle, immediately recognised me and was effusive in her welcome. She hugged my father, which hugely endeared him to her. 'Bien sûr, Nigel. Of course we have a place for you and your delightful family.'

She showed us to a really good spot – probably one of the best in the whole campsite – and we set up camp. Later that evening, I took us all to a restaurant in Argélès, where both Mum and Dad were highly suspicious of what we ate, but we all survived. Dad remarked that next time, he'd choose the restaurant.

Word had got round the camp staff that I was there, and over the next day or two, they all came around to say hallo. I was deeply touched. The camp owner, Monsieur JP, brought us a bottle of wine, and Wazzle constantly charmed my father. She told him that he looked like my brother, not my father. His virus cleared up pretty quickly!

Meanwhile, Mad Albert (the dustman) would stop and shake Mum's hand whenever he saw her. She kept saying that as flattered as she was; she didn't know where his hand had previously been, which meant she had to go and wash her hands each time she met him.

Dad loved to watch people and often gave them a nickname. Thus, Penguin was born – a guy whose tent was quite nearby. He told Dad he'd driven directly to the campsite from Calais all in one day, which Dad knew was complete cobblers. The guy was called Penguin because he walked around in tight swim shorts, his legs and body moving just like a penguin. He was quite hapless, which caused us a great deal of mirth. But he clearly thought Dad was his friend, as he came up to speak with him at every opportunity. Yeah, right!

I was in my element back at the campsite. I knew most of the staff. We were treated like special guests, and I fell into old habits, such as drinking directly from the water taps. Water in France at that time wasn't entirely potable, and Brits used to place little tablets into their water containers to purify the water. I'd obviously developed a resistance to the water bugs the previous year, but not so this year.

I woke up feeling queasy one morning and felt so rough I spent the day in bed. I was even worse the next day and stopped eating altogether. I had chronic diarrhoea and a temperature. I visited a doctor, who prescribed a diet of rice and carrots for a few days. Mum was a star and obtained and prepared the necessary ingredients. Within twenty-four hours, I was feeling much better.

We had a good holiday, lazing on the beach or around the pool. I think Hugh got a bit bored, given that most of my attention was focused on Jan and vice versa, but Mum and Dad took him out on day trips, including to Spain.

We eventually said a long goodbye to all the staff at the campsite and had a gentle drive back to the UK.

AUTUMN IN BRITTANY

1978

In September, Mum and Dad said they were planning a trip to Brittany in October – Brittany Breaks with Brittany Ferries. I casually mentioned I hadn't had a proper holiday that year. I was working at British Home Stores and had just secured promotion to the new BHS store at Bromley. I was due to start there in late October. I'd booked a week off beforehand, which just happened to coincide with the week Mum and Dad had planned their holiday. At the same time, Hugh was on half-term. He was in his A level year, and I think my parents were reluctant to leave him at home for a week in case he had friends round, parties, etc. They suggested to Hugh that he came along too.

So we both gatecrashed Mum and Dad's break. I remember the first night we arrived in France. We got to our hotel. Mum and Dad checked in to their room, and Hugh and I to ours. There was a significant difference in quality, which we later mentioned to Dad. He reminded us who was paying for the holiday, and that we were latecomers. Nuff said!

The food was good at all the hotels we stayed at. Hugh ate seafood every night. He had the knack of cutting off all the joints of the various fish (crab, lobster etc.), then noisily sucking out every morsel of meat.

He was also heavily into motorbikes. Although he didn't possess one, he probably knew more about Norton Commandos and Kwacky (Kawasaki) 900s than most and had a pile of motorbike mags in the back seat, which he read voraciously.

The holiday passed uneventfully and quite quickly until the final day. Hugh had been complaining of stomach-ache the night before, and the next day he was like a bear with a sore head. I was persuaded to take him to a pharmacist to seek an appropriate remedy.

This was going to be a challenge. I didn't have a French dictionary with me, so I took the plunge, assuming that as most French words ending in -tion are the same as their English equivalent.

I stood at the counter and tentatively said, 'Constipation?' The woman nodded, so I then said, 'Mon frère ici – il est constipé' *My brother is constipated.* Except I spoke as if I was constipated, pushing the words out with difficulty as if I was straining. Hugh looked seriously unimpressed.

'Ah oui,' the lady replied. And gave me some medication. Knowing the French were slightly different in their approach to medication, I wasn't certain if the tablets should be consumed orally, or via the back passage. Holding the packet in one hand, I proceeded to push it in the direction of Hugh's bum.

'Ici?' I asked.

'Ah mais non!' exclaimed the sales assistant. 'Par la bouche.' *In the mouth.*

Hugh, who'd gone a deep shade of red, looked relieved and couldn't wait to leave the shop.

The medication seemed to work, and the rest of the day passed peacefully.

We drove up to Caen to catch our ferry, to be told that there was a strike, and that the only crossing we'd be able to catch would be the following day, from Roscoff to Plymouth. This was going to make a substantial impact on our journey home, arriving late on the Sunday evening rather than Saturday night as planned.

Dad, although annoyed, took this with his usual aplomb and remained calm. He suggested we drive in the direction of Roscoff – a distance of some 200 miles – and stop for dinner en route. We found a restaurant and ordered food.

I remember Hugh and I feeling pretty disenchanted with the whole delay. To make matters worse, the food in the restaurant wasn't up to scratch, and the service was also quite poor. The tablecloths on the tables were made of paper, and towards the end of the meal Hugh and I vented our spleens writing our thoughts about the food and service all over the tablecloths.

Hugh was energised now the tablets had kicked in, and he wasn't finished yet in his frustration. As we came out of the restaurant, one of the chefs wheeled an enormous dustbin into the street, ready for collection the following morning. Hugh saw this as bait, and a suitable means for exercising his displeasure. He gave the dustbin an almighty kick, which resulted in it rolling down the road and crashing into a wall. The bin fell over with the impact, and its contents went everywhere. Mum and Dad looked a little shocked while I laughed my head off. 'I think it would be wise to make a move now,' said Dad, and on that note, we got into the car and started the long drive to Roscoff.

THE 1990s

DOING BUSINESS IN FRANCE

1992

It had been fourteen years since I'd been to France. During the 1980s, I was busy making a living, working hard, and following my ambitions. My holidays were more adventurous, in that I was keen to venture further than France, and instead went to Malta, Mallorca, and Lanzarote.

In February 1992, with the UK still stuck in recession, the company I was working for – BFN – was keen to explore all feasible routes of business to gain sales. As the company's Business Development Manager, I was tasked with finding new clients. At a sales meeting, one of the senior managers asked about the potential in Europe. It was discussed, and agreed that it would be worth exploring, but the MD commented that the business needed someone who could speak languages to help penetrate the key markets in France or Germany. The room fell silent.

'Well,' I said tentatively. 'I did French and German at A level.'

'So you can speak these languages?' asked another manager.

'Well – yes I can,' I replied. 'Although I haven't used them for many years.'

It was agreed that I should examine the potential in France to start with, given it was so close. I undertook some research. I needed to find someone who could boost our efforts through some form of partnership. During a wet Wednesday afternoon in February, I was searching in a European business directory, and came across a company called 'Sell in France'. I sent them a fax and received an immediate response from a chap called Conrad. He was British and lived in Paris.

After consultation with my MD and senior colleagues, it was agreed I should go to Paris and meet Conrad. At the same time, I planned to visit a former senior colleague, Mike, who had gone on to run a former French subsidiary of the group BFN was previously owned by.

I decided the easiest and cheapest way to travel was by car. I booked a ticket on the Dover to Calais ferry early one morning and drove down to Paris. I hadn't driven in Paris before, let alone the notorious Périphérique. After one very close shave, when I took a wrong turn and saw a large Saab 9000 hurtling towards me (which fortunately braked just in time), I managed to find Conrad's office in the north-west of Paris.

As soon as I arrived, he took me to lunch, to a small restaurant at the end of the road from his office. Conrad was an interesting guy, very eccentric, extrovert, and flamboyant. He spoke French fluently, but with the most appalling accent. A couple of months later, I commented on this, and asked him that if he spoke French so well, why he hadn't bothered to perfect his accent. He grinned and said that his bad accent was more memorable. He went on to explain that there weren't many British people who could speak French fluently, so that in itself was quite unusual. He discovered that if he could combine his French-speaking skills with a heavy English accent, it would endear the French to him, and in turn this would make him almost unique.

During our lunch, Conrad asked me lots of questions, and began to make notes. Except that he wrote his notes on the tablecloth, which fortunately was paper. He started to draw pictures and diagrams, which he explained helped him to plan. At the end of the meal, the waiter went to remove the tablecloth, which Conrad snatched back, folded up, and took it with us to his office. When we got back, he laid it out on his desk, complete with wine and food stains and breadcrumbs.

We talked for about four hours, and were regularly interrupted by his secretary Lisette, who made countless cups of coffee. Towards the end of our discussion, Conrad suggested the British Embassy might also be able to help. He made a couple of calls and secured me a meeting for the next day. As we wrapped up our meeting, I asked how practical it might be to leave my car at my hotel and catch the Metro to the Embassy. He looked at me in amazement and said I should drive. I mentioned how the traffic in Paris was somewhat mesmerising and tricky, and he simply told me not to worry but to go for it.

The following morning, I set off, initially to a shop fitting company near to Versailles who was known to us, and who we hoped might partner our activities. I then drove into Paris to the British Embassy. After that meeting, I drove back through Paris, out to the south, and down the autoroute to meet my friend Mike in Migennes.

IN JUNE, I went out to Paris again to meet Conrad. He was keen to work on a retainer basis, and I was equally keen to see what he'd do. We drew up a shortlist of companies who might be willing to become a distributor for BFN's range of products, and spent several hours discussing pricing, terms etc, so he could put together a meaningful proposal. We also went to meet a company in central Paris, who Conrad had spoken with recently. They seemed quite interested, and we agreed a date for their directors to visit us in July.

Conrad was quite crazy. He always wore the same suit (which smelt sweaty.). He drove a people carrier – a Renault Espace – at breakneck speed through Paris, in which he'd drink coffee from a large china mug which he'd brought from home. He also seemed to know a lot of people, especially women, to whom he'd wave and shout out to. He even gave a lift to one who he saw crossing the road, who climbed into the car and smothered him with kisses. Conrad had a complicated personal life; he was divorced with a son (his ex-wife was French) and was currently living with an English woman and her young children, whom he clearly adored.

He took me to an amazing restaurant – La Taverne du Sergéant Recruiter, near Notre Dame. We ate like lords, through several courses. He was thoroughly entertaining company. However, I did have a few misgivings about whether he would actually deliver for us.

The final time I saw Conrad was in October that year. He hadn't achieved very much, but there was a shop fitting exhibition in Paris. We agreed it would be good for us both to spend a few days there, to meet prospective partners/distributors. I arrived on the Monday morning, and just before we left Conrad's office for the show, his secretary rushed into his office, very agitated. It appeared she'd just taken a call from a client who was on the point of going bust, and who owed Conrad a significant amount of money. He asked her to book him a train to Bordeaux where his client was based and said he couldn't accompany me to the meetings at the exhibition, as he needed to extract a cheque from them. This was unfortunate. He gave me a list of the contacts he'd made and suggested I visit them once I got to the show.

I spent the next day, Tuesday, going around the exhibition, meeting these so-called interested parties, to discover that none of them had heard of Conrad. He hadn't actually been in touch with any of them. His only saving grace was that he'd developed a little further with the Paris-based company who came to the UK in July, and he'd arranged for me to tour around central Paris with their sales director the following day, looking at some shops with examples of their work.

After a fruitless day at the show, I was looking forward to the evening. My friend Mike was coming to Paris, and we'd arranged to meet that evening. Mike arrived, looking unusually flustered and annoyed. It turned out that his company was on the point of going into receivership. He'd also spent a few hours at the show and had to endure all the gossip and questions that his competitors were firing at him. Mike said he wanted a night on the town and to forget about his troubles.

He took me to a restaurant, and later on to a club, where he knew the owner. Within ten minutes, the owner had brought some girls to our table, and before long, Mike and one of the girls were engaged in serious conversation, then dancing, before cuddling up together. The other woman, who was about ten years older than me, started a conversation with me and then pulled me onto the dance floor. She wore a shimmering short dress, and let it slip she had nothing on underneath. If she asked me once, she asked me several times.

'Où est ton hotel?' It became pretty clear she was a prostitute. When I showed I wasn't interested, she stormed off.

Eventually, at around 2 a.m., Mike decided we should go to another club. Once more, he knew the people there. While we had a drink at the bar, an attractive black woman came up and started to talk to me. She too was a 'lady of the night'. She was quite pleasant and suggested we went to a room downstairs. By this time, all I wanted to do was go to sleep. I explained I had an early meeting planned – which was in six hours' time. She seemed to understand and suggested I came back another night when I had more time.

Mike and I left about five. He agreed he'd drive to my hotel. Except I couldn't remember exactly where it was. Eventually I recalled it was a Mercure near to Conrad's office. The Périphérique was not quite empty, but I'm sure Mike drove around it twice in his attempt to find my hotel. He finally dropped me off about 7.45 a.m.

I staggered up to my room. Fortunately, I hadn't had much to drink. But I needed to shower and change before Conrad arrived to collect me at half eight. When he did get there, he immediately saw how knackered I looked, and laughed. He took me to the French company's office and only told the directors what I'd been up to the night before! The MD laughed, but the sales director, who was about sixty years old, looked less than impressed.

We spent the morning visiting various shops. I found it incredibly difficult to keep my eyes open as he drove through Paris. Eventually, he took me for lunch in quite a smart restaurant. I'll never forget what happened next: we ate our way through a starter and a main course, and I couldn't resist profiteroles in chocolate sauce for dessert. That day, I was wearing a green silk tie. As I was eating my dessert, I managed to drip a large spoonful of chocolate sauce on to my beautiful tie. I dabbed at it. I made it worse. The tie was ruined. The guy I was with looked absolutely disgusted. I'm afraid I was a very poor ambassador for England that day. He paid the bill, walked to his car, removed my suitcase from his boot, handed it to me, and suggested I called a taxi to the airport.

NAJAC – ONE OF THE MOST BEAUTIFUL VILLAGES IN FRANCE

1992

Enthused and fired up by my reconnection with France, my wife at the time and I decided to go to France that summer. Our daughter Lucy was five, and my parents also expressed their interest in joining us. My good friend Alan owned a property in the Aveyron area, in the beautiful village of Najac.

We left home early on a Monday morning in mid-August, caught the ferry from Dover, and drove through France. Dad and I could split the driving, which helped. We stayed overnight in a Campanile about halfway down, and we arrived at Najac the following afternoon. Alan was there with his son, and he spent an hour showing us around before leaving to go back to the UK.

Najac is one of the 'plus beaux villages de France' (most beautiful villages in France). It has a ruined castle, and ramparts which we'd walk along to get to the village centre. Alan's house had a ground floor with two floors above. Off the first floor was a fantastic terrace, where we spent much of our time eating and sitting in the sun. We'd bought a litre of Aberlour malt whisky on the boat, and Dad and I spent many happy evenings on the terrace after we'd eaten, sipping whisky, talking, and looking up at the stars.

There was a magnificent outdoor swimming pool just outside Najac, which we decided to visit. We had the usual shenanigans however when we arrived, as in France, males can only enter a public swimming pool wearing swimming trunks (i.e., Speedo style). Swim shorts, which are worn in the UK, are forbidden at French pools, as they're deemed to be unhygienic! This meant I had to go back, walk into the village, and buy some trunks at an extortionate price, to gain access to the pool.

After a couple of days at Najac, we had a slight incident. Mum noticed that effluent was coming out of a drain hole just outside the front door, onto the road. We couldn't figure out why. I called Alan and explained. He suggested I contact a plumber he knew called Jules. I spoke to Jules, who said he'd come the next day, just before lunch. By that time, the situation had worsened considerably, and there was a pungent smell.

Jules duly arrived and had a look. 'Voilà' he said. He knew what the problem was. He asked me where the hosepipe was. I handed it to him, and he turned on the tap full blast. He pointed the hose into a drain on the terrace, which he explained was the main sewage pipe from the bathroom. After a few minutes, nothing seemed to be happening. So he inserted the hose into the drain and pushed the pipe deeply down. Eventually, he managed to clear the blockage.

He smiled and said, 'C'est fait.' *Job done.* He pulled the hosepipe out of the drain, which was covered in what you can imagine. He handed the hose to me and proceeded to shake hands with all of us. Mum's face was an absolute picture.

'I was in the middle of preparing lunch,' she remarked. 'And I know exactly where his hands had been. Urgh – disgusting man!'

During the latter part of our holiday, Lucy was keen to go to the seaside. We looked at the map. It looked doable to me. Probably a two- three-hour journey, maximum. But if we left early in the morning, we could be there and back in a day.

However, the traffic wasn't kind. We eventually arrived at Canet Plage on the Languedoc coast around two in the afternoon. As we walked to the beach, Lucy said she'd like to make sandcastles, so we bought her a bucket and spade.

We got to the beach and walked a fair distance towards the sea. We sat down, got out the new spade, and Lucy started to dig. I could see this was going to take her a long time, so I offered to take over. I pushed the spade into the sand, and as I started to dig, the shaft on the spade suddenly broke.

Cue lots of tears.

I returned to the shop, bought a much more robust tool to do the job, and we spent the rest of the afternoon building sandcastles, playing catch, and paddling our feet in the water.

The holiday went by quickly, but we ended in style. We'd booked a ferry just before midnight. After driving around the Paris Périphérique, we went north and arrived at Chantilly around 6 p.m. We decided to stop for something to eat. Dad explained Chantilly was quite upmarket. He and I changed out of our shorts at the roadside.

We found an absolutely superb restaurant, where we combined the rest of our cash and ate like kings over the most splendid dinner, before driving to Calais through a massive thunderstorm.

BUSINESS AND PLEASURE IN FRANCE

1994 – 1996

The mid-1990s were laced with both happiness and unhappiness.

My second daughter, Gemma, was born in June 1994, which was a hugely happy time.

I was also made redundant from my job at BFN that summer. The company was sold and acquired by an Aylesbury based business. Many employees were offered the chance to relocate, including myself, but the redundancy payments were generous, and I decided to take that option. I'd seen this coming and had started to look for another job earlier that summer. I found a job with a London based, family-owned company called LDS, who designed and manufactured shop display fixtures. They were looking for a European Sales Manager and given my shop fitting background and experience, and my ability to speak French and German, I was offered the job.

They were keen for me to find and develop distributors throughout Europe, principally in Germany. I disclosed that my German was quite rusty, and they agreed to contribute toward some brush-up German lessons before I joined.

The first couple of months were mostly spent in London and Germany, and then I was encouraged to look for distributors in France. I spent a week in Paris, and went back several other times to France, mostly in the Normandy, Loire, and Alsace areas.

In the summer of 1995, my marriage broke up. It was a difficult and sad time for all of us. I decided to throw myself into my job, and I travelled regularly throughout Europe. I moved out of our family home and spent the next fifteen months living with a former colleague (who was also separated from his wife) at his house in Gravesend.

It was a lonely time, and I felt I'd almost gone back to my early 20s when I first started work. LDS were very supportive of my situation and were encouraged to see my commitment to my job.

At the end of 1995, I endured a miserable Christmas. I was on my own, missing my children, with time on my hands over the holiday period. Some friends of mine invited me to a party on Boxing Day evening, and when I arrived, there was just one other guest present – Patricia. I knew her as her children went to the same school as Lucy. She was a single parent who'd been on her own for a few years. Suffice it to say, our mutual friends' matchmaking was a great success. We were two lonely adults who discovered we shared a lot in common – interests and values – and we gradually started to date.

I continued to travel extensively. I almost always drove, and by April 1996, my company car was changed due to the mileage I'd racked up. At the same time, I was informed I had a week's holiday remaining. I'd taken little holiday the previous year, apart from a week in the summer with my daughters and the usual extended Christmas/New Year holiday period. I was planning to take them for a week in the Easter holidays, but this didn't get approval.

My relationship with Patricia was beginning to blossom, so I decided to take her to France for a few days. She'd been to France for skiing holidays, but this was largely confined to the Alps. I suggested a short trip to Normandy, and off we went in the new company car.

I hadn't booked anywhere, so we were able to keep our plans fluid. We drove to Rouen where we spent a pleasant afternoon and continued towards Alençon. By seven we still hadn't found anywhere we fancied, until we drove into a small village, where we noticed an Auberge. We went in and spoke to the proprietor – a lady of around fifty something – who showed us a room with great enthusiasm and spoke encouragingly about their cuisine. I looked at Patricia; she nodded approvingly. The owner rubbed her hands with glee and then took Patricia's hands. She looked into her eyes and said, 'Do you have children?'

I replied, 'Yes, four.'

Meaning I have two and so does Patricia.

Madame eyed her up and down carefully and said, 'Quatre enfants? C'est pas possible!'

We laughed – it was too complicated to explain. Her voice was amazing – deep and throaty – almost like a cement mixer. We later discovered her husband, who looked at least ten years younger, was the chef.

We went down to the restaurant. Madame explained we were in the Calvados region, and Calvados cuisine was their speciality. She was right! Every dish was laced with Calvados in some form or other. We ate like lords, and when we ordered coffee at the end of the meal, she brought us a glass each of Calvados on the house. We slept incredibly well.

The following morning, we went down to breakfast. On our table was a large baguette, several home-made jams, and a large slab of butter with a menacing-looking knife sticking out of it. We were served coffee in bowls. A truly rustic French breakfast, which was completely new to Patricia. While we ate, various delivery vans arrived with meat, cheese, vegetables, bread, etc., and Madame – who we nicknamed 'Maman' – negotiated furiously with each of the reps/drivers, making sure she got the best possible food at the best possible prices.

We settled the bill and chatted as we prepared to leave. She gave us both a bear hug, and as her whiskers tickled my cheeks, I encountered stubble-burn for the first time.

We spent a couple of memorable days in Normandy, eating beautiful food, especially local cheeses such as Camembert, brie, and best of all livarot. We visited the Bayeux Tapestry, had early evening drinks by the harbour at Honfleur, and ended up with a splendid lunch at Dieppe, where we'd previously bought a giant size portion of livarot. It was a lovely trip, albeit too short, and we came away with fond memories of Madame (whose name was Solange), and who we'd meet again.

In September that year, Patricia's mother Lilo, sadly passed away after a long illness with cancer. She was only sixty-nine. Although I didn't know her very well, we had become very fond of each other in the short time since we'd met.

Lilo was German and moved to the UK in the early 1950s. She found a job as an au pair for a family living at Wimbledon. While she was there, she met her husband, Harry, who was the local postman. Patricia and her twin brother, George, were brought up in Morden, Surrey, and her parents continued to live there until they moved down to Kent in the 1980s.

Lilo was a warm-hearted lady, with a strong personality. She very much approved of my relationship with Patricia and we all miss her dearly.

Toward the end of 1996, we had a big family day out in France. My dad was seventy in the November. I found a restaurant in Ardres, just ten kilometres from Calais, and I called in on my way back to the UK after a business trip. I spoke to the owners and explained we wanted to celebrate my father's seventieth birthday. They offered to make a cake instead of a dessert and suggested a chocolate cake.

So my entire family – Dad, Mum, my brother Simon, his wife Julie and son Jamie, my other brother Hugh and his wife Mindy and daughter Rhiain, and Patricia, her two daughters Vicky and Jo, and my two daughters Lucy and Gemma all caught a ferry from Dover to Calais.

We arrived at the restaurant at half twelve, and were, in fact, the only customers there, so we had the whole place to ourselves. The food was excellent, and the chocolate cake was magnificent. It was hard stopping the kids poking their fingers into the icing!

We sang 'Happy Birthday' to Dad, and we had a wonderful time. The owners looked after us superbly. We stopped for some duty-free shopping and arrived back in Dover around 7.30 p.m.

THE FOLLOWING YEAR, in May 1997, I took Patricia back to France.

I mentioned before that one of my closest friends, Alan, owns a little house in a beautiful village called Najac, which is located in the Aveyron.

We had an interesting start. Our crossing was booked for 6.30 on the Monday morning. we got up early, left Patricia's house in Appledore, and drove to Dover. It was a beautiful, warm sunny morning. What could possibly go wrong?!

I exited the M20 and continued on the A20 towards Dover. Just as we approached the top of the hill, where we could see the sun shimmering on the sea, I suddenly swore very loudly and badly. It was a bit like the start of *Four Weddings and a Funeral* but without the 'ety'. This hill has since been known as 'Fuck Hill'.

'Fuck, fuck, fuck,' I shouted.

'What's wrong?' asked Patricia.

I'd suddenly realised I'd forgotten the keys to Alan's house. I had to turn around, drive the thirty-five minutes back to collect the keys, and drive back to Dover. I remember Patricia being incredibly relaxed over the whole thing.

'Don't worry,' she said comfortingly. 'Just look forward to a good English breakfast on the boat.'

After a fast drive back up the M20, I found the keys and shot back to Dover. We caught a slightly later ferry, where we were still in time for the magnificent, cooked breakfast P&O Ferries served. We arrived at Calais mid-morning and embarked on the drive through France.

I'd estimated that Najac was about an eleven-hour drive from Calais. I just wanted to get there before 9 p.m. There's an excellent restaurant in a hotel in the village centre, which I knew wouldn't accept orders after that time. The journey went well and we arrived at Alan's just before nine.

We didn't bother going inside, I just parked the car, and we walked into the village centre, which was about ten minutes away.

Patricia marvelled at the beauty of the walk along the narrow, cobbled streets, overlooking the ravine and hills on either side.

At around 8.55 p.m. we walked in and were directed to a table. Phew! It had been a long day. At least we had the house keys.

Patricia and I spent a few very enjoyable days in Najac. We didn't venture far from the village. The weather was glorious, and we spent most of time sunbathing on the veranda. We did go out one day, down towards the Gaillac wine-making area. We found an odd little restaurant, which was owned by a really funny guy. We were the only people eating lunch there, so he gave us his full attention. It turned out he was a former rugby player. He was huge, with massive shoulders and a big grin across his rather sweaty face. The three of us started to banter; he was flirting with Patricia, and he brought some pink roses to the table, which he assured us were edible. I think he was both surprised and pleased that we joined in and ate them. As a consequence, he returned with an amuse-bouche consisting of the pink rose petals stuffed with herbs and cream cheese. They were delicious.

After we'd finished eating, as a measure of his enjoyment of having us eat there, he gave me an enormous cigar. He insisted I lit it then and there and then persuaded Patricia to have a few puffs.

After leaving the restaurant, we visited a vineyard and were greeted by the owner's wife. She mistakenly thought we were loaded with money and proceeded to take us on a very lengthy tour and shared a ridiculous amount of totally superfluous information. Patricia and I looked at each other; we couldn't just leave – that would be far too rude. At the same time, we realised this was our last day and could feel the warmth of the sunshine outside while we led around the various wine cellars. Eventually, the lady asked us how many cases we wanted to buy. I explained I only wanted four bottles. She was mortified, and that was pretty much the end of it. She sold us the four bottles and sent us on our way with a scowl!

We had a lovely time at Alan's house in Najac. A few months later, when Patricia and I were reminiscing about our time there over a glass of wine one evening, I decided to play a joke on Alan. I knew he was in Najac that week and was accompanied by his sixteen-year-old son and his son's friend. I also knew that by around 9 p.m., Alan would have had enough of the two teenage boys, and he'd probably had a few glasses of wine, and would perhaps be enjoying a whisky on the terrace.

I telephoned him. When he answered, he did sound rather sleepy and slightly fuzzy due, no doubt, to a few glasses of whatever he was drinking. I greeted him in French, and proceeded to speak in French very, very fast, punctuated by some very heavily accented English. Alan asked me to slow down – he kept repeating, 'Lentement s'il vous plaît.' *Slowly, please.*

Eventually, I explained that the water was being turned off in the village for two days due to a major plumbing problem. Alan took a while to realise the implication of what I was saying, and suddenly seemed to sober up, when he understood the seriousness of the situation. I explained that all household appliances would be inoperative; no toilets or washing facilities. I paused to let him take this in.

'And for how long?' Alan spluttered.

'Deux jours, Monsieur.' *Two days, sir.*

I went on to explain that the hotel in the village would continue to have its water supply, and that residents in the village would be able to make use of its facilities.

'But, Monsieur' – I paused – 'there is one more thing you need to understand.'

'What's that?' asked Alan, who was sounding very weary and stressed.

'When you join ze queue for ze washing and er... ze toilets... please bring your own toilet paper.'

'Whaaaat?' exclaimed Alan.

It was at that point that I completely lost it and dissolved into helpless, uncontrollable laughter.

'Who is this?' said Alan.

I tried to speak but kept losing it and continued laughing.

'Is that you, Wilson? It is, isn't it?'

'Yes,' I wheezed.

'You bastard. You utter rotter. You really took me in there.' Alan started to laugh, as he realised the joke, and probably also in relief, in discovering the water wouldn't be turned off.

We still laugh about this over twenty years later!

MY FIRST BUSINESS trip to France on behalf of LDS was interesting! I drove to Paris to attend a trade exhibition called Equip'mag. One of my objectives was to hunt down a French shop equipment company, who had produced an unauthorised copy of my company's equipment. I found their stand and asked to speak with the boss, whose name I already knew. The boss identified himself – a tall, dark-haired man with a nonchalant air, and then began one of the most unusual conversations I'd ever had.

I introduced myself and said who I worked for. I drew his attention to some display equipment on his stand, which was a direct, but poor-quality copy. The guy just raised his eyebrows. Nonplussed, I went on to explain that copying my company's display equipment was a major contravention of our patent. He simply raised his eyebrows again. So I asked him if he understood that my company would take legal action against his company if he continued this violation. He looked at me and shrugged.

This was getting a bit difficult. It would have been a challenge if we were talking in English, but I was speaking with him in French. I asked the guy how much of the copied equipment his company had. He just stared at me, tilted his head on one side, and pouted his lips.

This clearly wasn't working. I decided to pull back a bit. I suggested we arranged a meeting at his office after the show, so we could have a proper conversation without the distraction of people coming on to his stand. He looked at me, turned down his lips, and shrugged again. I got my diary out to encourage him. He gave me a pitiful look and then turned away. I called after him and told him that due to his refusal to discuss the matter, we'd be in touch with our lawyers. The guy just walked away. During the entire, albeit brief, encounter, he hadn't spoken a word.

DURING THE NEXT year, 1995, I decided that business opportunities offered far greater potential in Germany and Holland, so I left France alone for a while.

However, I went back to France on a business trip in early September that year. This time I travelled down to Angers, then along the Loire, before descending to Dijon, and then coming back up via Metz. I stayed in various hotels, mostly Campaniles, which, while basic, offered a consistent standard of cleanliness and service, and the restaurant food was always good. These were days before satellite navigation. I used to plan the journeys using maps and atlases, writing the routes down on Post-it notes which I'd stick to the underside of the sun visor. France was always a challenge, especially Paris.

I REMEMBER ONE evening when I'd driven along the southern section of the Périphérique from a meeting in Versailles across towards Bagnolet in the east. The weather was atrocious, and the traffic just crawled stop-start all the way along. Eventually, after a couple of hours, I saw the exit for Bagnolet, and to my relief, the illuminated green sign for the Campanile was shining close by.

I exited the Périphérique and drove in the direction of my hotel, which I could no longer see. Every time I wanted to turn right I couldn't. When I finally turned left, I could see myself driving back towards another junction with the Périphérique, which I definitely wanted to avoid for fear of getting stuck in another traffic jam in the opposite direction. I drove round and round, occasionally seeing the hotel, but I just couldn't get near it.

In desperation, I turned into a very narrow side-street, then another and another, and suddenly found myself close to the hotel. I looked for a car park but couldn't see any signs. Eventually, I parked on the pavement outside the entrance to a building and ran into the hotel. I had to catch a lift to the reception on the third floor, and by the time I got there I had visions of my car being impounded or driven into. I waited five minutes to speak to someone who casually said the car park was beneath the hotel.

'But how do I get there?' I demanded. The receptionist looked at me coolly.

'You need to press the button, Monsieur,' she replied.

'Which button and where?' I almost shouted.

I was starting to panic about where I'd left my car. I was tired, hungry, and thirsty. It was 9.45 p.m., and I knew the restaurant would close at ten. She stared at me as though I was an idiot.

'It's on the wall by the shutter,' she said through clenched teeth.

'Where? Which road?' I roared. 'Left, right, or behind the hotel?'

'It's the first turning on the right to the left of the hotel.' she said, spitting out the words. At which point, she turned her back and walked away.

I ran out of the hotel and was relieved to see my car was still there. I jumped in, drove to where she told me, and lo-and-behold I saw the shutter and the button. I drove down into the car park, grabbed my luggage, and ran to the lift. By the time I got to the reception, it was 9.55 p.m.

'Please check me in,' I pleaded, and literally ran to the restaurant with my suitcase. I braced myself for an argument should I be too late. The waiter was fortunately understanding and helpful, though he did show some surprise when I asked for three bottles of beer (well – they are small in France) and a bottle of red wine!

Despite the frustrations of driving in urban France and finding my way (these were the days pre-satnav systems), as well as the apparent reluctance of French companies to express any interest in doing business together, I was still keen to find at least one distributor in France.

I renewed my intent and set about a plan of action whereby I'd spend a couple of months contacting a wide variety of French companies. I was prepared to travel through France. I spoke good French and was fascinated by the people, their customs, and the food.

I made another visit to a company at Angers, who had shown some interest. The owner of the business was quite engaging and had taken me out for a splendid lunch the last time I saw him. We agreed on a date to meet. He was delighted to see me and set about giving me a complete tour of his factory and offices. This took ages, largely because he shook hands with every employee he encountered. It was quite early in the day, around 10 a.m., and he'd obviously not left his office since arriving that morning. He told me there were around eighty employees working in the factory, and a further twenty or so in the offices. You can imagine how long it must have taken to get around. There were several female employees in the offices, so the greetings with them extended to 'les bises' – a kiss on both cheeks. And he also introduced me to several people, which naturally necessitated further handshaking.

I'm fascinated by the international process of shaking hands. In the UK, a handshake can be firm or floppy. Some men love the 'power handshake', which involves the squeezing of their hand around yours to the point it becomes painful, so that the squeezed hand quickly extricates itself from the handshaker. Round one to them!

Germans love a strong handshake, which is usually quite brief, consisting of just one shake. I remember when I was eighteen, visiting friends in Germany. I was introduced to an older, stocky man. He offered his hand, and I went into the handshake, except that one of my fingers was slightly bent (I clearly hadn't taken the handshaking protocol seriously enough). Rather than just accept my proffered hand and bent finger, he proceeded to move his hand away, and he actually straightened out my finger himself, before moving back into the handshake, and simultaneously giving me a grim stare.

I find that Americans will shake hands for longer than anyone else. They smile and talk and keep pumping away. That makes it hard to know when to pull away so that no offence is caused.

Asians, such as Indians and Chinese tend to have softer handshakes, which can feel quite insipid.

Most northern Europeans, such as the Dutch and Scandinavians have strong handshakes. And Russian men love the power handshake, staring you in the eye, willing you to submit.

The French love to shake hands. Sometimes it's a short one, other times it can go on for several shakes. In the countryside, where men are working outside, getting their hands dirty, they'll offer a wrist, or even an elbow. Almost anything – to maintain the physical act of touching as a greeting.

I MET WITH another French company, which actually became a distributor. The owner showed some interest in my company's products, and I invited him to come to London. He said he'd travel on the Eurostar and arrive the night before our meeting. He asked me to book him a double room in a decent hotel in central London. When I went to collect him the following morning, I found him with a female. I made the mistake of saying that this must be his wife. The lady shook her head and just said, 'Non'. It turned out she was one of the employees.

A couple of months later, I went to visit the company. As I went upstairs, the same lady came out of the owner's office and greeted me. She served me a coffee and went back into his office. While I waited outside, I could hear giggling and soft laughter. She eventually came out and took me into the office. The owner was friendly and welcoming, and looked a little ruffled.

I later discovered that they were both married, but not to each other. The female employee's husband worked for a company across the road, almost opposite. I wonder if he ever looked out of his window and saw them together. They were quite indiscreet. They took me out to lunch and sat next to each other, touching each other, and grinning like a pair of love-struck teenagers.

I MET ANOTHER Frenchman who was keen to become a distributor. He was a leading light in the trade industry (The French Shopfitting Association). He invited me to make a presentation to the panel of the Association's officers, who consisted of MDs from several shopfitting companies in France. This was a pretty big gig, and I prepared carefully. The meeting was in Paris, so I arrived the night before and stayed in a hotel close to the venue.

I got up early, had breakfast, and was about to make my way to the office when I received a call from the secretary of the Association. She explained there was a change of venue. She gave me the address, which was the opposite side of Paris, and said they were looking forward to seeing me in forty-five minutes. All my plans of getting there early, setting up my slide show, etc. were completely shot.

I arrived just in time, went through the endless routine of handshaking, and started my presentation. I was interrupted in the first minute by a large Frenchman who asked me something completely irrelevant. I replied, and carried on, when he interrupted me again, and asked me why I thought French companies might be interested in my company's products. I smiled and asked him to let me explain. A couple of minutes later, and another chap interrupted me to ask in which leading retail chains he could find the display equipment. I told him I was coming to that, and that became the form throughout the presentation. In a nutshell, they behaved like a bunch of badly behaved schoolkids, interrupting me, talking among themselves, laughing. and clearly taking the mickey.

I looked towards the guy who'd arranged the talk, and he just shrugged. It was one of the most difficult presentations I'd ever done, and it became hard to maintain any form of momentum, or patience for that matter. By the time my presentation had finished, I'd seriously had enough, and I was actually relieved that I wasn't asked to stay for lunch.

As I travelled through France, I mostly stayed in Campanile hotels. They all operated at a reasonable standard and price, and the restaurants were generally good. I had an unfortunate episode one night when I nearly set the place alight.

I was sitting alone at my table, and while I was waiting for my dessert, I was reading a newspaper – a large broadsheet – which I'd bought on the boat when I crossed the Channel that morning. I spread the paper out, forgetting there was a candle on the table. As I held the newspaper, I could smell burning. I was engrossed in whatever I was reading. What I couldn't see were the people opposite me, gesticulating wildly as my newspaper caught alight. Suddenly, the page I was reading started to disappear as the flames burnt their way through. I swore loudly and dropped the paper. I grabbed my serviette (which fortunately was linen), dunked it in my water glass, and blotted out the fire. There was carnage all over my table! Bits of charred, burning paper, water all over the place, and I managed to spill not just my wine glass but the whole bottle, which dropped onto the hard tiled floor and smashed. I had wine down my shirt and on my trousers, as well as all over my shoes.

People were staring at me as if I was completely mad. I must have looked quite crazy – reading a burning newspaper, and then flapping and scattering bits of paper all over the place. I'd made more mess than you'd find on the tray of a child's highchair. Then the waiter arrived with my dessert. He placed it in front of me and walked away. No help, no clearing up. Nothing. Nada. Rien. So, like any self-effacing Englishman, I picked up a clean napkin, placed it on my lap, rescued the scraps of newspaper, and laid them in front of me, as I continued to read and eat my dessert. The other guests shrugged and went back to their food. It was almost as if nothing had happened. After all, why should some weird Englishman spoil their meals?

As time went on, I had more meetings around France. A company in Marseilles expressed a great deal of interest, as well as another one in Lyons. I decided to kill two birds with one stone, and organised a rail trip from Paris to Marseilles, then on to Lyons the following day, and back to Paris. The train journey was wonderful, albeit the carriage down to Marseilles was absolutely packed. The only eventful thing that happened was a couple getting on to the train at the last minute. They had two large suitcases and struggled to find space to put them. Eventually, the male partner lifted one of them and rammed it into the luggage rack above the seats. It clearly wasn't rammed in enough however because when the train pulled out of Paris and went into a bend, the suitcase came flying out from the rack and on to the floor. How it missed any passengers was remarkable, which was very fortunate, as someone could have been seriously injured.

When I got back to Paris the following evening, I had to drive up towards Normandy for an appointment in Alençon the next day. I decided to stay overnight, 'chez Maman'. I'd already called ahead and booked a room. When I arrived, around 8.45 p.m., the place was almost empty. After a breathtaking bear hug from her, I was told the chef was off duty that night.

'Mais, pas de problème, Nigel,' she said. 'I'll cook something simple for you. Egg and chips?'

That was just what the doctor ordered after a long day's travelling. I ordered a carafe of red wine and waited hungrily. She appeared from the kitchen, carrying a large dinner plate and a bowl of chips. When she put the plate in front of me, I counted five fried eggs. Wow – all for me? Of course they were. Now I love fried eggs, always have done. But five?! Just as well I'd ordered a full carafe of red wine. I'd need something to soak up and neutralise the cholesterol. It was quite magnificent. I had a large slice of tarte tatin to follow, and after a couple of large glasses of Calvados I was more than ready for bed.

AS THE NEXT two years passed, I came to the decision I'd be better off concentrating my efforts in the Paris region. I also felt I should approach a few large retail chains directly, as I'd be in a better position to manage the process. After a lot of groundwork, I started to achieve some success. In the process, I learnt a lot about how business is conducted in France:

- Don't make appointments early in the day. The first hour is spent with the employees greeting each other, discussing what was on television the night before, and drinking coffee before settling down to work

- Whatever time the appointment is fixed for, always expect to be kept waiting – anything from ten minutes to an hour. During this waiting time, various employees will rush in and out saying 'desolé' (sorry), with endless small cups of coffee being delivered

- When the meeting starts, there is inevitably a glance at the watch, then another 'desolé' as it's explained that as the meeting is starting late, it's already backing into the next one. So conversation tends to be rushed. There is often a third-party who should be there, but who hasn't turned up, so further time is taken while they're found, before they rush in, shake hands, look at the watch, and rush out

- The best time for a meeting is around 11.30 a.m., because if things go well, there's likely to be an invitation for lunch, which at least gives time for some small talk and getting to know each other

- Everything is conducted at a slightly manic pace. The French love to talk – with their colleagues, and on the phone. Calls on mobiles are never ignored. Time disappears, and they then put themselves under intense stress to catch-up. The working day finishes promptly at 5 p.m. – no one wants to stay, so late in the day meetings are even more time-pressured

- The decision-making process takes ages, and written confirmation takes even longer...

Despite all this, I found the French to be friendly and informal in their business activities.

CYCLING FOR WIMPS IN BURGUNDY

1999

In 1998, I decided to come away from corporate life and employment, and instead set up in business on my own as a recruiter/head-hunter working in the niche sector of retail marketing. I operated mostly from home. One of the beauties of running my own business was the freedom. Although I obviously needed to work conventional business hours, I could also take time off when I wanted to and go on holiday when it suited me.

I worked long hours, daytime, evenings, and sometimes weekends. I made and received calls at all times – whether I was in the office, travelling, shopping, or on holiday. But it worked – for me, for Patricia, and also for my own two children who I saw on a fortnightly basis each weekend. At that time, Lucy and Gemma were living in Devon with their mum and her new husband, so I'd leave home after lunch on a Friday and get back late on Sunday evenings.

Patricia was enormously supportive. She also organised for her two daughters to spend the 'opposite' weekends with their father. This meant Patricia and I had every other weekend to ourselves, and these were really instrumental in enabling our relationship to blossom further.

In the summer of 1999, Patricia, me, and our four girls went on a camping holiday to a site called Sandy Balls (much to the amusement of our kids) in the New Forest. We had a great time, but the weather was typically English. When we got back, and I'd taken Lucy and Gemma back to Devon, Patricia and I talked about how good it would be to spend a week away on our own together before the schools went back. She arranged for the girls to spend that week with their dad, and we made some last-minute arrangements to go to France.

I'd been inspired by an article about a travel company called Cycling for Softies. At the first hotel, holiday makers would settle in before being given bikes by the CfS team, then the next day, they'd cycle to the next hotel while their belongings were taken in a van by the staff. They would ride between 20-30 km each day and the lure of an evening spent relaxing with great food and wine kept them all peddling without complaint.

Patricia suggested we did our own version of this, so on the Sunday night, we strapped our bikes on to the car, and also took a small tent. This gave us the choice between hotels or camping.

We left home and set off on the Monday morning, and decided to drive towards Burgundy, as we fancied combining some wine-tasting with our cycling! Key to our holiday was the *Alastair Sawday B&B Guide*, so accommodation could be booked en route. Towards late afternoon that first day, we approached Auxerre and decided to find somewhere to stay. Searching in the *Sawday Guidebook*, we found an old mansion in the countryside.

On arrival, we were shown to our room and then went back to Auxerre to find a restaurant for dinner.

We returned around eleven and the night was warm and tranquil. We went up to our room. The bed and mattress were almost ancient, but unbelievably comfortable. The windows and the shutters were wide open, and with the light out, it was pitch-black. All we could hear were the owls – there seemed to be loads around. I remember waking up around 3 a.m. to visit the loo. It was so dark, I almost got lost trying to find our room on the way back.

In the morning, we went down to breakfast. The hostess was friendly, and keen to speak English, which was very heavily accented. As she brought the breakfast in, including a selection of delicious home-made jams, she was accompanied by a troupe of dogs – Schnauzers. She also said she had many other animals. As we finished breakfast, we asked her what other animals she had.

'Oh many, many animal,' she said.

'Such as?' we asked.

'Oh cats, many many cats, and rabbits, and ants.'

'Ants?' we echoed.

'Oui, oui. Lots of ants. Many, many outside.'

Our expressions of disbelief must have rattled her, because she said to come outside, and she'd show us her ants. We walked into the garden, where there was a massive henhouse.

'Voilà!' she exclaimed. 'Ere are ze ants.'

We smiled politely. She meant hens. When we left, we laughed and laughed.

As we drove towards Burgundy, we decided that as the weather was so good, we'd camp that night. We found a campsite just outside a small town, and we saw a signpost for Avallon, which is Tenterden's twin town.

Tenterden is a small market town, close to where we lived in Appledore, and to where we'd move in August 2000. I suggested to Patricia that we set up camp, and then get on the bikes and cycle to Avallon. The weather was gorgeous, and the in-car thermometer showed 35 degrees. We set off, but after about three km, I could see Patricia was finding it tough cycling in the heat.

We stopped a few times and eventually cycled into Avallon. We came into an industrial area, which wasn't at all attractive, and made our way to the town centre. We found a bar and ordered some beers. As we emptied our glasses, Patricia said she had an idea. Rather than both of us cycle back, she should order another beer, and I should take a taxi back to the campsite and collect the car. I could see there was no way she'd willingly cycle back, so I found a taxi, and returned to the bar about forty minutes later. I assembled the bikes back on to the car, and that was the first – and last – time we cycled on our bikes that week. Cycling for Softies? More like Cycling for Wimps!

The following day we ambled about, had a good lunch, and spent the evening outside our tent with a bottle of wine. It was incredibly humid, and at around ten came a massive thunderstorm. It was quite spectacular, lying in the tent, looking out of the front opening at the lightning.

The following day, we decided to drive to some of the main vineyards – Nuits St Georges, Alexis Corton, etc. We had a superb lunch at a roadside restaurant and after visiting several vineyards, drove into Beaune. We consulted *Le Guide Alastair* and found a B&B nearby, which looked interesting. The owner was described as zealous.

We called to make a booking, then drove off. The B&B was in a rural setting, surrounded by lavender. A sprightly looking man in his early 70s came out and greeted us. He showed us into his house, which was beautiful and absolutely spotless. We asked him if he provided dinner, but he said he couldn't do that, and suggested we drove to a village about five miles away, where there was a castle, who provided evening meals.

It was getting late – around 8.15 p.m. – so we quickly got changed. Threw our clothes on the floor, showered, and rushed out. After arriving in time, we had a lovely meal and returned to our room at about 11 p.m., when Patricia said, 'Someone's been in here.' I asked what she meant, and she showed me that all our clothes, which had been discarded all over the room, were now either hung up or put into drawers. She commented that even her underwear had been put away neatly. There was also a red rose placed on her pillow!

We woke up the following morning to hear voices outside our room. We looked out and saw some couples breakfasting on the balcony below our room.

'Better not get amorous this morning' – laughed Patricia – 'or we'll be heard!'

We had a truly splendid breakfast, and afterwards chatted to the owner. We explained we'd found him via Le Guide Alastair, and he nodded, and mentioned to us that he had received a favourable review, but there was a word he didn't understand.

'Ah yes,' we said. 'You're described as zealous.' He still didn't understand, so I consulted a dictionary. Whatever the French equivalent is it can't be very complementary, as he was quite dismissive. But in view of the way he tidied away our clothes, we thought zealous was indeed the perfect description.

We drove off and headed towards the area where Pouilly Fuissé wine is grown. It was a particular favourite of my dad's and I was very keen to get him a couple of bottles, which I duly did. We agreed to find accommodation earlier that afternoon to save rushing out for dinner. We looked in the *Sawday Guide* and found a large family house just outside a small town.

The owner was a friendly lady. She showed us to a room on the top floor and said we could make use of the kitchen, which we'd share with some other guests. She described them as a young, sporty German couple.

We got changed and went out for dinner – another superb meal. When we got back, we fancied a coffee. We went into the kitchen and saw the German couple studying maps spread across the table. Patricia is half-German and speaks the language fluently. As my German is also pretty good, we addressed the couple in German. They were so surprised to hear English people speaking their mother tongue, they replied, and we started a conversation.

It turned out they'd caught a train from their home near Frankfurt to the French west coast and were in the process of cycling back to Germany. The guy said he'd noticed our bikes on our car, and explained he felt we had something in common. We smiled. He asked how many kilometres we were doing. I said about nine km.

'What?' he exclaimed. 'Only nine km each day?'

'No,' I corrected him. 'Nine km for the whole week.'

They just couldn't get over the fact we'd brought our bikes all the way to and through France, only to cycle nine kilometres. His partner asked if we were injured or unwell.

'No, just lazy,' replied Patricia. We laughed, but the Germans didn't. They must have thought we were very strange.

WE WENT THROUGH an incredibly sad time in the autumn that year. My father had been feeling unwell for a couple of months and was diagnosed with liver cancer. Although the prognosis wasn't good, Dad continued to live life as normally as he could.

Ten days before he passed away, Patricia and I went up to Norfolk to spend the weekend with my parents. Dad was in good form, and he looked great. It seemed impossible to believe he was so ill. Earlier that year, I'd watched a TV series featuring Rick Stein, and he demonstrated a fish recipe which really caught my eye. I'm no cook – it was something that had never interested me – much as I adore good food. But ably encouraged by Patricia, I cooked this a couple of times. I decided to prepare this dish that evening at my parents' house. Dad bought a beautiful bottle of Chablis, and he genuinely loved the meal.

Poignantly, it was the one and only time I would ever cook for him. A week later, his condition suddenly worsened. He was taken to hospital and passed away that evening. He'd been very ill, but perhaps due to his inner strength, this hadn't been so obvious. At least the sudden deterioration meant he didn't have to endure the pain of cancer for too long. But it was a shock to all of us and the cause of great sadness.

Dad was a huge inspiration to me – and indeed our whole family. I still miss him hugely. In the short time he knew Patricia, they came to adore each other, and it's a big regret they weren't able to spend more time together.

Dad's passing was especially difficult for Mum. She'd been married to him since she was twenty-one. His death at the age of seventy-one was certainly premature. Over twenty years later, Mum's life is incomplete without him. But it's a testament to her own character and strength that she's got on with her life and made the very best of things.

Dad would be proud.

THE 21ST CENTURY 2000 ONWARDS

A Family Holiday, A Marriage Proposal, and Oysters

2000-2001

In the summer of 2000, Patricia and I fulfilled a dream we'd long nurtured. We took all the girls on a camping holiday to France. It's something we'd wanted to do for a while. As a child, I'd had some wonderful camping holidays in France. In fact, for many years, the words 'camping' and 'France' were almost naturally tied together. One of the best things about campsites is that they're generally very safe places for kids to run around, play, and explore. Although we'd been camping in the UK, there's something about camping in another country that takes it to another level. Kids will gravitate towards each other, despite any differences in nationality, culture, and even language. Plus, of course, the food. Our girls couldn't wait to run to the on-site bakery each morning to buy the bread and croissants.

We decided to camp in Brittany. It wasn't too long a journey, and the weather is typically better than the UK. Rather than make the investment into buying our own tent and equipment, we decided to hire a tent from Canvas Holidays. There's also absolutely no way we'd have been able to bring anything more with us. Our Saab 9-3 was packed to the gunnels, and we towed a small trailer too.

We were also accompanied by my youngest brother, Hugh and his wife and daughter, and also my mum. So all in all, there were ten of us, equally split into two cars.

There was huge excitement. We caught an early morning crossing from Dover and drove down to Dol-de-Bretagne in Brittany to Camping Les Ormes. The campsite was large – one of the largest in Brittany. It catered for tents, caravans, and motorhomes. In addition to Canvas, there were also pre-erected tents from two other companies.

To say our children loved it was a huge understatement. With three swimming pools, a massive playground, a lake, shops, a small zoo, tennis courts, and a family bar, what was there not to get excited about! But most of all, it's the freedom that kids like best of all. To go where they want, and be independent of their parents, who can relax, knowing it's a safe environment. Eating outside, en famille, and being able to leave the washing up to parents as the kids continue to explore and play is great fun. Bedtime is naturally extended until at least ten.

We also had various trips out, to seaside resorts such as Dinard, to Mont St Michel, and to various markets. It was all great fun.

While we were there, Hugh celebrated his fortieth birthday. Patricia said she'd cook a big family meal that night, and we waited for Hugh, Mindy, Rhiain, and my mum to come over from their tent in another part of the campsite.

Prior to the holiday, Patricia saw a joke product for sale in a local shop. It was called – and I kid you not – Shit-in-a-Can.

Basically, it was spray-on look-alike shit. No smell, but very, very authentic looking. Patricia felt sure we could put this to good use on our holiday.

Funnily enough, there was a small dog which belonged to a French family in a tent very close to Hugh's. In fact, Hugh often moaned that the dog would run in and out of their own tent. It could have been planned.

Once Hugh and his family had installed themselves at our tent that evening, Patricia and I disappeared under the pretext of going for a quick shower. We shot off to Hugh's tent, armed with the shit-in-a-can. We opened the main entrance door and started to spray – everywhere – on the floor, on the beds, the pillows, even on top of the fridge and the stove. The stuff just froze in shape and stayed put.

We went back to join the family and enjoyed a wonderful evening of eating and drinking. Around eleven, Hugh and family decided it was time to go back to bed. Although we hadn't told the kids what we'd done, in case one of them inadvertently blurted it out, we said we'd accompany them back and use the loos on their block, which were less busy than our own toilet block.

As we got to their tent, Hugh pulled out his torch and suddenly shouted out.

'Watch where you're walking.'

'What is it, Hugh?' I asked. He pointed to a large 'turd' in the doorway.

'It must be that little dog you're always comparing about,' remarked Patricia.

As they entered the tent, Hugh shouted out again.

'Oh, my God. It's all over the place.'

'Urgh, Daddy,' said Rhiain. 'It's on my bed, too.'

'And mine,' said Hugh.

'Oh no. This is awful,' said Mindy. 'It's everywhere.'

'You haven't been feeding the dog, have you?' I asked. 'Or maybe it's nicked some food.'

Hugh began to look really stressed. He'd had a fair bit to drink. He was ready for bed, and the sudden thought of having to clear up and disinfect everything was not attractive. Although our girls were innocent parties in this. They joined in too.

'Look, there's another bit here. And here too. Oh wow. It's on top of the fridge too.'

Patricia and I started to explode with laughter. In fact, we became helpless. The kids looked on with amazement.

'It's not funny,' said Hugh sternly. 'Just think how you'd feel if it happened to you.'

'Don't worry,' said Patricia. 'I'll help you clean up.'

And with that, she scooped some up with her hand and sniffed it before putting it into her dress pocket. Now it was our girls' turn to express their disgust.

'Urgh, that's revolting,' they shrieked.

Hugh and Mindy looked on with horror.

'Come on, Hugh. Don't just stand there. Get your hands dirty,' I said, with tears of laughter rolling down my face. As he and Mindy continued to stare at us, Patricia produced the offending article – a rather depleted can and gave it to them.

'You rotten bastards,' said Hugh – fortunately, with a smile on his face. 'Where did you get that from?'

We all started to fall apart laughing, and given the late hour, tried to suppress the noise so as not to awake other campers. Eventually, we slowly walked back to our tent. We lay in bed, still giggling at their reaction!

We had been at the campsite for almost a week and were due to leave on the Tuesday morning. We had to vacate the tents by midday. The night before, after another great evening of eating and drinking outside, Hugh and his family went off to bed.

'Don't drink too much more,' he warned. 'We've got a long drive ahead of us tomorrow.'

He's really grown into a responsible adult, I thought.

As Patricia and I cleared up, we said goodnight to a couple opposite, who we'd spoken to a few times during our time there. We got into conversation, and before we knew it, we'd offered them a drink. It was only around 11 p.m. The girls were all asleep in bed. What harm could another drink do?

Conversation flowed easily. The other couple – Sally and Don from Sunderland – were friendly and interesting. Don mentioned he liked whisky. I announced I still had a drop left. By the time we'd finished that drop, it was 2 a.m.

I woke at 8 a.m., and felt OK, just a bit tired. We slowly packed up and were eventually ready to leave by midday. I suggested we stopped for lunch at a restaurant just outside the campsite, and then we could drive straight to Calais – roughly a five-hour journey. We had a typical French four-course lunch. I declined any alcohol, and then we embarked on the long car journey ahead. We were about ninety minutes from Calais and were about to go through a motorway toll booth. I was driving ahead of Hugh. As I paid the toll, I noticed some Gendarmes waiting just past the booth. I didn't give it a moment's thought, and after paying, I pulled forward and stopped to wait for Hugh.

Now, as far as the Gendarmes were concerned, they obviously thought I'd seen them, and that in my nervousness to hide something, I'd paused to think. So, they directed me to pull in at the side.

Hugh drove through the tolls and naturally followed me. One of the Gendarmes signalled for me to open my window and asked me if I'd been drinking. I could honestly say no, but my mind immediately cast back to the previous late night of whisky drinking.

The officer produced a breathalyser kit and asked me to blow into the bag. I very tentatively took the bag and slowly breathed into it.

'Plus fort,' *stronger*, said the Gendarme.

As I blew harder, all I could think about was how we'd all get back if the crystals in the bag turned red, and my car was impounded. Plus, the embarrassment in front of my children and my mother. I nervously handed the bag back, feeling the sweat run down my T-shirt.

The police officer inspected the bag. 'Oui. OK. You can go,' he said.

I looked behind, only to see Hugh also handing a breathalyser bag back. Apparently, the other officer didn't understand why Hugh had followed my car and stopped but decided that if I was going to be checked, then he'd follow suit, much to Hugh's delight! That could have been a disastrous end to the holiday. But thanks to the fact the alcohol had passed through my system, no doubt helped by a large lunch, it meant that all was OK.

SHORTLY AFTER RETURNING from our holiday, we moved house to the nearby town of Tenterden. Patricia's house at Appledore, while sitting in a beautiful location in open countryside, was in need of some serious repair. In fact, had we had the cash, we'd have pulled the house down and rebuilt a new one (which is what the eventual buyer did). Her girls were at school in Tenterden, and Patricia also taught at school there too. The obvious and logical thing to do was to move to Tenterden. We eventually found a suitable house and moved there at the end of August.

We'd enjoyed our holiday at Dol so much that we all decided to come back the following year. This time, Hugh and Mindy made sure they booked a tent next to ours. Prior to leaving the UK, Patricia and I arranged for T-shirts to be printed, which we ceremoniously handed out once we'd arrived and unpacked.

We had Nigey Bossi, Daisy Cooki, Hughey Baldi, Mindy Hungri, Betty Nanni, Lucy Sleepi, Vicky Tricki, Joeey Crazee, Gemmey Funni, and Rhianey Titchi.

My nickname for Patricia is Daisy. I've called her that since the start of our relationship. Maybe it's due to the plethora of daisies growing in the field in which her house in Appledore was situated.

I remember the weather not being great for the first few days; it was quite cloudy and overcast. The girls were delighted to be back on familiar territory, with all the freedom, and we all settled quite quickly into camping-mode.

We'd arrived on the Saturday evening. On the Monday evening, we ate outside our tents as usual, and after the meal, it was the turn for Hugh and me to wash up. We went to the 'wash up' area at the toilet block. On the wall in front of us at the sink was a poster, which simply said *Will You Marry Me?* The words were surrounded by flowers (which I subsequently realised were daisies).

'What's that all about, then?' asked Hugh.

'Don't know, mate,' I replied.

I looked at the posters again. They had a certain familiarity about them but given that the wash-ups Hugh and I did usually end up in a water fight, I had one eye on what he was doing.

Hugh continued looking at the posters with a puzzled expression on his face.

'Maybe it's for you,' I said.

Hugh and Mindy had been together for around fifteen years but hadn't yet got married.

'Oh no, mate. Not for me,' said Hugh with just a hint of nervous bravado in his voice.

We completed the washing up, took the clean dishes back, only to be given various pots and pans to be washed. As we complained, Patricia pointed us to a nearer wash up point, which had just become free.

'Go over there. It won't take long.' We wandered across, only to find another poster above the sink, saying the same thing: *Will You Marry Me?*

When we got back to the tent, Hugh and I mentioned we'd seen these posters. Nobody said much. So we sat down, opened another bottle of wine, and talked together.

After a while, Patricia said she'd seen one of the posters on another toilet block wall. We just laughed and carried on talking. After about half an hour, I noticed Lucy seemed a bit different. She'd gone quiet and kept staring at me. Eventually, she stood up.

'Dad, don't you get it?' she cried out. 'Will you marry me? Daisies all over the posters.'

She burst into tears. I started to get a hint of what was going on. I looked at Patricia, who was grinning from ear-to-ear, and quite flushed in the face.

'Have you got something to say to me?' I asked. She nodded.

'Are you going to do it in the traditional way?' I laughed.

So, Patricia got down on one knee, looked me in the eye, and asked, 'Will you marry me?'

'Of course I'll marry you,' I replied in sheer delight.

Everyone shouted and cheered. There were hugs and kisses all around, plus a few tears. In all the excitement and commotion, I looked up and noticed that several other campers who were sitting outside their tents were watching. 'Congratulations!' shouted a Dutch family opposite. Then another family stood up and clapped. We'd certainly made a big impression.

I later discovered that Patricia had 'asked' my mum at Christmas time and told her she wanted to propose to me. We'd often talked about getting married, but Patricia said she wanted to wait until she knew she was completely ready. Having been married twice before, she clearly wanted to make sure it was third time lucky. And sensibly, she wanted to make sure the girls were all settled and happy together. That day, after breakfast, she confided in the two eldest girls – Lucy and Vicky – but didn't dare tell the younger two – Jo and Gemma – in case they unwittingly blurted it out.

As we gathered round celebrating, I noticed Hugh was carefully filming everything with his expensive new video camera. However, it wasn't until the next day, when we asked him if we could see the video, that he confessed, deeply embarrassed, that he'd forgotten to remove the lens cap. So all we had was audio. Oh well. It was a wonderful evening which I'll remember forever.

The following day, Patricia and the girls went round to all the posters and stuck another one over them, which said, He said Yes! Those posters stayed up all the time we were there.

The rest of the holiday seemed almost quiet in comparison to our engagement. We had some more funny moments, though. That year, in 2001, both Lucy and Vicky turned fourteen. According to them, they knew everything about modern life, unlike their parents, who were completely out of touch and knew very little.

Which reminds me of one of my favourite proverbial stories about a fourteen-year-old boy who thought his father was a complete idiot. By the time the boy reached the age of twenty-four, he couldn't believe how much his father had learnt during the past ten years!

THE CAMPSITE HAD a nightclub. There didn't seem to be a minimum age requirement. After being told several times the previous year 'next year', Lucy and Vicky pestered Patricia and me constantly to go. Eventually, we relented. It was going to be inevitable and save us a lot of grief in the long run. We gave them permission, providing they got back at midnight. If they were late, they would be grounded for the rest of the holiday, and bedtime would be 10 p.m. with Joanna and Gemma.

On the agreed day, the two oldest girls spent all afternoon getting themselves ready. Hair, make-up, clothes, several changes of clothes, and finally around half eight, they were ready. Patricia and I were given strict instructions not to go to the nightclub, which they felt would be unfair and tantamount to spying. Off they went, almost tripping up on their high heels.

At around ten, Patricia and I decided to wander up to the main camp bar, which was next to the club. Hiding ourselves discreetly, we managed to peek around the entrance to the dance floor. We saw the girls dancing together. They looked pretty glum. There were few other people dancing, and certainly no boys. We giggled, finished our drinks, and went back to the tent. Good to their word, the girls crept into the tent on the stroke of midnight. Phew!

TWO THOUSAND AND one was the year thongs became popular underwear for young women. The two eldest girls would wash and hang theirs out on the washing line. This was a source of amusement to Hugh. He couldn't believe how anyone would want to wear something that, in his eyes, looked like a catapult.

Eventually, the girls tired of his silly jokes. One evening after dinner, Vicky had had enough. She saw a pair of Hugh's large Y-fronts on the washing line, and pulled them off, and threw them at him. Hugh threw them back, and this went on for a few minutes. Vicky then decided it would be funnier (which it was!) if she wiped them around the saucepan used to cook the curry. At this point, Hugh expressed some mild anguish. Apparently – although we'd never have known – these were his new white pants. He got up and went to grab them. So Vicky threw them up on to the roof of the tent, much to everyone's amusement.

That was the end of Hugh's pants – or so we thought.

Three years later, Hugh and Mindy finally got married. I was asked to be the best man. As I was searching for stories to include in my speech, I remembered about Hugh's pants. I explained to Patricia what I was planning, and she confirmed it wouldn't be tasteless but funny and acceptable for the range of guests, which would include children. So the next time I was in London, I bought a giant pair of underpants from a street vendor on Oxford Street. When I got them home, we placed them in a bowl of water containing a couple of tea bags. Just to give them that 'used' look. On the day in question, I wrapped them up, and took them to the wedding.

I'd primed the youngest girls, and at a chosen point, I asked Rhiain to collect a parcel from me, hand it over to Joanna, and asked her to open it. The parcel contained a thong, much to everyone's amusement. I then explained the underwear story of our holiday,

I asked Gemma to come up, and gave her another parcel, and she walked across the floor, and gave it to Hugh. I described the situation when Vicky had had enough, and after wiping the curry pan with the pants, she threw them on to the tent roof. I explained that Canvas Holidays contacted me at the end of the holiday when they took down the tents and posted me Hugh's pants. Hugh opened the parcel and discovered some extremely large pants. His missing pants. The place fell apart with laughter.

I'm not sure if Hugh's ever got over it!

THERE WAS ONE more episode I should recount about that year. It's regarding oysters. Up until 1998, I don't think I'd ever eaten an oyster. I had a friend with whom I had collaborated as a consultant on some projects. He was very much a Francophile, and occasionally we'd pop across the Channel for a spot of lunch. He was an oyster lover. I queried this, knowing that oysters had a reputation for occasional food poisoning. My friend laughed it off. He told me of a few occasions when he'd eaten what he called a 'duff oyster' and after being horribly sick with both ends burning, he'd got back in the saddle the following day and eaten oysters for lunch. Mad!

The first time we had lunch together in France, he gave me a gentle introduction, and we ate oysters poached in vermouth. I found them to be quite pleasant, and actually enjoyed chewing them, unlike my friend who would swallow them whole.

We went back to France for another lunch nine months later. This time we ate raw oysters – six each – and I didn't suffer any aftereffects.

The final lunch we had together was at the end of the following February when we visited a town very well-known for its oysters – I believe they were called St Vaast. Our lunch became a bit of a macho thing. We confidently asked for six grade one (or whichever were the largest) oysters each. Then my friend had a change of heart.

'Why don't we order a dozen oysters each?' he suggested.

'Go for it,' I replied encouragingly

The oysters arrived and were duly consumed. The following day, around twenty-four hours later, I started to feel queasy. Although I wasn't sick, I spent that day and the entire weekend feeling extremely bilious. On the Sunday evening, feeling no better, I telephoned my friend. His wife answered the phone. I asked to speak with him, and she told me he was in bed. In fact, he'd been in bed all day, comparing of severe queasiness. I explained I too was feeling distinctly unwell.

'It must have been those bloody oysters,' his wife remarked. 'I just don't know why he persists in eating the damn things. Don't tell me he's got you hooked too?'

'Never again,' I replied. 'Never, ever again.'

My biliousness continued throughout the entire month of March. I wasn't actually sick – I just felt constantly queasy. It wasn't until Easter that I began to pick up and feel better. Although this episode was over twenty years ago, I still very occasionally notice this bilious feeling return, especially if I'm feeling under the weather. I did some research several years ago and discovered that the bacteria from duff oysters can linger in the gut for many years and resurface from time to time according to one's general state of health, or after consumption of particularly rich food or an excess of alcohol, especially spirits.

Another life lesson learnt; avoid raw oysters like the plague – at least eating them!

MY STAG WEEKEND IN PARIS

2002

In the spring of 2001, Patricia and I went back to Najac to spend a long weekend at Alan's house. We had some memorable moments, sitting on the veranda at night-time in the dark, sipping whisky, as I'd done with my dad several years ago. We also had the most splendid Sunday lunch at the local Hotel Belles Rives. We sat outside on a terrace and decided to spoil ourselves. Delightfully and charmingly, the waiter replaced our wine glasses when we ordered a bottle of Pomerol and placed two beautiful massive crystal glass wine goblets on the table. we were the only diners rewarded with such glasses.

In 2002, Patricia and I got married in the March. We had a small wedding ceremony and celebration at a local stately home, Great Maytham Hall. It was a place that held a certain significance for both of us; we were both on the local fundraising committee for Macmillan Cancer Relief (Patricia spent almost twenty years on this committee), and over the course of several years, during the summer months, our committee put on tea and cakes on selected weekends at Great Maytham Hall as part of the 'open gardens' scheme. They had just obtained their licence to hold weddings there, and in fact our wedding was the first they held. It was a beautiful, sunny March Saturday, and the garden was full of daffodils. We were joined by around thirty-five family members and close friends, and a wonderful day was enjoyed by everyone present.

Before our wedding, I wanted some kind of stag night and asked my two brothers and a friend of mine called David to join me for a weekend in France in mid-February. England were playing France at rugby at the Stade de France. My youngest brother Hugh managed to obtain tickets, and then two weeks before our weekend away, said he couldn't go. The timing clashed with a theatre trip Mindy had booked tickets for, to see… Postman Pat. Clearly no contest! Although, in fairness, they'd promised their young daughter they would go.

I arranged to collect Simon from his house at Hemel Hempstead on the Friday afternoon, and we'd drive to Heathrow and catch an evening plane to Paris. We got there about eight thirty, and caught the RER into Paris, and made our way to our hotel – a ubiquitous Ibis. I'd booked a double room with twin beds. Naturally, we were shown to a room with a double bed. I went back to reception and complained. While the person on duty was quite charming, there was nothing they could do to help, as the hotel was full. But they promised to move us to another room the following evening.

It was getting late, and we decided to let it go.

'Come on,' said Simon. 'Let's go and find some food with a bottle or two of wine.'

The following morning, we went to for breakfast, and made our way to Gare du Nord to meet my friend David. He's sixteen years older than me. He went to the same school, and we met at a school reunion some years before. David is a lifelong bachelor. He enjoys living on his own. He's very anti any form of technology. This includes TV as well as computers and mobile phones. He also doesn't have a car. He is quite loveable and very eccentric and happens to be a Doctor of German. He's also a life-long Chelsea fan.

I spotted him at the station and greeted him in the familiar way. 'Hallo you old bastard.'

The three of us then made our way to a bar just outside the station and ordered beers. In fact, we ordered several beers. The bar filled up with both French and English rugby fans. Food was being served, and we filled up with steak and chips. Eventually, we followed the crowd and made our way to the stadium. The weather was freezing cold – about two degrees Celsius, and a few snowflakes fluttered down.

We found our seats. During the national anthems, David remained standing and joined the French singing the Marseillaise. He was word perfect and received some admiring glances from the French fans.

At half-time we went to the bar. There was the usual scrum, and I managed to work my way to the front. I was the first person to be served. As I staggered through the crowd with six beers, a couple of French guys heard me call out, and said, 'Anglais,' disparagingly.

England lost the match. Jonny Wilkinson had an off-day, and a French flanker – Serge Betsen – really gave him a tough game. We walked back to the Metro station and travelled into central Paris. I remembered the restaurant I was taken to some years before when I was on a business trip – La Taverne du Sergéant Recruiter. We stopped at a bar. Simon and I had had enough cold beer. It wasn't so enjoyable in cold weather. We ordered a couple of coffees and cognacs while David amazingly managed to quaff through another few beers.

We turned up at the restaurant. Simon and I ate the recommended menu of several courses, while David ordered a steak. It wasn't to his satisfaction, and he moaned about it constantly. In fact, he's never let me forget 'what a terrible restaurant' I took him to.

Simon and I ate like lords, and we had a couple of bottles of excellent wine. As I mentioned, David is a bit of a loner. And when we left the restaurant, he made his way back to his hotel, and Simon and I walked back to ours. We had a few more drinks. Simon's capacity for alcohol is staggering. It's always been like this, ever since he was a teenager. He could drink large quantities of beer, followed by a bottle or two of red wine, and finish up drinking several glasses of his favourite – Rémy Martin cognac. He'd recently given up smoking, but it certainly didn't stop him from having a good time!

The next day was warmer and sunny. Simon said he fancied going up the Eiffel Tower. I'd never been up it either, so that's what we did. We had some lunch and finally made our way back to the airport. We'd had a great weekend together.

In the autumn of 2002, Patricia and I went back to the beautiful village of Najac. We decided to travel by train, and after catching the Eurostar from Ashford to Paris, we caught the TGV to Toulouse, where we hired a car. The weather was chillier, more typically autumnal, and although we had a great time, Najac's allure was slightly less charming, with several shops and bars shut.

On the day of departure, we had to leave at 6 a.m., to get to Toulouse in time to catch the train at 8.35. The journey would have been around an hour and a quarter, so we assumed we had plenty of time. However, we didn't allow for rush-hour traffic in central Toulouse, to say nothing of the never-ending roadworks in the city centre. We eventually managed to reach the hire car parking at 8.30 a.m., and I shot into the bureau and threw the keys on to the desk. We dashed into the station concourse. It was 8.33 a.m. We located the correct platform and rushed up and down the steps, only to see the train leave.

I almost went into meltdown. The stress of the traffic jams and the fear of missing the train had clearly pumped volumes of adrenalin into my system. I eventually started to calm down and went into the ticket office to find out the time of the next train. Naively, I explained our circumstances to the ticket clerk.

'Ah non, Monsieur,' she said. She went on to say that our tickets were only valid for the trains we'd booked. As we'd missed our train, we'd have to buy new tickets, including Eurostar too. I was apoplectic. This was going to cost about €350, which was more than we'd originally paid. I argued the toss, but the ticket clerk remained resolute. We couldn't just catch a later train with our existing tickets. We'd have to shell out an exorbitant sum for replacements. I was furious, but there was no alternative. She even told her colleague at the barrier gate that under no circumstances were we to be let through with our old tickets. So I had to swallow it. One of what would become several future brushes with unyielding French officialdom.

IN THE SUMMER of 2003, Patricia was diagnosed with breast cancer. It was quite sudden, and a massive shock to all our families. She was operated on very quickly, and as a testament to both her physical and mental health and strength, she recovered swiftly. As a consequence, we decided to book a holiday in Spain with Vicky and Jo, and we hired a house in a beautiful village called Gaucin in the hills behind the southern Spanish coastline. We had a lovely week together. It was important family time for all of us, and Patricia's recovery was no doubt accelerated as a result.

It wasn't possible for Lucy and Gemma to come with us. My summer holiday dates had already been agreed with their mother, and couldn't be changed, as she herself had booked a holiday away while the girls were with me. Being self-employed, I could organise my time and holidays quite easily. I also wanted to take Lucy and Gemma away; the additional workload of having all four girls at home for a fortnight would have placed an unfair strain on Patricia.

So I contacted Alan, and to the girls' delight, I took them down to Najac for ten days.

They loved Alan's house. The weather was great. They shared a bedroom at the very top of the house, and both liked a lie-in. This meant I could get up early, make a coffee, and sit outside in the small garden, which was also at the top of the house, and relax reading in the sun until the girls got up.

As I've said before, I'm no cook, so other than breakfast and a snack for lunch, we ate out most evenings. There were plenty of inexpensive restaurants around. There was also a fabulous outdoor swimming pool just outside the village. We spent many happy afternoons around the pool. Gemma was keen to practise her swimming and managed to extract several Euros off me during the week, as she proved she could swim ten lengths, then twenty lengths. Both girls were and are great book readers (just like their dad) and we'd sit and read, watching Gemma complete her never-ending monumental swims.

During one of my early morning coffees in the garden, I looked at the map and noticed we could get down to the coast near to where I worked at Camping Bois Fleuri quite easily. The drive was long – just under four hours, but it was mostly motorways. I mentioned this to the girls over breakfast, and they became very excited.

We decided to go the following day. We left at 6 a.m., jumped into my Saab convertible, lowered the roof, and took off. We stopped for croissants en route and arrived at Camping Le Soleil around 11 a.m. I decided to go there first; the site had its own beach, and if we were discreet, we could use the showers and get changed. We could also eat at the on-site restaurant.

We had a wonderful, memorable day on the beach. We all swam in the sea, we had a late lunch in the restaurant, then went back to the beach. We left about 6 p.m., and I drove up to Camping Bois Fleuri to show the girls where I'd worked. They seemed to understand very quickly that this was a special place for me. We walked around the campsite and then began the long drive back to Najac. Little did I know that I'd unwittingly set in motion a train of events that we'd pursue for many years.

BUYING OUR HOUSE IN FRANCE

2004

This was a massive moment in my adventure with France. Patricia continued to recover strongly from her breast cancer. But it had shaken us; we'd only been married a year. We realised that nothing was forever, and to get on with our plans for our life together. We'd often spoken about how much we'd like to buy a property abroad. We're both great Europhiles. With Patricia being half-German, we'd previously thought about buying a holiday home in Germany. However, we'd come to the conclusion that Germany was in many ways quite similar to the UK in terms of lifestyle and climate. Property there would no doubt be expensive too. More recently, our pipe dream had been about buying a property in France.

When we first got together, we arranged a meeting with Susan, our longstanding Independent Financial Advisor. One of the things she recommended was that we took out Critical Illness Insurance. After Patricia's operation, we contacted Susan and told her what had happened. She said she'd pursue an insurance claim on our behalf. To be honest, neither Patricia nor I had attached much thought to this. Our main concern was her recovery.

In February 2004, a letter arrived from our insurers to advise us that a cheque was on its way, for a not inconsiderable sum of money. Enough, in fact, to buy a modest property in France. We didn't need telling twice. After banking the cheque, we started to go down the path of considering the property purchase. The first decision was whereabouts we wanted to look for a property. We agreed that we'd want to go sufficiently far south to attract good weather, in particular hot summers. However, we also wanted to find somewhere that we could realistically drive to within a day.

During my holiday in Najac with Lucy and Gemma the previous year in 2003, one of the books I read was by an Englishman. He'd bought a very run-down house north of Limoges and described his adventures. I especially enjoyed the book, as I found several parallels with the author. He was about the same age as me and had been through a divorce. He used to regularly catch the train from Kent into Charing Cross in London. It just got me thinking.

On the way back from Najac, we stopped off at Limoges, and we also went to a porcelain factory shop just outside Limoges at Aixe-sûr-Vienne. After shopping there, we sat on the riverbank at Aixe, and I remember thinking what a wonderful place it was. It just felt very right.

We did some research and found out that Limoges and the area around in the Haute Vienne were about seven to eight hours drive from Calais, so it was doable. So Patricia began the property search. We contacted several estate agents in our chosen area, booked flights and accommodation, and in March we went for a five-day recce trip.

Buying property in France is very different from the UK. For starters, you can't just walk into an estate agent and expect to visit a property the same day. Mais non! This is France. Appointments have to be made. So we prepared a short document detailing our key requirements, and also our budget range. We also confirmed we'd not be interested in buying a restoration project.

The first night we arrived at our B&B. This was a magnificent house, owned by an English guy and his Russian wife. They were friendly and welcoming, and the food was excellent. After a hearty breakfast the next day, we set off to our first estate agent. We'd already been in touch and corresponded in French, as her English was quite poor. She offered to drive us to five properties.

The first property we saw was an old barn, which had been very poorly converted. It was a complete restoration project. We weren't interested and disappointed that our list of needs had been ignored. The second property was very small. It had a garden, about fifty metres away on the other side of the road. The third property we saw was just awful – small, poky, in a horrible small town. The fourth wasn't bad, but it would have required a lot of money to be spent on it. Finally, she took us to a property owned by a Dutch family, which looked OK. The house was surrounded by a decent sized garden, and the interior looked in reasonable condition and about the right size. We had a walk-through, and then it struck me: where was the bathroom? We asked the estate agent, who asked the owner. She replied that the toilet and shower were in the garden. She said it got a little cold in the winter, but that meant people didn't spend long in there!

'There is no way we're buying a house with a toilet in the garden,' I growled. Patricia nodded in agreement.

So that was it. A disappointing and rather wasted day. We said goodbye to the estate agent, and drove down towards Brive, to a B&B where we'd spend the night. This was a magnificent, converted barn owned by an English couple. It turned out the husband was a DIY supremo. He'd certainly done a great job. We explained how frustrated our house-hunting had been that day, and then the wife mentioned that they'd converted a small stable block which they were looking to sell. This piqued our interest, and in the morning, after breakfast, we went to have a look.

Once again, the conversion and building work was immaculate. The house was also fitted out with kitchen appliances and basic furniture. The couple told us they were intending to rent it out, but that they would sell for the right price. Much as we liked the house, it was a bit small, and a little too close to their own house. The asking price was right at the top end of our budget too, so we decided not to pursue.

It was my birthday that day, so we drove into Brive and found a fabulous coffee and cake shop. We bought some lavishly decorated creations, and Patricia popped a candle on top of my cake and wished me a happy birthday. After wandering around Brive, we drove back towards Limoges, where we had an appointment with an English estate agent in nearby Chalus the following morning.

We had booked a room at a small hotel between Limoges and Chalus, and after parking the car, we went inside. A man of similar age to myself, with a 1970s style moustache, was behind the reception. I said *Bon Soir* to him and said we had a room booked. He seemed to have some difficulty understanding my French, so I repeated what I said. He had a strange accent when he spoke and seemed very flustered. He looked for the key and muttered to himself in English.

'Are you English?' I asked.

'Oui,' he said. 'I mean yes. Sorry.'

It turned out he'd recently taken over the hotel. Very recently, we thought, as he lost his way twice as he tried to locate our room. He seemed a friendly chap, and we said we'd be down to dinner shortly. When we got downstairs, the dining room was full. He showed us to our table and gave us some menus. He was the only person waiting at table. Almost all the other customers seemed to be French. The owner was dashing about from table to table. It seemed he was having difficulty understanding what his customers wanted, and he kept going back to confirm their orders.

Eventually, he came to us. He apologised for the wait, but we told him not to worry, and gave him our order. As our meal progressed, he became less frenetic, and when our desserts arrived, the restaurant had mostly emptied. We had a brief conversation with him, and it transpired that he and his wife had only taken possession a week ago. They were from Liverpool, and I asked him if he had a background in catering. He replied he was an engineer, and his wife was a bookkeeper. They'd long held a dream of owning and running a business in France and decided to buy this hotel. He admitted his French wasn't good, and that his number one objective was to hang on to his chef, who'd developed a good reputation. Obviously, the reason the restaurant was full.

This chap did have a sense of humour, especially when Patricia said she'd have to call him Basil, although in fairness the hotel was better run than Fawlty Towers. I think it was the moustache – a definite likeness to Basil Fawlty.

After breakfast, we drove to Chalus. The estate agent was charming. She was English and told us she'd lived in France for twenty-nine years. She cut to the chase and explained she only had two properties that would match our needs, and that one was already under offer. So, she volunteered to drive us to the available one, which was about fifteen minutes away. She was a bit of a mad driver, but we got there OK. The house was in a small hamlet called Pellac. She stopped outside the house, and then we went in.

There was some furniture in the house, and some of the cupboards contained various items. The estate agent, Janice, explained the house was owned by a Parisian couple who had the house as their holiday home. However, the husband had died about ten years ago, and his wife had since gone into a care home in Paris. The house had been on the market for almost two years, and two nephews had power of attorney over the sale.

The downstairs of the house, which was completely and almost immediately habitable, consisted of a very small bathroom, a small galley kitchen, a lounge-cum-dining room, an entrance hall, and a large bedroom. There was also a garage, from which there was a ladder which led to an attic upstairs. Although this was floor-boarded out, there were two massive beams about waist height. Janice said that her ex-husband who was a surveyor had seen this attic and confirmed that the beams could be cut and re-installed at ceiling height if required. So there was considerable potential for additional living space upstairs.

We probably saw the house at its worst. It was a cold, dank March day with mist in the air. The house smelt musty, with cobwebs everywhere. But once Janice opened the shutters and the windows, we could start to see the potential. There was only one window overlooking the rear of the property, as the land behind the house belonged to a neighbour. However, there was a large, enclosed front drive and garden. Opposite was an orchard, with a wood barn which also belonged to the property.

We breathed and took stock. The place had potential. But the asking price was considerably more than our budget.

As we drove back to Chalus, Janice said it was highly likely that the vendors would accept an offer. I pushed a little harder. What would they be likely to accept? Janice advised us to just have a think and put in an offer. She would say no more. When we got back to Chalus, she recommended a restaurant opposite her office, where she and her ex-husband would be having lunch together. We found a table separate from her, so we could start to talk and play around with some numbers.

After lunch, as we got up to go, Janice asked us if we'd come to a figure which we'd like to propose as an offer. I said that we had but went on to say it was quite a bit less than the asking price, and I didn't want to embarrass her or irritate the vendors.

'Just give me your figure.' She laughed. 'And I'll contact the vendors and submit your offer.' We gave her our figure.

She said it might take a few days to make contact and get feedback.

So Patricia and I decided to drive to Limoges, and have a look round the city centre. We parked our car and walked into the Galleries Lafayette department store. As we ascended to the first floor on the escalator, my mobile rang. It was Janice. She said she'd been in touch with the vendors and asked me if I could increase my offer by €1,000? I immediately said yes, and she replied, 'Then the house is yours.' I couldn't believe it. Patricia and I stepped off the escalator at the next floor and just hugged each other.

'Oh my God,' she said (or something like that!) 'What have we done?'

Janice told us that the process would start and explained again the mechanism of buying a house in France. She asked if we had a Notaire (solicitor), and as we didn't, said she'd put us in touch with someone with whom she worked regularly. Sure enough, within a week, a pile of documents arrived, and things began to move forwards. We had to submit a whole raft of stuff, including birth certificates, marriage certificates, and details of bank accounts, copies of utility bills, even references. It was even more confusing for Patricia, as she's been married three times, and at one stage she received a document addressed to her with all four surnames including her maiden name.

The process continued back and forth over the next two months, until Janice advised us that the formal signing of documents would take place at the solicitor's office, similar to a completion in the UK. She said we didn't have to be there, and either she or someone else could represent us. We had some friends living locally, and they kindly agreed to sign on our behalf.

They called us later that day, to confirm everything had gone OK. They mentioned the Notaire had said he hadn't yet seen sight of the final payment (which was the balance amounting to 90 per cent or so of the transaction), but he didn't seem unduly worried. I knew the money had gone through, as I'd faxed through all the details to our finance brokers in London, and they had in turn confirmed back that all had gone ahead OK.

A week later, I called Janice to check the money had been received. She contacted the Notaire, and called me back with some concern, to say it hadn't yet come through. She agreed to follow up as a priority. Generally, I sleep soundly, but that night I had one of the very few sleepless nights I've endured. This was a lot of money. What on earth could have happened?

Janice called me the next day. Someone at her head office had given me the bank details for another Notaire, with whom they also regularly worked. Apparently, the money had gone into this person's bank account. She went on to explain that all Notaires in France share the same bank, so it would simply be a case of transferring the money to the right one. I was astounded the original recipient hadn't realised that there was a large, unexplained amount of money sitting in his bank account. But hey-ho – at least the money had been traced and found.

The following week, Patricia, my mother, and I drove to Pellac to take delivery of the keys and see how much work awaited us. Was the house going to be habitable during July when we planned to go across with Vicky and Jo?

We arranged to spend the first night at a B&B in the village, which was owned by French people. We also asked if they could provide us with an evening meal, which they seemed a little surprised at, but agreed to. As a consequence, we were joined by the entire family while they too ate their evening meal.

The following morning, we drove into Chalus and collected the keys from Janice. We opened the front door of our new house, to be greeted by cobwebs everywhere and lots of big spiders. However, everything was pretty much the same as we'd seen back in March. Most of the furniture was still there. And, as we opened various cupboards, we found a complete dinner set of Limoges porcelain, various bottles and jars of peculiar looking substances. When we opened the cupboards in the bedrooms, we discovered various items of clothing, including underwear, and some tiny shoes, all presumably belonging to the previous owner!

We embarked upon some basic cleaning and encountered our first problem: there wasn't any running water. I called Janice, who contacted the Mairie, who advised we called the water authority. They agreed to turn on the water supply and informed us this would take a few days. That pretty much put paid to the cleaning. So, we explored a little more, and drove across to spend the night at a B&B near to Limoges where we'd previously stayed in March during our initial recce trip.

TOWARDS THE END of July, Patricia and I returned with Vicky and Jo. We decided to leave immediately after school broke up on the Friday afternoon for the summer holidays. We caught an early evening ferry and drove through the night.

We eventually arrived, after a few stops, at about 9.30 a.m. We drove into the driveway and opened the front door to the house. Vicky and Jo stared in shock and horror. All their excitement seemed to ebb away. Maybe Patricia and I had built up too much enthusiasm for our new holiday home in France. The reality was a sparsely furnished house, which badly needed redecoration. It was dark inside – until we opened up the shutters, which actually didn't help, as the girls could then see the reality. No proper bedrooms with beds, a very shabby lounge, no sofa, and worst of all, no TV! The bathroom was tiny, with one rather grotty loo, and although there was running water, it wasn't hot.

The girls were looking forward to a shower after a night in the car. But that would have to wait until we worked out how to use the very old-fashioned water heater on the kitchen wall, which seemed to heat about two litres of water at a time.

One of the biggest problems was that there wasn't a mobile phone signal. This was an absolute disaster for Vicky. She very reluctantly had to be parted from her boyfriend back in Tenterden for the week we were in France. Without any facility for texting, let alone speaking, this was going to be a long week!

Suddenly, we heard someone calling. It was our next-door neighbour – a lady in her seventies, called Solange. She was tiny and chattered away in a very strong local accent. We learnt she'd lived in the village all her life. Her husband, who'd passed away some years beforehand, had been the mayor, and was a highly respected member of the community. Her cousin Maurice – a bachelor in his late fifties – lived adjacent, and we exchanged the usual shaking of hands and kisses as we introduced ourselves.

Solange seemed absolutely delighted she had new neighbours. She was under the impression we had moved into the property on a permanent basis, and it took several days before she understood we had bought the house as a 'maison secondaire'. She was friendly, and offered all sorts of useful advice, and introduced us to a local handyman called Yves, who quickly made himself indispensable as he got the hot water working and showed us how to switch on the oven.

After unpacking the car, we decided to start cleaning the kitchen and bathroom. After a few hours, the house began to look more orderly, so we decided to drive to Limoges for a mammoth supermarket shop for food, cleaning, and decorating materials. Patricia was an absolute star, and wasn't at all fazed by the old, dirty cooker which ran on a gas cylinder, and she prepared vast quantities of spaghetti bolognaise.

Over the next few days, we carried on cleaning, and started some basic decoration, mostly painting. Solange turned up to lend us her steam cleaner to help steam wallpaper off the walls, and at one point, was found up the ladder herself! The interior began to look less like a bombed outbuilding in Beirut. Gradually, with curtain rails up and curtains in situ, the house started to look more homely. The girls had a makeshift bedroom in the hallway, and we bought a portable TV/DVD player which improved the girls' lives 100 per cent. Vicky managed to find a phone signal high up one wall; as soon as she heard the familiar ringtone, she would shoot out of the front door as though there was a pack of tigers chasing her, and she'd run at full pelt through the village to the green, where she could occasionally get one bar of signal.

On the fourth night, we waited for our double bed to be delivered. We'd previously tried ordering some furniture online from French retailers, but it proved almost impossible to organise. Patricia searched further online and came across a company run by a British chap called Bruce. We could order from a wide range of UK-manufactured furniture, and Bruce then took our order and arranged personal delivery as he does for all his customers.

Earlier that evening, we had a call from Bruce to say he was running late and could deliver the following day. However, after three uncomfortable nights on camp beds, we told him it didn't matter how late he arrived. Eventually Bruce arrived around ten, accompanied by his wife Diana and two of their sons. He explained he was in the process of moving his family to live permanently in France at their newly acquired property further south near to Brive.

We immediately got on well with Bruce and Diana, and I'm delighted to say they've since become some of our closest friends.

The rest of the week passed without too much drama. We found it was easier to eat out and found some interesting local restos. Vicky started counting down the hours until we'd be back so she could see her beloved boyfriend. The only drama that did ensue – and we still talk about this – is that during the final evening, Jo, who was fourteen, spent a few hours washing, conditioning, drying, and brushing her long blonde hair, then walked through the lounge and straight into a flycatcher suspended from the light-fitting. The girls had been driven mad by the flies that week and had hung up sticky fly catchers. Unfortunately for Jo, the flycatcher she walked into was particularly sticky and covered with dead flies, several of which became caught up in her newly washed and groomed hair. The angrier she became, the funnier the rest of us found it...

The only other amusing anecdote we recall is that when we arrived at Boulogne the following evening to catch the Speedferry, we were told there was only one operating due to mechanical failure. This meant our journey would be delayed by up to four hours. Vicky was almost frantic with frustration (boyfriend again). We decided to go to the bar, and Vicky said in a loud voice that she needed a large martini to cope with her stress. Unfortunately, the barman heard this and told her he couldn't serve her as she was underage. She'd not worn any make-up all week (clearly no need to!) and looked a couple of years younger than her actual age of seventeen. As the steam began to pour out of Vicky's ears, with her fists clenched tightly and eyes watering up, I ordered her a coke, winked at the barman, and said I really ought to order her mother a martini as well as a glass of wine. That did the trick. Vicky sipped the martini in the car and proceeded to spend the next four hours applying make-up in preparation to meet her beloved, who had texted to say he'd meet her when we disembarked at Dover.

RETURN TO CAMPING AT ARGÉLÈS

2004

During the summer holidays in 2004, I took my two daughters, Lucy and Gemma, camping in the south of France. Since our short visit there the previous year, they'd both said how much they'd like to stay at Camping Le Soleil for a week. So, we arranged to drive to Pellac and spend the first night there so they could see the house and drive to the south coast the following day.

Both girls were excited, and as we approached the house, Gemma literally squealed with excitement and delight at seeing the charming little property which was our house in France.

We drove off to Argélès the next day, and upon our arrival, drove to our designated space and put up the tent. I'd already explained to the girls that as a reluctant cook at the best of times, there was no way I was going to embarrass myself in front of neighbouring campers making a fist of whatever I was cooking, and that instead we'd eat out every night, either at the campsite restaurant, which was good, or elsewhere.

We settled into the camping vibe very quickly; mornings spent on the beach, which was five minutes' walk away, and afternoons around the large swimming pool.

As a lifelong Chelsea fan, I'm delighted my girls have followed in the dad's footsteps; both Lucy and Gemma had brought their Chelsea shirts, which I washed out and hung on the little washing line by our tent.

There was a family next door – the guy sounded Liverpudlian – and the next morning, he stopped by as he walked to his tent on his way back from the showers.

'I noticed the shirts (shairts),' he said.

Oh, here we go, I thought, *clearly a Liverpool fan, or an Evertonian.* Except that Jim was actually a Chelsea fan! He lived in Wrexham and had supported Chelsea all his life. He began recounting various matches he'd seen. He was clearly a bit of a character. He had two sons, neither of whom supported Chelsea, much to his chagrin. He was clearly in his element, being next door to us.

On the Sunday, Chelsea were going to play Manchester United in what was then the Charity Shield. Jim came over and suggested that there must be a bar in Argélès where we could watch the match. So he and his two sons, myself, Lucy, and Gem all caught a bus into Argélès and eventually found a bar. Jim was hilarious; he couldn't concentrate on the match and kept telling us about his memories of matches during his lifetime.

'Do you remember that game in 1992 against Newcastle? We scored in the last minute of extra time to win the game.' Or 'Do you remember such-and-such player?'

After the match, we all walked back the three kilometres back to the campsite. Jim talked non-stop all the way. He was a big guy – tall and burly. He ran his own building company, and drove a Land Rover Discovery, which pulled an enormous caravan. Attached to his caravan was a massive awning. He'd installed two fridges in the caravan for beer and wine. He was someone who clearly liked his space and his creature comforts.

One night we had a thunderstorm, and as a result, the electricity supply failed. The following evening, there were a few rumbles, and in order to ensure his beer remained at the correct, refrigerated temperature, I saw Jim later that evening at one of the main switchboards, pulling plugs out and swapping sockets around.

'What the hell are you doing?' I asked. 'You'll electrocute yourself.'

'Nah, I'm OK, mate,' he replied in his Scouse accent. 'Just making sure the supply to our caravan is fully protected!'

Lucy had made friends with a family a couple of tents away in the other direction. She'd obviously explained to their teenage children that her dad wasn't much of a cook, and one afternoon, as we walked past, the mother asked if we'd like to have dinner with them that evening. I didn't need asking twice. There was another couple with them who had a son aged about nineteen. When they discovered I was taking the girls to Barcelona the following day, they asked if I'd mind taking their son with us. 'It would be a pleasure,' I said. That was another evening meal in the bag! Shameless or what!

One of the funniest moments was when the space opposite Jim's tent became vacant. We'd been to have dinner with him and his family the previous evening, and Jim had complained that his designated space wasn't large enough to properly accommodate his car, and that he had to leave his 4x4 partially parked on the road adjacent to his caravan. When the campers opposite left a day early, Jim wasted no time parking his Discovery in the space. The following morning, his wife grabbed him as he returned from the shop with his breakfast baguette in his shopping bag and pointed out that people had arrived to set up their tent opposite them – a small middle-aged man with large spectacles and a beard, together with his wife, and that he'd have to move his vehicle. Jim was less than pleased. After parking his car in its former spot on the road, he shouted across to me,

'That's a waste of bloody time. Having to move me car for that bloke over there. Not only does he look like Harold Shipman, he's also a bloody German.' Not one to mince his words our Jim!

After a wonderful week of camping, we drove back to spend a couple of nights at Pellac. While Gemma was delighted at this, and was keen to help with cleaning and decorating, Lucy was less than enamoured. She'd had a great time at the campsite, making friends and nightclubbing, and what made things worse is that the weather in the Limousin had changed and it rained solidly for the next two days.

Autumn in the Limousin

2004

Patricia and I couldn't wait to return to Pellac in late September. Frankly, we couldn't get enough of the place. Patricia had given up her job as a teacher. The stress of the job, teaching in an enormous, comprehensive school, with all the inherent politics, was simply too much to bear, and it was so good to see her relax and her health recover fully. We'd decided to call our house 'La Tarte dans le Ciel' which translates as 'Pie in the sky'. When we first got together, there was a Sunday evening TV drama series called *Pie in the Sky* featuring Richard Griffiths, about a policeman whose retirement plan was to open a restaurant with this name. We both liked the sentiment behind this pipedream, and we agreed that should we ever buy a house abroad, that's what we'd call it.

We got lots of jobs done that week, including getting a telephone installed. A couple of guys from France Telecom came out to run wires from the poles outside and put some sockets in the house. This means that in addition to having a phone, we could also get access to the Internet.

The weather was good, and we had a wonderful week there – apart from the penultimate day. The front of the house was covered in ivy, and we decided it was neither attractive nor good for the brickwork. We spent the afternoon pulling it off the walls and found that easiest way was for me to cut the stems at the top near the eaves, so we could then easily haul the ivy down.

I started at one end and carried on cutting stems across the front of the house. Towards the end I found one stem to be particularly tough, so I applied greater pressure, only to discover I'd cut our telephone wire. I was absolutely furious with myself, and cursed loudly, 'Shit, shit, shit.'

Patricia suggested I went next door to ask our elderly neighbour Solange what I should do. Her response was that I needed to call France Telecom.

'But I can't,' I exclaimed.

'Ah oui, je comprends.' She laughed and offered me her phone to make the call.

I got through and explained my problem. They said they would give it their immediate attention. Never in a million years did I think they'd get anything done until we were back in the UK. To our amazement however, the following morning at ten thirty, there was a knock at the door. A telephone engineer stood there grinning. I went outside and explained the problem.

'Oh là là,' he said, and went on to say that installing a new cable was one thing. Repairing a cut cable was much more difficult. He shook his head and said he'd give it a go.

About an hour later, he knocked at the door.

'C'est fait, Monsieur.'

He took me outside to show me he'd completed the work. I was delighted. He asked me to sign his timesheet, and I noticed he'd inserted he'd done three hours' work, which I assume I'd be billed for.

'But hang on,' I said. 'This isn't correct.'

'Look here, Monsieur,' he replied, waving the form at me. 'See what it says here.'

I read that the work was completed free of charge. In return for me signing that he'd completed three hour's work, he'd indicated that the repair was due to a fault. Result – win/win. I shook him by the hand and passed him a €10 note.

'Merci Monsieur, et bon appétit.' He winked as he drove off.

A HARSH WINTER AND A WARM SPRING

2005

After that visit, we weren't able to get back to France until February the following year. It was half-term week, and Jo – Patricia's youngest daughter – who had just turned fifteen came out with us. We left England on Monday, 28 February in heavy snow, and actually missed our ferry crossing from Dover due to snow blocking the road towards Ashford. We eventually arrived in France around lunchtime.

Although it continued to snow lightly in northern France, I decided to go via Paris, on the assumption the roads there would be clear. They were, and traffic ran reasonably freely. We continued south on the autoroutes, which were also clear. We came off the A20 around 9 p.m.

There had been heavy snow in the Limousin although all the roads were passable. I remember driving on the country roads, and seeing a massive lorry loaded with logs driving towards us at high speed. We all shuddered as we thought of what might have happened had the lorry driver skidded out of control.

We arrived at Pellac at about ten. The village looked very picturesque, and we were relieved to see the street lights – the few that were there – working. At least there was electricity in the village. We parked in the drive and entered the house. It was absolutely freezing and felt bleak. We decided to make a hot drink and go straight to bed. Patricia suggested that all three of us slept in our bedroom, with Jo on a camp bed. That way, we could turn on the massive electrical radiator we had and heat the room throughout the night.

I woke up around 4 a.m. The temperature was unbelievably cold. I got up and noticed the radiator wasn't switched on. I turned it back on. No response. I decided to go back to bed and leave matters until daylight.

When we got up, we realised the electrical supply had tripped. I turned it back on and switched on the radiator. It worked for about twenty seconds before blowing out the trip. I turned it back on, and the same thing happened. The radiator was clearly too powerful. So that left us with a problem, as we had no heating.

We all went into the lounge and stared at the fireplace. It was open and empty. I knew we had a large supply of wood in the wood barn. Jo and I went across the orchard and carried back as much wood as we could carry. We placed a pile in the fireplace. It was so dry we didn't need firelighters (not that we had any!) It took off like a rocket. We all turned to each and grinned.

Easy peasy!

Or maybe not.

Suddenly, smoke started to pour back into the room. It was awful. We quickly opened the large windows to allow the smoke to disperse, much to the consternation of one of the villagers who was walking past. They simply stopped and stared. The temperature outside was around minus ten degrees. They must have imagined we were weird, opening our windows in such cold weather.

We let the flames die down, and tried an alternative way of lighting the fire, this time standing the wood lengthways upwards. At first it seemed it was working, but then smoke billowed back into the room. The chimney must be blocked.

I plugged in the landline, which thankfully was working, and telephoned Yves – the local handyman. I left a message with his wife, who said she'd try to get Yves to come round that afternoon.

As the house was so uncomfortably cold – we were still wearing yesterday's clothes to stay warm, we decided to drive to a local town, where we could get a coffee and some croissants, and then go supermarket shopping. We got back at lunchtime to a freezing, inhospitable house, and made some soup.

Yves arrived just after two and I explained the problem with the electrics and the radiator. He explained the radiator was too powerful for the power supply. He had a look around and reported back that the wiring in the house was old and needed upgrading. He told me he was busy for the next few weeks, but that he'd be able to put in a new fuse-board around the end of March. He also suggested he install a new immersion heater, which would be much bigger and more suitable for our needs. However, again, this couldn't be done until the end of the month.

I asked him about the fireplace. He had a look up the chimney and couldn't see a blockage. He recommended we got it swept and added he could do it – you guessed – at the end of the month! So positive news for the future, but nothing that could help us now. Yves thought that given the chimney hadn't been used for many years, it could be very damp, which would cause the smoke to pour back into the house. He suggested we could persevere if we didn't mind leaving the windows open.

After he left, we tried lighting the fire again – several times. It was actually less cold outside, so all three of us stood in the garden watching the lounge fill with smoke. After an hour or so, nothing had really changed; the house really stank of smoke. So, we decided to give it up as a bad job and went back inside.

I popped out to a local town to buy a smaller, less powerful electrical radiator. They were in very short supply, but I returned with a small convection fan heater. This at least took the edge off the coldness in the lounge, although we continued to wear our coats and scarves inside.

That evening, the three of us sat in the lounge, watching old videos on the tiny portable TV, wrapped in dressing gowns, socks, scarves etc. We'd all managed to take a shower, but as the water would need re-heating after each shower, this was a lengthy process.

We managed to stick it out over the next couple of days, but by Thursday evening, Patricia and I agreed this was a miserable existence. We were on the point of packing up to return home on the Friday, when Patricia suggested we telephone one of the B&Bs we stayed in when we initially came to the area to house hunt. Amazingly, they had a couple of rooms available, so we booked ourselves in for a couple of nights, then returned to the UK as planned on the Sunday. There was still a lot of snow on the roads, and driving was quite hazardous. I promised myself that one day I would buy a 4x4 vehicle.

As promised, Yves started to carry out the work of re-wiring and installing the new immersion heater, and in mid-April, Patricia and I decided to go across for a weekend. We thought it would be fun to catch the train, so we caught an early Eurostar on the Friday morning, spent a couple of pleasant hours in Paris en route, and arrived in Limoges late afternoon. We collected the hire car and drove to Pellac. Spring was in full-force, and although there wasn't much sun, everything felt different.

A massive new immersion heater was fixed to the wall in the tiny bathroom. This meant we could have proper showers – joy! All the power sockets downstairs had been changed, and thankfully the large radiator worked. With that switched on, plus the other heater I'd bought, the house gradually started to warm up. We didn't do much else that weekend and caught the train back from Limoges on the Sunday evening.

Our next visit took place in May, again for the half-term week. We went back with Jo and Gemma, plus our dog Billy, and drove down on the Friday. The weather was glorious – hot and sunny. We arrived late afternoon. The garden was like a jungle, but I'd anticipated that, and brought with me a new Stihl petrol strimmer I'd recently bought.

We didn't do much for the first few days other than do some more cleaning and general tidying up as well as a massive amount of gardening. We put all the old furniture and artefacts in the garage, which created lots of additional space in the house.

After a few days, Patricia started to feel unwell. Overnight, her temperature shot up, and she woke up feeling very out-of-sorts. I was quite worried – she really was quite ill. When our next-door neighbour Solange popped across mid-morning with some vegetables from her garden, she suggested I called a doctor. Within a couple of hours, a doctor arrived. He checked Patricia out and prescribed various medications. It was a nasty, flu-like virus.

While she stayed in bed for the rest of the day, I decided to take some of the stuff from the garage to a local dump (or recycling centre as it's called these days), which was about a twenty-minute drive away.

I arrived at the dump and joined the queue of cars. As I entered the site, I noticed a man standing on a platform which was like a bridge between the various skip containers. This was the man responsible for running the place. He was wearing reflective sunglasses, like a gangster. He stood menacingly, with his arms folded. As I approached, he pointed at me, and then beckoned me to drive up on this bridge. I parked the car and got out. He stared at me and raised his chin slightly in a mildly challenging way.

'Monsieur?' he remarked.

I showed him what I'd got in the boot of the car, and he proceeded to give me a tour of the site, pointing at the various containers, and where I should deposit my stuff, depending on whether it was wood, metal, textiles, etc. He was intrigued by both the quantity and weirdness of what I'd brought with me. I explained we'd bought a maison secondaire.

'Non, Monsieur. Vous avez achetée une musée !' *A museum!*

I emptied the car. As I drove out of the exit, I noticed a sign to a 'lac'. I decided to investigate. I drove into the entrance where it was located and indeed discovered a massive lake. There were pedaloes and other types of play-boats, and a number of people were swimming in the water. I spotted a beach on one of the banks where people were sunbathing.

As I started to drive back, I called the house phone, and spoke to Jo. I explained I'd found this lake and told her and Gemma to get their swimming gear together. When I got back, Patricia was reading in bed. The girls were excited; they'd had enough of playing in the garden and needed something different. While they got into the car, I loaded up the second lot of stuff for the dump, and I drove back to St Mathieu.

The girls were delighted. I bought them some ice creams, and they found somewhere on the beach to put their clothes and wandered off for a swim. I drove back to the dump for the second visit and joined them afterwards. The atmosphere was wonderful – in fact, it was like being on a beach by the sea.

CAMPING LE SOLEIL – MARK 2

2005

In July 2005, I fulfilled one of my biggest dreams – to return to the south of France for a family camping holiday. The plan was that Lucy, Gemma, and I would spend a week at Pellac, and then travel down to the south coast, back to Argélès to Camping le Soleil. We would set up the tent, and then Patricia and Jo would fly out a couple of days later to join us.

Lucy, Gemma, and I arrived at our house on the Sunday evening. One of my tasks that week was to build a new side gate, to replace the existing one which had virtually rotted away. I went to M. Bricolage to buy the materials and spent a few contented days making the gate and painting it before I proudly installed it. The girls were happy to laze around in the sun.

I probably drove them mad in the evenings; apart from having to put up with my very limited cooking skills, I had a video I wanted to watch each night. It was a journey called *Long Way Round*, featuring Ewan McGregor and his friend Charlie Boorman. They went on a motor-cycle trip around the world, travelling from London to Europe, through eastern Europe/Asia through Mongolia and parts of Russia, finally ending up in the US. My problem was that I kept falling asleep before the end of each episode, so each night, I'd have to go back to get to where I remembered before continuing. I suffered some serious mickey-taking!

The night before we left for Argélès, we went to dinner with some friends – Walter (Walt) & Hilary – who had a house about thirty minutes away in the woods near Nontron. They were also going to look after our dog Billy while we were away camping. They had some friends staying, one of whom played guitar, so he, Walt, and I played guitar together until late in the evening – or until our fairly limited repertoire of songs had been used up.

Lucy, Gemma, and I left early the following morning. It was a Saturday; the weather was once again gorgeous, as it had been all week. It took a while to get down to the campsite. We forgot that the French only travel on the weekends during the main summer holiday period. This means the autoroutes are absolutely chocker full of cars heading south – and also north as families head back after their holidays. After suffering a multitude of traffic jams, we finally arrived at Camping Le Soleil around seven thirty pm, which was about two hours later than our intended time.

We'd decided to buy a new tent that year. We'd outgrown the previous tent, and one of the main zips also failed the year before, so I bit the bullet, and ordered a massive new tent online, which arrived in late April. Patricia, Gemma, and I did a dummy installation in the garden, which seemed relatively straightforward. I assumed that the two girls and I would have the tent up by 9 p.m., which would enable us to get to the campsite restaurant in time before it closed at 9.30 p.m.

We unpacked the tent, and then Lucy said she needed to visit the loo. Gemma and I carried on putting up the tent. Eventually, after about half an hour Lucy reappeared. She nonchalantly strolled up and asked if I had any spare change, as she needed to call a friend. 'Which friend?' I asked in a rather bad-tempered way. I was knackered after a long drive down, and I was hot and tired putting up the tent.

'We need you here, helping us,' I said.

'I will,' replied Lucy. 'I just need to make a quick call, unless I can use your mobile…'

'No way,' I replied. 'Knowing you, you'll never get off the phone, and it will cost a fortune.'

Lucy persuaded me she'd be back in ten minutes. I begrudgingly gave her a pocket full of change, and Gemma and I continued putting up the tent. We actually worked really well together. When I'm hot, hungry, and thirsty, my bark becomes far worse than my bite. But Gemma was able to read me easily, and she just got stuck in. By 9 p.m., the two of us had managed to get the tent up and the car unloaded. Lucy turned up just as we were finishing, with a can of beer for me, and a bottle of Orangina for Gemma. That helped to take the heat out of my fire. By then, I was exhausted and needed to eat.

Over dinner, I asked Lucy who her friend was. I'd mentioned it to Gemma earlier, but she remained discreetly silent. It turned out it was a boy back home, from Burnham-on-Crouch, called Phil. She didn't say much, but said he'd just got home from holiday. I commented he must be a bit special for her to be on the phone for so long. Little did I know then how special he'd become. They got married seven years later!

With full bellies, and with me having consumed the best part of a bottle of red wine, we went to bed and slept in late the next morning. We pottered about on the Sunday, getting shopping and preparing for Patricia and Jo to join us.

On the Monday morning, we left the campsite after a quick breakfast, to drive to Girona in Spain to collect Patricia and Jo. Although they could have flown to Perpignan, the cost of flights to Girona was considerably cheaper. Unfortunately, we got delayed at the French/Spanish border and arrived at Girona airport to find the two of them waiting outside. We were all delighted to see each other. I'd really missed Patricia. We drove back to the campsite and the girls all went off to the swimming pool, while I introduced Patricia to the campsite. I'd bought some food for dinner that evening – basic stuff like pasta and sauce and offered to cook.

Patricia was quite horrified (actually disgusted, I think) to see how primitive my cooking arrangements were. I had a two-ring Camping Gaz burner, which I propped up on a couple of large stones I'd found. This meant that to cook, you had to squat down. I had very few cooking utensils. Yes – I agreed, it was pretty rough! I then shot myself in the foot by explaining to Patricia that the previous year, we'd mostly eaten at the campsite restaurant.

'Why aren't we eating there tonight then?' she asked me.

I explained I wanted to cook for her and the girls and apologised and opened another bottle of wine. I think I ended up doing the washing up as well that evening, while Patricia sat outside the tent polishing off the wine. Hey-ho!

She and Jo settled very quickly into campsite life, and we spent lots of time on the beach and at the pool. We also went to the main bar most evenings. Back in the 1970s this was more of a bar/disco, but there was now a separate nightclub in a cave type dwelling below ground. The main bar had family entertainment most evenings – kids singing and dancing – and it kept the girls happy and amused. I'd noticed that Lucy was slow to join in; she spent a lot of time texting on her phone – to Phil no doubt.

After a couple of days, Patricia told me how much she was enjoying the camping, and said she'd like to come back the following year.

'However,' she told me firmly (and sternly, although Patricia doesn't really do stern, so this was as firm as it got) – 'Things will change next year. We will have proper cooking facilities, with proper utensils, and we will do this properly!'

Opposite our tent were two caravans occupied by two French families who'd come together. One family had three children – a teenage son and daughter, and another son aged about ten. The other family had a daughter of similar age, and a son aged around eighteen whose swarthy looks occupied Lucy and Jo's attention from time to time. We nodded to each other across the little road dividing our tents and said Bonjour or Bon Appétit a few times. Patricia had spotted their magnificent barbecue and suggested we buy a small throwaway barbecue. The following evening, as I was trying to light our rather pathetic barbecue, one of the Frenchmen opposite popped across and explained that small, disposable barbecues were forbidden due to fire risk. We got chatting, and I commented on his barbecue. He immediately offered to lend it to us the following evening.

That broke the ice. The next evening, he and the other Frenchman carried across their barbecue, said 'Bon Courage', and left it to us. When they returned from the restaurant they'd visited, I took across a couple of bottles of wine to say thanks. We got chatting, and they invited us to join them for apéros the following evening.

We weren't aware of the misunderstanding that the word 'apéros' creates when French people invite you for a drink. Earlier that day, I'd asked what time they'd like us over. They shrugged and said six or 7 p.m. I suggested six-thirty and they looked at me quizzically and replied, 'Comme vous voulez.' *As you wish.*

So we had an early dinner, much to their amusement as they looked across while we ate. Patricia and I washed up, and we all went across at 6.30 p.m. punctually.

After the usual ritual of introductions, handshakes, and kisses, we pulled up chairs, and they offered us drinks – pastis, whisky, wine, or beer. I started jabbering away in French as usual – none of them really spoke English, apart from their kids, who said a few phrases in the typically embarrassed way that teenagers do. Our girls – naturally for English kids – didn't speak French, apart from Gemma, but she was only eleven.

The 'Frenchies' as we subsequently called them, were absolutely amazed to learn we had a house in France. They didn't know many English people, and certainly no one who owned property in their country.

We had another drink, and the kids drifted off to the campsite play area. Patricia was able to understand some of what I was saying, and we managed to keep a conversation going for a good hour. Eventually, one of the men said he was going to light the barbecue. I looked at Patricia and suggested we should take our leave and leave them to eat.

'Mais non?' they exclaimed, and insisted we join them for dinner. We couldn't say no. Food was prepared, cooked and served, and we tucked in.

We ate and chatted away for another hour, and then the Frenchies said they were going to the nightclub. They asked if we'd like to accompany them. Patricia and I were a bit surprised; we thought it was just for older teenagers. The age range was from sixteen upwards, so we settled Jo and Gemma back at our tent. Lucy wasn't over-keen to come, so she too stayed back at the tent.

We queued up outside the club, which hadn't yet opened, with our new French friends. They introduced us to some more French people – friends of theirs. They were pretty weird; a woman in her late 50s, wearing a very low-cut minidress, who clearly fancied herself, and any other man looking in her direction! Her husband had greasy hair and a smarmy, furtive look, especially as he eyed up the teenage girls. Eventually, we got into the club. To say it was awful was an understatement. It was about twenty per cent full, the drinks were expensive, and the music was terrible. The Frenchies all started dancing together and included us. Patricia and I aren't keen dancers. In the twenty-five or so years we've been together, we've still never been to a nightclub together or a disco. Conversation was impossible. The leery man tried to get close to Patricia. His weird wife kept giving me the eye. Eventually, having put up with this for about half an hour, we went to get a drink. We hung around for about an hour, then made our excuses and left.

The following evening, Patricia and I and the girls went to the campsite bar. There was some kind of talent competition going on. Some teenage boys from Liverpool got together and sang/danced a routine and won their level. Interestingly, Jo spotted one of them on TV a couple of years later on a programme about kids suffering from Tourette's.

Earlier that day, we had all hung around the pool. Jo had made some friends, and she joined them on a large platform overlooking the pool, where a lot of teenagers hung out. We all gradually drifted back to the tent, apart from Jo. After we'd showered and changed, Patricia began to get concerned. She went looking for Jo, and after fifteen minutes came back looking worried. She couldn't see her at the pool, and said she'd go for a wander around the campsite looking for her. After about an hour, Jo turned up at the tent. She didn't say much about where she'd been, and I told her that her mum had gone looking for her. When Patricia got back to the tent and found Jo, she absolutely wiped the floor with her. I'd rarely seen Patricia so angry.

She'd clearly been very worried. We decided to ground Jo that evening, which led to tantrums and tears. Eventually, after apologising to us all several times, we relented.

The next day, it was time for Lucy and Gemma to fly back to the UK to Stansted, where their mum was going to collect them. I drove them to Girona, and we said an emotional goodbye at the airport. It's so sad when holidays come to an end. I slowly walked back to the car. I started the engine, and as I put my foot on the accelerator, there seemed to be a loss of power. The car slowly picked up speed, and I drove out of the car park and onto the Autostrada.

Within a mile, I could sense a major problem. The loss of power kicked in again. I was crawling along at about 20 mph. Fortunately, I saw a garage and pulled in. I parked the car and called the RAC. I explained the problem; the guy at the end of the phone sounded a little hesitant when I said I was in Spain. He went on to say that if there was any way I could cross the border into France, assistance would arrive much more quickly. We agreed I would wait there and talk again in forty minutes.

I was still feeling pretty low after saying goodbye to Lucy and Gem. I tried Patricia's mobile, but it was switched off. Calls at that time were horrendously expensive to both make and receive. I waited in the car for about half an hour, then restarted the engine. This time, the car fired correctly, and there was no loss of acceleration. I decided to go for it and drove back on to the Autostrada. After around twenty minutes, the RAC called me back, and I explained I'd got the car running, and I was approaching the French border. The RAC suggested I carry on and call them if the problem recurred.

I managed to get back to the campsite not much later than I'd said. Patricia and Jo had packed up the tent, and it was all ready to go into the car, ready for our drive back that night. I'd already decided not to say anything to Patricia. She would only worry and given the car had operated ok since the initial problem, there seemed little point in mentioning it.

We set off from the campsite at around 7 p.m., after a last pizza together, sitting on a bench at the camp entrance. I began the 6-hour drive back. En route we didn't say much. I was apprehensive should the problem recur, and Patricia and Jo were tired after a long day in the sun. We arrived back at Pellac around 1 a.m. Jo went to bed, and I poured myself a very large whisky.

'Are you OK?' asked Patricia. 'You seem a bit on edge.'

I downed the whisky, and poured another, and explained about the car. Patricia agreed that she would have been really worried and gave me a big hug and thanked me for getting us all back safely.

We were meeting Walt and Hilary the next day at a local restaurant. They were bringing back our dog Billy who they'd been looking after. As we drove away from the resto after lunch, I suddenly, without warning, experienced the loss of power I'd had the day before in Spain. We limped back to Pellac, and I called the RAC again. They moved quickly, and within two hours, a British mechanic turned up. He diagnosed that there was a problem, although couldn't say what it was. He explained he'd make arrangements for the car to be collected and repaired, and also organise a hire car for us. He said he'd be back in touch the following morning.

By 9 a.m., the phone was ringing. First of all was a garage, who told me (in English) that a pick-up truck was on its way. Second was a call from a hire car company, to say they'd arranged for a taxi to collect me at midday to take me to them to collect a hire car. Finally, the taxi company called to confirm they would collect me. I was so impressed! The RAC really had done their stuff and pulled all the stops out.

Accordingly, the pick-up truck turned up, and we waved our 5-series estate goodbye, hopefully on its road to recovery. Then, an hour later, the taxi driver arrived. He was a live wire! He shot off at about 60 mph along the winding country lanes, and jabbered away in very fast, heavily accented French. During the drive to Limoges, he took lots of calls on his mobile, which he held to his ear, including several from his wife. He asked me loads of questions, such as why we owned a house in France, why I owned a BMW (a brand which he seemed to love), and he recommended a couple of good local restaurants which I wasn't aware of. He then dropped me off and sped away.

It was lunchtime, so the car-hire office was shut until 2.30 p.m. I wandered down to a supermarket and grabbed a sandwich. I then collected the car and drove back.

The next few days were pretty uneventful. Jo became bored, so we decided to drive to Périgueux on the Saturday morning. Given it was mid-August, the market wasn't up to much, so we drove back via a fete in Thiviers. On the Sunday, we had a call from our French friend Jacques. We'd met Jacques earlier that year, as we walked through the village one evening. He lived there with his partner Marguerite. He was friendly and warm, with a good sense of humour, and we became close friends. He explained that an English family, who lived in the village several years ago, were back in the village that day, and so he invited us all round for drinks and apéros at lunchtime. It turned out that they lived in Canterbury, and Jo quickly became friends with their youngest daughter.

I had a called from the BMW dealer in Brive on the Monday. The car was repaired and ready to collect. I called the hire car company to confirm it was ok to drop off the car in Brive not Limoges. I then drove to Brive, dropped off the hire car, and took a taxi to the dealer. They didn't say much, except that all was well. They explained what the problem, but frankly, if they'd told me in English, I still wouldn't have understood, not being remotely interested in the technical aspects of cars. Unlike in the UK, when cars are returned washed and valeted, my car looked dirtier than it was when it went off.

The following day, I took Billy to the vet. This was a ritual; while it was simple to bring a dog into France, there was a certain protocol that had to be followed prior to departure. We would have to visit a local vet, who would verify the dog's identity chip, and then dispense an anti-tapeworm tablet for which we'd be charged between 30 to 35 Euros. The vet would then stamp the pet's passport to signify the animal had been given the drug, and that it was fit and able to travel.

In the early days, the dogs would receive an injection instead of a tablet, which would often cause discomfort due to the contents of the syringe stinging. But over the past ten years, the injection has been replaced by a tablet.

We began to develop a good relationship with the vets. The two principals spoke some English and possessed a good sense of humour. Many of their clients were from the UK and they explained they had to speak English, as so many Brits didn't speak French. Once they discovered I understood French, we've enjoyed a good laugh together over the years. The vets are almost bemused that English law dictates this protocol, and they admit they're quite happy to take our money if our country insists on this process.

There was one vet who caused Patricia's heart to beat a little faster when we went. He was built like a rugby player, with a huge chest and enormous shoulders. He had piercing blue eyes and a deep voice, and while he didn't say much, he would just stare. But as Patricia admitted, she would no doubt get bored simply staring back at him, and when the guy eventually moved on after a couple of years, I don't think she missed him too much.

In recent years, we've been having an annual break in the Black Forest. As in France, we have to visit a local vet before our journey back to the UK. We found a vet some years ago, who is absolutely charming. He speaks fluent English, has the most organised and spotless surgery, and charges just 12 Euros. The second time we went, I casually mentioned that we pay up to three times the amount in France.

'Ah, it's just bollocks,' said the vet in his perfect English. 'They are ripping you off.'

I had a similar conversation with the French vets the following year, when I mentioned what we're charged in Germany. The French vet simply smiled and said it was all part of their service. It was hard to argue!

The next day, we started to pack up and clean the house. On our final night, we went to a local resto nearby. Jo was on good form, laughing and joking, and we had a lovely meal. When we got back, Patricia and I sat on the front doorstep sharing a whisky, and I wistfully commented how easily I could stay for another couple of weeks. But we had to go home, and the following day we drove back to the UK.

BILLY'S LAST TIME IN FRANCE

2005

Our next visit to France was in October, and we took my mum with us. She hadn't seen the house, apart from the very first time, when we took possession of the keys. She was impressed with the various changes, and we spent a very pleasant week together. We visited one of the restaurants that Joel, the taxi driver had recommended. I called to book, and we arrived at 7 p.m.

The resto was in a private house, with no more than four or five tables. There was no menu – dishes simply arrived. To Patricia's disgust, the starter was gésiers (gizzards) on a warm salad, but the meal picked up after that. The owner would only accept cash – no cheques or credit cards – so we scraped all our various notes and coins together, and just about afforded the bill.

We also decided to drive down to the centre of the Dordogne one day and stopped off at Sarlat. Being October, there weren't many tourists, and we enjoyed a very pleasant wander around and lunch in a little bistro.

Before we left the UK for France, we'd taken Jo to Stansted Airport the weekend before. Her school had a two-week half-term, and during this break it was work experience time for the GCSE students. Patricia and I had stayed in touch with the owner of the B&B where we stayed in March the year before, when we came to look for property. Patricia contacted the owners – an Englishman married to a Russian woman – and asked if Jo could stay and gain her work experience. This was a great idea – she could work in all areas of the business – the kitchen, waiting tables, changing beds, etc.

Jo (then aged fifteen) said a tearful goodbye to us at Stansted – she did look very young as she walked through the barrier. We arranged to collect her from the B&B at the end of our week. On the Saturday afternoon at the end of our stay, Patricia, Mum, and I (with Billy our dog) drove over, which was about an hour away. It was good to see Jo, who looked happy and confident. She'd clearly had a good time. The arrangement was for us to stay overnight there and drive back to the UK on the Sunday.

The owner had got a dog earlier that year. It was huge and looked and sounded really menacing. It had clearly become a bone of contention among the owners; the wife liked the dog, but the husband felt it would put off their customers. Gradually, a row ensued between them as the evening went on, and they tried to involve us to take sides. We went to bed feeling somewhat uncomfortable and left early the following morning to drive to Calais.

A couple of weeks after returning home, we very sadly and suddenly lost our dog Billy. He fell ill, and within forty-eight hours was staying overnight at the vets. He stayed there over the weekend, and never returned home. We were absolutely devastated. Losing a dog is always very upsetting, especially as it was so unexpected. Billy was only seven years old. We'd had him since he was a puppy, bringing him home from the Blue Cross for unwanted pets. He was a gentle, sweet-natured dog, a mixed-breed about the size of a cocker spaniel. To be honest, he didn't really take to France. As soon as he was let out into the garden, he'd jump over the wall and run off. This meant we had to keep him on a long chain by the front door. He was at his happiest at our home in Tenterden and going for walks in the local woods.

OUR DISCUSSION GROUP – LEARN REAL FRENCH

2005

In the autumn of that year, we started a new initiative. For the past two years (2004 and 2005), Patricia had studied French at night-school. Although she speaks fluent German, having had a German mother, her French was very basic. She stuck at the course and seemed to have more than a basic understanding. However, during the summer, when we returned to Pellac after our holiday at the campsite, she asked me one evening after dinner what I thought of her French. 'Pretty crap,' I replied, much to her disappointment. I went on to explain that while she professed to understand what was being said, she showed no willingness to join in conversations and speak. She agreed, and we reflected that a lot of English people probably felt the same. It was the embarrassment or awkwardness in speaking up and not being understood.

'It's given me an idea,' I expressed as I started to uncork another bottle of wine.

'Why don't we set up a French discussion group in Tenterden? We could put together a quick and dirty website and see if there's any interest.'

Thus started a brand-new adventure as we embarked on this new project. We called it Learn Real French. The idea was that people would come along to our house for an hour and a half one evening each week, and we'd talk purely in French on a pre-designated topic. We prepared six different themes: travel and holidays; food, wine, and eating out; shopping; work and leisure interests; buying a property in France and DIY; and finally, dealing with the unexpected.

We would prepare the vocabulary and phrases, and the idea was that we'd speak the French that the French speak, spoken as it is these days, colloquially. We thought that as we could only accommodate a small group of around six to eight people, we'd run a 6-week programme covering these topics, and we'd then start up the programme again with new people. I would lead the discussions, and we'd all share a glass of wine together to make the evenings more convivial.

We stuck an advert in the local newspaper. Within a week, we had our first 'students', and we had enough for a reserve list for the next course.

People arrived on the first Tuesday evening in October. There were six of us, plus Patricia and me. I set the scene, and we began to talk. People were less hesitant than I'd imagined, and the conversation began to flow. By the third week, the group had started to get to know each other. At the end of the fifth session, I explained that the following week would be the last.

'What happens after that?' one of them asked. 'Can't we keep coming to talk about other topics?'

Patricia and I were a little taken aback. We'd always gone with the premise that it was a six-week programme. We didn't expect people would want to keep coming back. But they did!

The next question was what to do with the people on the waiting list? We decided we could bring in two more people and told the others they would remain on the waiting list. My work was then cut out. I'd imagined I'd just need to prepare the six different sessions, which we'd use again and again. But given the demand to continue, I had to think of, plan, and prepare additional subjects.

By the beginning of 2006, our French discussion group started to take off. Gradually, we discovered that people would come and go. As the level of French within the group improved, some people who were less confident fell by the wayside as they felt out of their comfort zones. Equally, we received an almost continual demand from new people to join in. We decided to set the benchmark for joining, in that any newcomers had to be able to speak a reasonable level of French confidently within the group. We'd moved beyond simply encouraging people with very basic French to attracting people who would be able to make a real contribution to the discussions.

We also noticed that the group members were becoming friends. We organised a summer party for them and their 'other halves' and by the time of our Christmas French party in December, Patricia and I realised quite what we had achieved.

As the years rolled on, Tuesday evenings with Learn Real French were ever present in our calendars. We said goodbye to a few members, and welcomed some new ones, until we got to a point where we had about a dozen people who came on a regular basis. Fortunately, they didn't all come at once every week. There were a few occasions when this did happen, and we struggled but managed to find chairs and additional glasses (and wine) for everyone.

We evolved and changed the format, and as we got to know each other, there was almost a desire to know more about what was going on in our respective lives. In order to get everyone fully focused and talking, I started each week by going around the table, asking people what they'd done at the weekend, or since we'd last met. One lady had a mother in her 90s living alone in Derbyshire, and as her mother's health deteriorated, she spent most weekends travelling back and forth to see her. Another member had similar issues going on, with elderly parents living far away, and the subsequent passing of each of them. In that sense, the group had almost become therapeutic.

There was a lot of information that was usefully shared. For example, several group members had second homes in France, it was helpful to share experiences, problems, pitfalls as well as ideas, initiatives, etc. On this basis, we agreed to extend the principle of sharing information among the group members to create a spreadsheet of useful contacts in the local Tenterden area, with a variety of recommendations for electricians, plumbers, builders, tree surgeons, dentists, mechanics, etc.

I always said that to join the group, you had to have a strong sense of humour, and a very broad mind. We would discuss anything and everything – always in French of course. We wouldn't speak English at all for the whole ninety-minute duration. Sometimes conversations would go down some challenging paths; given our average age range, when most of us grew up in the 50s and 60s, political correctness in our discussions often fell by the wayside.

I remember one evening; it was early summer, and by some quirk, only men were present that night. As soon as this was realised, one of the guys said, 'Right, Nigel, let's learn the swear words and vulgar expressions.'

I had a couple of very colloquial dictionaries, and there was a lot of ribaldry and laughter that night. At that time, Patricia was running a weight-watchers group, and could only attend the last half-hour. She got back at 8.30 p.m. to find us collapsed in hilarity!

I recounted an interesting story to the group that a French friend Jacques had told me about. Apparently, he went to see some friends who had some elderly relatives from Canada staying with them. Jacques explained that French-Canadians often speak in a more old-fashioned way, using vocabulary that was rarely used in France. During the evening, Jacques noticed that one of the French-Canadians had left the room, so he asked where he was. The reply he received was, 'Il se branle dans le couloir.' This was intended to mean *he's rocking (in the rocking chair) in the hallway.*

Jacques however was horrified. The verb se branler in idiomatic French means to wank. So, Jacques initially interpreted this as meaning *the friend was masturbating in the hallway*!

We had one unique group member – he was the first person to respond to our initial advert. He was a widower in his mid-80s. He and his wife had lived in the south of France during the early 1980s. She didn't take to the lifestyle out there, and much to his sorrow, they returned to Tenterden. He was a charming little man, very dapper, politically incorrect, with a penchant for hugging ladies a little too close for comfort. He had an ancient *Collins Gem Pocket Dictionary*, which he'd use to search for words, and would come out with old-fashioned French. He was quite lonely, and when we talked about our weekends, he often invented stories from his vivid imagination about weekend trips to exotic places such as Argentina, or the Middle East, and he'd talk of meeting equally exotic ladies. The first time he did this, we sat open-mouthed with incredulity!

We were also a very social group. In addition to the two parties we held each year – one in July and the other in December, we had some trips to France together. We'd go across mid-afternoon for a spot of shopping, and then go to a restaurant which was pre-booked, before catching the last Eurotunnel train back home. Some strong, lasting friendships were forged. One party in particular was very special: the oldest member of the group (previously mentioned) was ninety. We celebrated his birthday by hiring a troupe of belly dancers. They arrived while everyone was in the garden. We sat the birthday boy in a chair in the conservatory, and as the ladies made their way outside, they all kissed the top of his head. His face was an absolute picture, and his eyes were on stalks. Eventually, we all ended up belly dancing, wearing sashes, and being taught by the ladies, to much mirth and laughter.

The French discussion group ran for a total of twelve years. They were happy times. Every Tuesday, the doorbell would repeatedly ring as seven thirty approached. Our dog Freddie, who we acquired in 2007, would always bark excitedly, and then make a fuss of whoever arrived.

Coats would pile up in the hallway, cries of 'Bonjour or Bon Soir' as people walked into the dining room. Faces would be kissed, hands would be shaken; wine would be poured, crisps would be munched as we settled into conversation. We always, always had a laugh. We inevitably ended up talking about food and wine, and politics was often on the menu with a healthy cross-section of views both left and right. Some people would leave promptly at 9 p.m., while others were happy to stay and finish off the wine. Occasionally, there would be European Champions League games featuring my own team Chelsea on TV, and I'd be itching to steal away to grab the closing minutes.

We finally decided to call a halt in 2017. By then, I'd set up my yoga business, which took up a couple of evenings with classes.

In conclusion, we felt, like so many things in life, that the French group had run its course, and that it was time to move on.

HOME COMFORTS AND PROPER CAMPING

2006

In March 2006. I celebrated my fiftieth birthday. The month before, I'd had a car accident near Heathrow Airport, and had my car written off. I was between cars, waiting for the insurance company to pay out, so we took Patricia's Vauxhall Corsa to France. We were pleased to discover the car coped admirably with such a long trip, and it was a more comfortable journey than we anticipated. We had a quiet week, topped off by our friends Paul and Stephanie arriving from Nottingham for the weekend.

We went back in May in our new car. I was tempted to get something smaller, but various friends talked me out of it, saying we really needed something substantial on what were eight-to-ten-hour journeys. We also needed space to accommodate the hundred and one things we always seemed to need to take. We bought another estate car, this time an Audi 6, which was diesel. This was very economic as diesel at that time was markedly cheaper in France – around thirty per cent less than UK prices. It also fulfilled my dream as it was the Quattro 4x4.

Patricia and I had decided to break a major resolution; we'd always agreed we wouldn't have a TV set in the house. But there were a number of occasions, especially during cold evenings, when a TV would have been good. The final straw was when I tried using the existing TV aerial to watch the Lions play rugby in New Zealand. Despite the fact it was on French TV, the view from the little portable TV/DVD player we had was insufferable.

We weren't at all impressed by French TV, so we arranged for a satellite dish to be installed. The guy was recommended by Solange, our next-door neighbour. He arrived at 10 a.m. on the dot, a chap in his late 60s with a cheeky look and a roving eye. At this point, I should add that Patricia is a stunningly beautiful woman. He took one look at Patricia and said to me in French, 'Is this your wife?' I replied that she was, to which he retorted the equivalent of 'You lucky bugger!' As he set about installing the dish, he couldn't resist constantly looking over his shoulder at her as she made him a coffee.

Incidentally, the French just can't understand why we Brits drink coffee in mugs, whereas all they want is a couple of teaspoonfuls in a tiny cup.

He went home for lunch and returned an hour later to tune the TV. I explained we wanted English TV and the name of the satellite channel – Astra 2, I believe. This poor chap went through almost every satellite channel imaginable during his search. We saw channels pop up from the Middle East, from Russia, from Africa. It literally took him all afternoon, before eventually he came up with what we were looking for. We paid him, gave him a bottle of wine in recognition of his efforts, and with a last cheeky glance at Patricia, he drove off.

The TV really enhanced our lives out there. We could catch-up with the news, watch our favourite dramas and films, as well as sport. A couple of years later, we bought a second TV set to watch upstairs in the newly converted loft.

We were discovering that every time we went out there was invariably work to do in either the house or garden. We had an orchard opposite the house, which contained various fruit trees. The front garden/driveway was mostly gravel, but the grass in the orchard was overgrown. The year before, Solange suggested the village 'cantonnier' (road mender/gardener/odd-job man). He turned up with his tractor, and completely demolished the grass – one hour's work for forty Euros, and a decent-looking orchard as a result seemed good value. We asked for him the following year, only to learn he had sadly committed suicide.

I decided to invest in a petrol strimmer, which helped me to get the orchard back into shape. It was hard, hot work but it had to be done. The front driveway wasn't too bad, and I could get that strimmed in about an hour.

We also came to the conclusion we needed decent Wi-Fi. We had coped – just – with an old-fashioned modem, but we decided to upgrade. That also made a massive difference to our lives. We could both work from there, which was essential for me. It also meant that our youngest daughter, Gemma, who regularly came out with us during school holidays, could use her laptop. Setting up home Wi-Fi wasn't easy in France, especially as we're Mac users. Eventually we got there. The cost too was staggering – forty per cent more than what we were paying for in the UK. But it was a necessity.

Patricia, Gemma, and I went camping again at Camping Le Soleil in the summer. Following Patricia's comments the previous year, we did 'proper camping', and bought a proper camp cooker, a cupboard style storage unit, and a gazebo under which we could cook. Over time, we also invested in a decent paella set complete with a gas burner. That year, we were joined by Hugh, Mindy, and their daughter Rhiain. They rented a mobile home which was a five-minute walk from our tent. We also were delighted to find that our friends – the Frenchies – had returned. Their tents were less than twenty metres away. We all had a great time.

I do however find there are often some very odd people who go camping too. Opposite us was an English family from Romford. The husband/father was quite stocky, and covered in hair, apart from his head, which was bald. He would stand outside his tent and scratch himself like a bear in the woods.

There was another English family who arrived after we'd been there for a week – mother, father, and two young children. The father came up to our tent the first evening. He walked almost right into our tent. Now you just don't do that when camping. There's a certain protocol, that you gently approach someone else's tent if you don't know them and keep your distance before even considering walking on to their emplacement. Definitely camping virgins!

This guy was overfamiliar, and immediately asked where we were from, what I did for a living, how long I'd had my car, how much our tent cost, etc. We humoured him, and he eventually left. The next day, he went up to Patricia and asked her if she had an iron he could borrow. Patricia just laughed. 'An iron, on a campsite? I don't think so,' she said. This guy became quite irritating. One evening, on his way back from the toilets, he just sat in one of our chairs. I'm surprised he didn't pour himself a glass of wine.

We were there for ten wonderful days and resolved to go back for two weeks the following year. The booking process was quite quaint, especially by today's standards. Every Tuesday and Friday morning, the camp owner would sit in his office between 10 a.m. and midday. Campers would queue up outside, sometimes for over an hour, until it was their turn. They would enter the office, sit down, and book their spot for the following year. The owner would write down all the details. It was possible to look at the site-plan to see which spots would be available during your dates. Once the booking was made, it was cast in stone. No email confirmation. The owner's word was his bond. He'd take a small deposit, and that was it. This was a far better way of making a reservation via telephone or letter.

We left on a Saturday morning, which would be for the first and last time, given the traffic jams we encountered in the usual weekend holiday travel. We had to vacate our patch by 10 a.m., and then queued for an hour to get on to the main road which led to the motorway twenty miles away. We'd decided to go back a different way and go over the newly constructed Millault Viaduct. The traffic was awful – queue after queue after queue. The autoroute was at a standstill. We arrived at Millault around mid-afternoon. For such a magnificent bridge, the toilets were some of the most primitive we'd ever encountered in France, and the restaurant prices were extortionate. The journey this way seemed never-ending. We finally arrived in Pellac at around 1 a.m., having been on the road since ten that morning. Never again would I drive on a Saturday in August, I resolved to myself.

A couple of days after we got back, Jo and her then boyfriend, Paul, flew out. Gemma was pleased to have company closer to her age, and we had a few good days out at the lake at St Mathieu. The highlight of the week was the Mechoui. This took place every year in Pellac, always on 15 August, which is a French public holiday. We'd heard about the Mechoui from Solange – it's basically a Moroccan barbecue, where mutton is cooked over large pits in the ground. There's a committee of helpers in the village, who do everything from putting up the huge marquees then preparing and serving the food, clearing away, and organising the entertainment.

There must have been around 300 people there. It all kicked off at midday with drinks, and people sat down at 12.30 p.m. for the lunch. It was a five-course meal – melon served with generous quantities of port, followed by ribs, then the main course of mutton, with beans and salad, then cheese, and finally a fruit tart for dessert. There were bottles of wine and water on the table, but a drinks trolley also came round, from which you could buy better quality wines, beers, soft drinks, etc.

The meal itself took around three hours. Everyone sat on long benches at trestle style tables. You could reserve where to sit, or just take potluck.

At the beginning, we met several English people, none of whom lived in the village. They were all ex-pats, living locally. They swarmed around us like bees to a honeypot. Word got round that we were relatively new. They were generally friendly. We did however spot some serious drinkers among them.

After the main meal, there were games, including a tug-of-war (English v French naturally), sack races, and dancing. The music was mainly traditional French, with some lesser-known disco hits. There was the archetypical middle-aged Frenchman, with a cigarette hanging from his lips, who was unshaven, with lank, greasy hair, wearing super skinny trousers, eying up in a really creepy, pervy way all the young girls who were dancing. Jo and Paul were delighted to win the sack race – two people in the same sack (this is France remember!). We went home around 6.30 p.m. and collapsed for the rest of the evening.

The kids all flew back to the UK the next day, and Patricia and I had a couple of days on our own before driving back to Tenterden. On the Friday that week, we went to Brantôme. This is a beautiful little town, only forty-five minutes away. It's called the Venice of the Périgord, as the entire town is surrounded by water. Each Friday there's an interesting little market there. It's not the biggest or best of markets, but the location is lovely, and the atmosphere is superb. After wandering around the market for a couple of hours, Patricia suggested we drove on to a village called Bourdeilles, which has a chateau. We arrived at lunchtime, found a nice restaurant, and ate in the courtyard outside.

After lunch, we walked around the village. We entered the chateau and went up the stairs to the first floor and then on to the roof at the top. On the way up, I noticed a couple on the first floor. The woman looked vaguely familiar, but I couldn't think where from. As we went down, the couple had gone, but I remarked to Patricia that I thought she looked like the wife of a cousin of mine, who we'd met at a recent family funeral. Indeed, it was the first time I'd seen him and his wife for over twenty years. Anyway, my powers of recognition are pretty awful, and I paid no more attention to it.

We carried on wandering around Bourdeilles, and then I needed to make a business call. We went back towards the car, and I sat on a bench, feeling very relaxed and unhurried, and made a couple of calls. I then stood up, and we approached the car and climbed inside. I didn't realise at the time, but Patricia commented afterwards that it felt I was doing everything in slow motion.

I started the engine, carefully reversed out of the parking space, and slowly drove back down into the village. 'Look,' shouted Patricia suddenly. 'There's your cousin.'

Sure enough, the couple who I'd seen earlier were walking towards us. I wound the window down and called out, 'Chris!'

My cousin looked up. It was indeed my cousin Chris and his wife Nerissa. I stopped the car, and we greeted each other. I then parked my car back in its space, and we got out. What an amazing coincidence. We all went to the nearest café for a drink. It turned out they were on holiday and staying in a gîte about an hour away. They'd just hit upon Bourdeilles by chance, as had we.

Chris's father, Fred, was a cousin of my father. They were of similar age. Fred had died when I was about thirteen, and my dad had passed away in 1999. As Patricia said afterwards, it was almost as if Dad and my uncle Fred were trying to get us to meet. We'd missed the first opportunity but got there the second time.

The 'slow motion' that Patricia had noticed was bizarre; under normal circumstances, I'd have made my calls back at the house, where I'd have had my laptop. But for some reason, I decided to make my calls at Bourdeilles, and did everything very slowly.

The conclusion we drew was that it gave Chris time to catch us before we left. I'm not a religious or particularly spiritual person, but looking back, it did seem as though certain forces were working with us.

Whatever, it was a memorable occasion, and once again, one of those examples that wherever you are in the world, you should never be surprised to bump into someone you know.

WE WENT BACK to Pellac in October with Mum again. This time, we went out for the day with Jacques and his partner Marguerite. Knowing that Patricia is half-German, they took us to an Alsacien restaurant in Limoges.

The food consisted of popular German dishes, including pork knuckle with lashings of sauerkraut. Very different to typical French restaurants.

After that, they took us on a tour of Limoges, including a porcelain factory, where Patricia added to her continually growing collection of porcelain dishes.

Discovering Nice and the French Riveira

2007

At the start of 2007, we decided to book a long weekend in Nice. We wanted to go somewhere different. Patricia's birthday is in February, mine is in March, and our wedding anniversary is also in March, so there were several opportunities to celebrate. Our flight arrived mid-morning, so we made our way to our hotel, and then found a restaurant for lunch. Our hotel was in central Nice, quite close to the Promenade des Anglais. The weather was beautiful, and we spent the rest of the day just pottering about.

We had an interesting encounter at a branch of Credit Agricole, with whom we had a French bank account. I wanted to transfer some money into our account. The easiest and least expensive way to do this at that time was to make a cash withdrawal using my UK bank debit card, and then walk into the branch and pay the cash into our account. It was perhaps unconventional, and I had to present my passport, but it was a method that worked, and always conducted with the appropriate seriousness and formality found in French banks,

I wanted to put around €500 into our account, so outside, I made the appropriate withdrawal, then went into the bank with my paying-in book. After queueing for ten minutes, I presented myself to the cashier and explained what I wanted to do. When she saw the address of our bank, she informed me this wouldn't be possible. I asked why not and was told that in that area, Credit Agricole was a different company to Credit Agricole in the rest of France. As a consequence, I wouldn't be able to pay in the cash. That was it – no further conversation.

I cursed as I walked out. I now had €500 in cash, which I didn't want or need. I also didn't want to walk around with €500 in my wallet all the time. Crazy!

On the Friday, we did some shopping, and had lunch at the magnificent Hotel Negresco. We had a simple salad outside and felt utterly charmed by this unique building. The following day, we caught a train to Monaco, and after visiting the casino and admiring the range of jaw-droppingly expensive cars outside, we had lunch overlooking the harbour – beautifully arranged salad niçoise.

On the Sunday we caught a train in the opposite direction, and visited Cannes, which we weren't overimpressed with, and then stopped at Fréjus. Later that afternoon, in the hotel bar, we watched England play France in the Six Nations Rugby in Paris. I became very animated in the bar; Jonny Wilkinson wasn't having a good day. Suddenly, a large glass of beer arrived on our table. I looked up; I hadn't ordered this. The waiter pointed to a smartly dressed man at the bar and said that he felt sorry for me as England were losing the match, and he decided to buy me a beer. How utterly charming. I raised my glass and toasted both him and the French team warmly.

The next day, Monday, 12 March, was my birthday. Patricia wanted to treat me to lunch, and I had one of the most memorable meals of my life; we had lunch on the beach, at an open-air restaurant, at a table with a beautiful starched white tablecloth, highly polished cutlery, and crystal glasses. We sipped a glass of fizz before enjoying a truly excellent lunch. We then caught a taxi to the airport, where to cap it all, Patricia bought me a gorgeous watch in the duty free. What a lucky man!

A COUPLE OF weeks later, we returned to France for the evening, with several members of our French discussion group, where we had a fabulous dinner at the elegantly old-fashioned Hotel Atlantique, on the north French coast, just twenty minutes outside Calais.

IN LATE MAY, we introduced our new dog Freddie to France. We went out with Gemma for the half-term week, along with Freddie. He was another rescue dog from the Blue Cross, also mixed-breed, similar size to a border collie, and blessed with a ginger coat of fur and handsome looks. He seemed to settle in at Pellac very quickly. Although he jumped over the garden wall a few times to chase cats, Gemma had him well trained, and he always came back pretty promptly.

Patricia has a friend called Jacqueline, who had spent some time living in France with her husband Dennis. Jacqueline regularly said how much she'd like to see our house, so Patricia mentioned about going in July, just the two of them. I agreed it was a good idea. Meanwhile, I was having an extremely busy and stressful year, and I asked Patricia how she'd feel if I went out for a week beforehand to relax on my own. I also explained I could take some larger items out with me, such as the gas barbecue, a lawnmower, and my bike.

I went in early July. It was indeed quite strange being there without Patricia. I found myself doing the things we generally did together, such as going to our favourite supermarket, and also the weekly market at Piégut, which is one of the biggest for miles around. I went on a few bike rides too and tried to relax, but not entirely successfully, as I couldn't resist taking my mobile phone with me.

Later that week, Solange popped round with some vegetables from her magnificent potager and told me that one of the English men living in the village had fallen off his bike and broken his ankle. She reminded me she'd introduced him to us the very first day we arrived after buying the house.

I remembered him – he was a Yorkshireman in his 60s called Desmond. He and his wife Cassie had lived in the village for around fifteen years. He spoke fluent French and had said that if we needed any help with anything to ask. He, Solange, and I chatted for a few minutes in French, and when he discovered that I spoke reasonable French, he seemed quite surprised. He asked how that was and went on to say that he was constantly having to help English people living in the village for translation. He muttered that he probably wouldn't be of much use to us and disappeared. I'd seen him a few times, but never had cause to ask him for help.

Solange was a wise woman. I think she sensed perhaps a gentle frisson in that we hadn't been in touch with Desmond, and suggested I gave him a call to see if I could be of help to him. I thought about this and decided to telephone him. He suggested I pop round for a cup of tea that afternoon – which I did – and introduced me to his wife Cassie, plus various cats and dogs. We had a good conversation together and got on very well. I came away thinking that Desmond (who was a typically down-to-earth Yorkshireman) perhaps had a feeling that I was a bit snooty from our first meeting, and that equally I had the impression he was a bit of a busybody helping out hapless Brits with their lack of ability to speak conversational French. Clearly, we were both wrong. We've laughed about it since. I'm pleased and proud to say that Desmond and Cassie have become very dear friends, and we inevitably get together whenever we go out.

WE WENT BACK to Camping Le Soleil at the start of August. My eldest daughter, Lucy, flew out and joined us for a few days. We spent a lovely day and evening in the fishing village of Collioure, which never ceases to entice me. I remember going there thirty years earlier, and really nothing had changed very much. I can understand why Picasso was so inspired by living there.

Once again, the Frenchies were at Camping Le Soleil. We had a couple of get-togethers. I got on really well with the two husbands/dads – Leon and Thibaut. We shared a lot of banter together. Leon was an avid Arsenal fan, and he and I were constantly winding each other up about the football. Their wives really welcomed Patricia and encouraged her in conversation, which boosted Patricia's conversational confidence enormously.

We returned to Pellac, and once again we were delighted to be joined by Jo and Paul, who flew out especially for the Mechoui.

HORRIBLE FLIES AND A BROKEN WRIST

2007

In September, Patricia and I planned to go out to Pellac for a week. We decided to fly this time – the journey was just too long to make so soon after the summer holiday. We booked our tickets and arranged car hire. Three days before going out, Patricia was walking Freddie in Tenterden when he suddenly pulled her forward. She caught her foot on an uneven pavement slab, fell over, and broke her wrist. She was pretty shaken up, but OK. She's made of strong stuff my wife! The main downside I could see was that I might have to cook!

We had an irritating situation at Stansted airport before flying out on the Thursday afternoon. We checked in our luggage at the Ryanair desk, as was the custom at that time. My hand luggage was deemed to weigh almost eleven kilos. The limit was ten. I was subsequently told by the officious employee that I would have to put the case into the aircraft hold and pay an additional £40 for the privilege. 'Oh hang on,' I remonstrated. I explained as that as Patricia's luggage weighed only eight kilos, I could transfer some of my luggage into her case. The person on the Ryanair desk refused point blank, on matters of security. I argued the toss, but it was no good. As my laptop was in my hand luggage, I removed it to avoid any potential damage. This meant that in addition to paying £40 to put my bag in the hold, I'd also have to buy an extra bag to carry my laptop on-board. To say I was furious was an understatement. I remember grumbling to Patricia that if there was a repeat performance at Poitiers airport for the return flight, I'd simply take all of my clothes out of my bag and wear them. Patricia nodded as I said this. She knew me well enough that this wasn't an idle threat – she could visualise me looking like a Michelin man as I boarded the plane.

We duly landed at Poitiers and drove off to Pellac. At around 8.30 p.m., shortly before arriving, I stopped the car at a village en route, to make an important business call. I had a Dutch client, who ran a major business in Holland, and was keen to acquire an English company, from which they could spearhead and develop their activities in the UK. I was familiar with the style and culture of the Dutch company, and one of my UK clients sprang to mind. I rang the owner, Martin, and after exchanging the usual pleasantries, I asked him if he'd ever considered selling his business. He replied he was always open to new initiatives, and that it would depend on the price. I felt encouraged by this. I introduced the two companies together and helped to broker the deal which was eventually sealed ten months later.

Martin and I have remained great friends. During the process of selling his company, he introduced me to his accountant, Chris, who has since not only become my accountant, but also a very good friend too. He, Martin, and I generally meet three times a year for an extravagant lunch, which we call our 'Gentleman's Lunch'.

Patricia and I arrived in Pellac at around 9 p.m. We parked the hire car in the drive, unlocked the front door, and entered the house. Patricia walked into the downstairs loo and rushed straight out.

'Oh my God,' she exclaimed.

'What's up?' I asked.

She opened the door. On the wall opposite was a black mass, the size of a football. It was moving. It consisted only of flies.

Clearly, some flies had got in via the window frame, which was not in great shape. They'd reproduced many, many times, and the room was just full of them. We quickly shut the door. It was almost vomit inducing.

'OK,' I said. 'We need fly killer spray.'

We hadn't got any, so we quickly popped down the road and knocked at the door of our friend Jacques. He wasn't aware we were coming out and was surprised, although pleased, to see us. 'Entrez,' he said, and then he saw Patricia's cast around her broken wrist. He ushered us inside.

'What can I get you to drink?' he asked.

'Actually, Jacques, we'd like some fly spray if you have any, please?' I laughed.

I explained the problem, and Marguerite went into the kitchen and came back with two massive canisters, called '*bombes*'. We said thanks, and that we'd be up to see them the next day and went back to the house. Fortunately, the flies hadn't spread beyond the bathroom, but it was carnage in there. It took both cans of spray to exterminate them, and then we spent the rest of the time (and for months afterwards) sweeping up dead flies. Fixing that window frame became a top priority that weekend.

The rest of our time out there was pretty uneventful. Patricia survived my cooking, although she was quickly back on top of things and cooking again (thank goodness!). However, the short time there gave us the chance to do some thinking and give serious thought about what we wanted to do with our house there.

When we bought the house, we were attracted by the fact it wasn't a ruin, and other than some serious redecoration, no major DIY was required. The loft upstairs was empty, and we parked that for the time being, deciding it would be a retirement project.

Retirement, however, was still many years away – ten to twelve at least. We were using the house as fully as we could, and were becoming frustrated at the lack of space, especially when the girls came out. We talked about what we'd like to do, which basically meant extending the living area upstairs. Beyond that, we hadn't thought about it much.

But Patricia made a very valid comment; she recalled when, after recovering from cancer in 2003, she didn't want to unnecessarily wait for anything. To that end, we'd accelerated our plans to buy the house.

'Is there any way we could afford the building work to make the property larger and more liveable?' asked Patricia.

We talked and chatted. I was having an extremely good year. My recruitment business was continuing to grow, and 2007 revenues were proving to be twice as much as previous years. On that basis, we could afford to do a certain amount. We hadn't a clue what it would cost, and we agreed to make some enquiries.

I contacted an English surveyor who was based locally. He confirmed he could sub-contract and project manager the building works. But his estimates were slow in coming forward.

I also contacted a French builder, Serge, who was local and who came highly recommended. He responded positively and came round for an initial discussion.

Over the next couple of months, Serge stayed in touch.

We went back in November for a long weekend, and during this time, he arranged for a draughtsman to come out while we were there to measure up and formulate some ideas.

The area upstairs was large enough to accommodate four bedrooms and two bathrooms. But Patricia and I agreed we didn't need that many. Two would be enough, plus two bathrooms, so visitors could have an en suite. We wanted the rest of the space to be open and used for leisure.

I could also have a desk up there to work from.

By December, Serge had enough information to draft some plans and costs, and we decided to go out after Christmas and spend the New Year looking at these in detail.

The proposals were largely in line with what we wanted.

The draughtsman, Pascal, had understood our requirements well. The figures weren't too bad either. Based on an exchange rate of around €1 equalled 70p, they looked affordable.

Things were coming together nicely.

Planning Our Renovations

2008

In March the following year – 2008 – Serge contacted me, and asked if I was planning to be at the house that month, as he was keen to organise a site visit with the various sub-contractors – electrician, plumber, plasterer, tiler, joiner, etc. We agreed a date, and for expediency, I flew out on my own for a couple of days for the meeting.

Patricia normally would have accompanied me, but her father, Harry, had been very unwell and had been in hospital. We agreed that I would go alone and get there and back as quickly as possible. Sadly, Harry passed away at the age of eighty-three just after I returned from my short trip.

I was attracted by the idea of using only public transport to get from Tenterden to Limoges airport. So I caught a bus a five-minute walk away from home in Tenterden to Headcorn, then a train from Headcorn railway station to London Bridge, then the Tube to Liverpool Street, and a train to Stansted, where I'd catch a plane to Limoges. As there aren't any public transport links from Limoges airport, my friend Jacques kindly offered to collect me from the airport, and take me back a few days later, when I'd do the whole outward journey in reverse.

Jacques duly collected me at the airport on the Monday afternoon, and as his partner Marguerite was away visiting her daughter in the south of France, Jacques invited me across for dinner on the Monday evening. I was very fond of Jacques. He was a good friend, and we had a solid understanding between us. He had two adult daughters, and he too had been through a difficult divorce. We shared similar values, and the conversation between us flowed as usual.

I pottered around the house on the Tuesday, and on the Tuesday evening I was invited to dinner by our friends Desmond and Cassie who lived in the village, just a few minutes' walk away. I spent a very pleasant evening with them. Desmond is an excellent cook – out of all the men I know who cook, Desmond is without doubt the best. He's able to combine English classics with French cuisine, and the result is always quite excellent. He also likes a whisky to follow, and we enjoyed a few whiskies together. Both Cassie and Desmond are great conversationalists, and we shared lots of stories as we got to know each other better.

Jacques and I went out to lunch at a local restaurant on the Wednesday lunchtime, and as we perused the menu, he looked around the restaurant, and to the amusement to all the British contingent there, he loudly pronounced, in heavily accented English.

'I sink I am ze only froggie in 'ere.'

At 2.30 p.m. on the dot, Serge and his men arrived. Jacques offered to stick around, which I certainly appreciated, as some of the technical building terms were lost on me! After the usual handshaking and greetings, which as always seemed to go for ages, we went into the house.

Serge immediately took the lead and walked around, explaining what was going to happen and where. The questions became technical – where did I want the electrical sockets? A single or double? At what height? Exactly how wide did we want the archway to be in the kitchen; where did we want the staircase – straight or dogleg; where did we want the bath to be; which wall would the shower be on; what sort of central-heating boiler and how many radiators etc. etc. The questions were endless. Thank goodness Jacques was there. The site meeting carried on for a couple of hours. It was certainly very thorough, with lots of notes taken.

After they'd all gone, I was exhausted. My brain felt shot to pieces! I had a beer with Jacques before he too went home for the evening, as Marguerite was back. He confirmed he'd collect me at nine the following morning to drive me to the airport.

As I sat and reflected that evening and made notes of the materials Patricia and I would need to choose – kitchen units, bathroom suites, wall and floor tiles etc. I recognised that Serge was a born leader. He was the sort of man you would be happy to follow into battle. Stocky and strongly built, with a no-nonsense approach coupled with a good sense of humour. I liked him a lot and felt we could trust him to do an excellent job.

One of the issues we needed to get our heads around was the central-heating system. There was an ancient boiler in the garage, and a few old, rusty radiators downstairs. We weren't sure if the boiler was oil-fired or electric. There wasn't any gas in the village. Solange told us that many years ago, the heating pipes had burst, and there had been a terrible flood in the house. As a consequence, the heating system was useless and had never worked since.

Serge had brought to the meeting the chap who we knew as Yves, the local handyman, who had done some small jobs for us, including re-wiring and the installation of a new immersion tank. Yves had made some proposals for an incredibly sophisticated boiler and central-heating system, which amounted to almost 25 per cent of the overall building costs. I'd heard that Yves was planning his retirement and seemed to want to make as much money as he could during his final months. While I don't blame him for that, we weren't going to fund this with a way 'over the top' heating system for our needs.

I discussed this with Jacques on the way to the airport. He mentioned that he knew an excellent plumber and asked if I'd be happy for him to bring this plumber over to the house and take a view of our heating needs.

I'll never forget the call I received from Jacques on Friday, 17 April 2008. I was driving back to Kent having collected Gemma to stay for her usual fortnightly weekend with us, when Jacques called around 6.30 p.m. He sounded a bit breathless and very excited; he went on to say that he'd had the plumber over to our house that afternoon. After a good look around, the plumber had discovered an oil tank in our driveway, and after some considerable effort, he had managed to get the ancient boiler working. Jacques was genuinely delighted, and so was I, especially when he told me that there were one thousand litres of heating fuel in the oil tank.

When I got home, and told Patricia, she reminded me that the previous year I'd considered having a bonfire in the very spot where the oil tank was lying undetected deep in the ground. That would have been the end of our dream!

A few weeks later, we came out to Pellac. We got into the habit of calling Solange the day before, as we knew how much she looked forward to our visits. As we arrived, she spotted us and came straight round. 'Voilà Nigel et Patricia,' she exclaimed. She kept smiling and looked as if she was hiding something. 'Viens,' she said and took my hand and led me into the house. She'd already unlocked the front door. We stood in the hallway, and she just looked at me. Eventually, she asked me if I noticed anything about the temperature. I must have looked puzzled, as she took my hand again, and pressed it against a radiator. It was warm. 'Aha,' I said and laughed. Solange was like a little girl – she was so excited – and said she couldn't believe that after all this time, the boiler and radiators were working again. It was indeed a special moment and a lovely surprise.

PATRICIA AND I went out again in June when we caught up with Serge again. We then drove to Pellac once more at the end of July, before travelling down to Argélès again for another camping holiday. This year, both Vicky and Lucy flew out for a few days. It was Vicky's twenty-first birthday, which we celebrated in style, with balloons and bunting all over the tent on her special day.

We were delighted to see our French friends there again. That was also the holiday when we made friends with several Dutch families. First was a chap called Johan who'd been opposite us the previous year, with his wife and daughter. Through him, we met a guy called Patrik who was there with his wife and two teenage children. Patrik was a kindred spirit. We hit it off straight away. He was a self-employed business consultant. He was also very funny and a little crazy especially after a few drinks. He was highly intelligent, and fluent in English. We spent a few very enjoyable boozy evenings together.

There was also a group of four Dutch lads almost opposite. They'd been eying up Vicky and Lucy as soon as they arrived, and had stopped by a few times, chatting to the girls. On the Sunday, which was Vicky's birthday, we invited them over for a drink. They were charming lads, and amazingly we are still in touch with them, albeit on Facebook. One of them, Thijs, was a trainee chef, and he's since opened his own restaurant, which has become very successful and developed a reputation as a top restaurant in Holland.

Lucy and Vicky returned to the UK a couple of days later. The Dutch boys continued to stop by for an occasional beer with us. On their final night, they brought across two crates of beer, and together with Patrik and Johan, we drank the lot. It did get a bit noisy, and around 1 a.m., we received a visit from one of the camp's security guys to say there had been a complaint and asked us to keep the noise down. The Dutch lads knew immediately who it was from – a Frenchman camping in a tent next door. We will never forget, that as they left to walk across to their tent, they picked up their crates of empty beer bottles and rattled them loudly outside the Frenchman's tent!

THAT WAS ALSO the year we spent two full weeks at Camping Le Soleil. I have so many wonderful memories of lying on the beach reading and listening to a wide range of music. We had a couple of days when the weather wasn't great, with rain and wind. We decided to drive out to Fitou on one of these days. It was about an hour's drive, and we thought we'd go for some lunch.

We found a restaurant, which was almost empty, and as it felt so chilly outside, we all had a massive bowl of cassoulet each. We ordered a bottle of wine, which was really good, so we asked the waiter where we could buy some. 'Next door,' he replied. It turned out that the vineyard owned the shop and restaurant. I bought half a dozen bottles and asked that if I was to place an order, would they deliver? They confirmed they would deliver free of charge anywhere in France if a minimum quantity of sixty bottles was placed.

Just to continue that theme, Patricia and I decided that we really enjoyed the wine, and that we should place an order for sixty bottles, which we'd get delivered to Solange's address next door. When we went out in October, we collected our wine from Solange's barn.

We shared a bottle with Mum who was also with us, and she didn't seem hugely impressed. Nor were we. I assumed – and very much hoped – that it was perhaps a rogue bottle, and that when we got back to the UK, it would taste better. In fact, it didn't! We tried several bottles, and we were pretty disappointed. Although the cost per bottle was €6.50, it was still a substantial investment. We started drinking the wine as a run-of-the-mill midweek wine. We gave several bottles to friends to try, and several more as charity or tombola prizes. Gradually, the stock whittled down. We had about a dozen bottles, which we left untouched in the wine cupboard for about six months.

One wet Sunday lunchtime I decided to open a bottle as we just fancied a glass of something red. As we took our initial sip, Patricia and I just looked at each other over the rims of the glasses.

'Wow,' we both exclaimed. 'This is unbelievably good.'

The wine was in fact completely different – and tasted just as it did at the restaurant in Fitou. What we subsequently discovered is that after the various transportations, the wine needed time to settle down. Talk about buyer's remorse! We kept the remaining bottles to ourselves and savoured every single drop. A major lesson learnt!

AFTER RETURNING FROM our holiday at Argélès, we went to the village Mechoui on Friday 15 August. It was a quieter affair this year, and we sat with various friends, including Jacques and Marguerite and also Desmond and Cassie. We consumed quite a lot of alcohol.

An English lady was there, staying with some English friends in the village. We'd seen her a few times before. Her personal life was apparently complicated; as a consequence, she became more and more morose as she became drunk. She was very tall and thin. We nicknamed her Long Tall Sally. Towards the end of the afternoon, she was having difficulty standing. She went to sit down on one of the long benches. Unfortunately, she sat on one end. Sadly for her, the other end tipped up, and she found herself sprawled on the grass. She wasn't hurt thank goodness. But it was difficult not to laugh!

The weather was really hot that day. One lady fainted in the marquee, and someone called the local Pompiers. Now the Pompiers are effectively firefighters, but they're also trained in first aid, and are generally the first people to arrive on the scene.

Four or five hunky Pompiers turned up. They went up to the lady who'd fainted; she was lying quietly on the ground, with a friend in attendance. So the Pompiers proceeded to greet their friends, exchanging handshakes and kisses before returning to attend to the lady in question. Only in France!

Towards the end of the afternoon, I was wandering around talking with a few people, and came across the Maire. I knew who he was, although I didn't actually know him. We greeted each other and shook hands. He'd also had a fair amount to drink. He seemed friendly and convivial. He had a strong local accent and the difficulty in understanding him was compounded by the amount of booze he'd had to drink.

He asked me where I lived, and I pointed out our house. We then had a strange conversation, which had we been sober, would have caused me some consternation. He told me he knew where our house was, as planning permission had been applied for regarding the expansion upstairs and the building work. He then told me that planning permission had been refused.

I was gobsmacked, and somewhat aggressively (thanks to the alcoholic 'confidence') demanded to know why. He told me not to worry and clapped his hand on my shoulder. He said it wasn't a major problem, and that with a slight amendment, planning permission would be granted at the next meeting of the local council.

I emphasised my concern, as work on replacing the roof was due to start in September. He gazed at me in surprise and told me not to be alarmed. He explained it was a formality and shrugged, saying, 'C'est normal.'

I asked him what the issue was – something technical?

'Non,' he replied, and said it was something about the balcony.

When I pressed him for more information, he waved his arms around and spluttered a bit, and told me, 'Parlez avec votre architecte.'

Clearly, he was having difficulty remembering the specifics through his alcoholic haze.

I was concerned about this. When we got back to England, I telephoned Pascal who was the interior designer/architect. He laughed and said it was nothing to worry about. He'd make the amendment to the drawings. I confirmed with him that the balcony would still be built. This was something that was quite important to Patricia and me. It was actually an idea which came from the English surveyor who we originally spoke to about the extension upstairs. He'd suggested we had a balcony outside our bedroom, so we could sit outside in the early morning and drink our coffee. It was a glorious, quite romantic idea. When we originally sat down with Serge at the planning stage, we outlined our desire for a balcony, and this was included with the plans and estimates.

Pascal duly sent me an amended plan, which I glanced at, and which looked pretty much as before. I just guessed it was a technicality and thought nothing more of it. But to complete the story, some months later, when I received the final invoice from the joiner, I queried why the cost of the balcony had increased by €800. He explained it was because it was now two metres longer than originally planned. He told me to look at the plans and the revision. Sure enough he was correct. The shape had changed, with angled ends, so Pascal had decided to enlarge the balcony. Win-win-win. Only in France!

When we arrived in early October for a short break with Mum, we were greeted by a huge pile of roof tiles. The work was due to begin! We had a pleasant week, which was pretty non-eventful apart from the return journey.

On French autoroutes, the system is that as you enter a motorway, to pass through the barrier, you take a ticket from the machine. Then, when you exit the motorway, you insert the ticket into a machine, which will calculate how many kilometres you've driven on the motorway, and charge accordingly.

On our way back, we followed our usual route – up the A20, on to the A71, and then on to the A10. Patricia was sitting in the passenger seat, so when we approached the barrier for the A10, she opened her window to take the ticket from the machine. She then placed the ticket on the dashboard, and as she closed her window the wind rushed in, causing the ticket to blow towards the windscreen. I made a grab for it, but too late! The ticket dropped through the gap between the dashboard and the windscreen and disappeared. There was no way we could retrieve it.

'Oh brilliant!' I exclaimed. 'You do realise that means that without a ticket to present when we exit, we'll be charged for the full extent of the motorway.'

'What does that mean?' asked my mum.

'Well, the normal charge for this stretch is about ten Euros, but given this motorway goes from Bordeaux to Paris, we'll probably get charged about one hundred Euros.'

I was really cross – bloody angry, actually. At this point, Mum and Patricia started to laugh. They became almost hysterical – well not quite, but they had tears running down their cheeks. One was setting off the other. The more they laughed, the more I fumed.

'If you both think it's so funny, you can pay for the ticket between you.'

Part of my frustration was that I knew there was no way I could get the operator at the exit barrier to understand my situation. They would simply think I was trying it on, especially a car with a GB plate.

When we arrived at the exit point, I thought it was worth a try. I got out of the car, went round to the operator's booth, and explained what had happened. I was met with a blank stare, which became stony. I apologised and said I was happy to pay for the onward leg all the way to Paris and tried to convince the operator I'd only joined the motorway at Orléans not Bordeaux. Then I had a stroke of genius (or so I thought). I'd stopped for fuel on the A71 just before Orléans. I pulled the receipt from my wallet. This would surely prove I hadn't travelled up from Bordeaux.

I think the operator finally gave up trying to understand. She simply said, 'Twenty Euros.'

I whipped out my credit card and drove off before she could change her mind.

After that, I applied for what is known as a 'Badge'. This is a small gadget which is 'flashed' at the ticket machine when approaching and exiting the motorways. The motorway authority called Sanef will then debit the credit card they hold on file and issue a monthly statement. This makes driving on French motorways much easier and quicker. Weirdly, it seems the majority of French motorists don't possess a Badge, and so they form queues at the barriers, which at peak times can get very long. I speak from experience; a forty-minute wait in August is not unusual. The thing to remember is not to do as advised, which is to place the Badge into a placeholder on the inside windscreen. Because this alerts thieves, who will happily 'smash and grab' and travel the length and breadth of France's motorways at the Badge holder's expense.

PATRICIA AND I couldn't wait to see what progress the builders had made, and we went back in November. The roof was complete and looked absolutely fabulous. Inside the house, the builders had started. It was agreed they would start working upstairs, building the new interior. The two massive waist-high beams had already been cut and raised up towards the roof. The plasterer had started to create the walls for the two bedrooms and bathrooms.

While we were there, the plumber – the guy who got the old boiler working – arrived. He was a very switched-on guy, in his thirties. We explained we wanted the spare en suite bathroom to be more of a shower room, with a large shower cubicle to be the focal point. It was pretty cold during the few days we were there, as although the central heating was now working, the massive hole in the hallway ceiling to the upstairs resulted in some major draughts.

It was a strange time. We'd just come through a massive global financial crisis, aka the 'credit crunch'. When I received Serge's first invoice just before Christmas, it was quite a shock. At the time he quoted, the Euro was worth around seventy pence. By Christmas, the £/€ rate was almost parity. Patricia and I had a few sober conversations about how we might afford the inevitable additional cost, and we agreed that we were in too deep to change our minds, and that we'd just have to swallow it.

BUILDING WORKS AND FRENCH TRADESMEN

2009

The New Year in 2009 started slowly. The workmen restarted the work from the second week of January, and it was all fairly quiet. In early February, I received a call early one morning from the joiner, who we knew reasonably well. He had previously replaced the front gates, and around eighteen months later, he replaced all the downstairs windows. He was a short, cheerful chap, and although difficult to understand due to his strong local accent, we got on well with him.

I picked up the phone.

'Monsieur Wilson,' he said and went on to explain that work had progressed well upstairs in the former attic. He said that the rooms had been created and confirmed the bathroom floors were being tiled. However, there was already a wooden flooring in the attic, which had been covered by a strong plastic sheeting.

Marc, the joiner, said that he was in the process of removing the plastic covering, and noticed that the wooden floor needed some work, and asked if I'd like him to give it a thorough sanding. He went on to explain that if we wanted him to do this, now was the time before any furniture was taken upstairs. I asked him how much, and he said around one thousand Euros. I thought for a moment, then agreed, and told him to go ahead. He cheerfully said goodbye.

Five minutes later, the phone rang. It was Marc the joiner again.

'Bonjour, Monsieur Wilson.' He coughed, then laughed rather nervously.

He said he'd made a mistake.

'OK,' I said, thinking what's coming up now.

He then told me he'd forgotten to provide an estimate for the cost of creating a hole – in fact a very large hole – through the ceiling in the hallway to allow for the staircase leading to the upstairs.

'So,' I challenged him, 'when you say you've made a mistake, what exactly do you mean?'

'Well, I've already created the hole. The staircase is in position. I just forgot to estimate the cost of doing this,' he replied.

'So it's too late,' I said, stating the obvious, and he laughed again.

'Did you not include the cost of this when you gave me the figure for the staircase?' I queried.

'Well, not exactly,' said Marc. 'If you look at the estimate, it just says to build and fit a staircase made from oak. There's nothing about creating the hole.' He laughed again.

I asked him how much this extra cost was going to be. 'Let's call it €750 Euros,' he replied.

It wasn't too bad, I thought. Had it been anyone else, I might have been suspicious or less accommodating. But knowing Marc as

I did, I could see how he might have overlooked this. He was an excellent joiner, and his prices were always keen. Administration and running a business however were not his forte. When Marc called, I'd just come out of the shower. As I went downstairs to breakfast, I came to the conclusion that this was an expensive day; I'd just 'spent' €1,750 Euros without any forewarning. C'est la vie!

AT THAT TIME, I was in Germany on a business trip. I was working alongside some German friends running management training courses for a major multi-national company. Given the state of the economy, and the lack of recruitment opportunities, I was glad of the chance to do something else.

Later in February, Patricia, Gemma, and I went out to the house for a few days during the half-term holiday. The builders had largely completed the work upstairs and wanted to start downstairs. This involved knocking through walls and rebuilding what used to be the garage. We needed to move the downstairs furniture upstairs. I'd ascertained through discussions with Serge that the house wouldn't be habitable, but Jacques and Marguerite very kindly offered to have us stay with them for the three nights.

When we arrived, it was around 6 p.m., and it was still light. Our neighbour, Maurice, saw us and came out to greet us. This was quite unusual, as Maurice was quite reserved. It usually took a few days before he'd come up to us and say hello. Maurice asked us if we'd been inside the house yet. I explained that we'd just arrived, and that we didn't have a key, as we'd given it to the builders. Maurice simply walked to the side of the house, picked up a flowerpot, retrieved a key, and let us into our own house. He even walked around with us. This really was unusual. He'd not once entered our house, despite us asking him several times if he'd like to come in for a drink.

As we walked around, we could see the extent of the work. And the amount of work we'd have to do over the next few days, moving our furniture and belongings around.

We walked up to Jacques' house and were greeted by a glass of wine and a lovely meal. We really were lucky having them as friends. It was also good for Gemma, as she could practise her French. She had really taken to learning the language, and after her GCSEs, she went on to study, and pass, French at A level.

The next day we went back to the house and moved our bed upstairs, then the lounge furniture, and all the stuff from the kitchen – crockery, saucepans and cooking utensils, plus pictures, ornaments. It was quite staggering how much stuff we'd accumulated there during the past five years.

The next project was to empty the garage. Jacques said we could store whatever we wanted to in his large barn, which was an absolute godsend. Back and forth we traipsed, carrying garden equipment, bikes, camping equipment. By the end of the day, we were totally exhausted.

Jacques and Marguerite joined us at our house at the end of the day. They were keen to look around. As they entered the garden, another neighbour – an elderly lady who we called Madame la Duchesse, who we knew but not terribly well – simply strolled across and joined us as we walked into the house. She explained that our balcony overlooked her land (which it did), and she wanted to be able to see what we'd see from our balcony.

Patricia and I wondered, given the fascination among the villagers, and the ease with which Maurice found the key and came in the night before, how many other people either had, or would, come for a nosey around…

On the final day, we made a list of what we'd need to bring out next time, in terms of decorating and cleaning materials, and other pieces of furniture.

By the Friday night, we were ready to collapse. I recalled another difference between the English and the French. When we got back to Jacques' house, he offered me a glass of wine. I was actually gagging for a cold beer. In fact, I could have drunk several. He searched around, and presented me with a small 25cl stubby, which was lukewarm having been in a cupboard. I gratefully accepted and downed it in one. Jacques remarked that was something he almost never saw a Frenchman do. They would sip a pastis or a wine, but not drink a beer like I had.

We enjoyed another splendid meal by Marguerite. We'd already agreed we'd provide the wine each night, and that final evening, I asked them if they would like to try an Australian red, which we'd brought across from England. It was a full-bodied Shiraz, quite a good one. Jacques looked a little sceptical. Marguerite was very eager. She was from Bordeaux and had a very well-developed taste.

She sipped the Shiraz, and pronounced it to be very different, but extremely good. Jacques, on the other hand, found it hard to believe that a country such as Australia could produce a serious wine. Italy, Spain, and Portugal perhaps, but Australia? Really? He tried the wine, then shrugged, and said it was like an average red wine from Bordeaux. I roared with laughter, and replied it was nothing like a Bordeaux, but he wouldn't have it. He poured himself a glass of French wine, while Marguerite looked as if she relished every drop of the couple of glasses of the Aussie Shiraz she drank.

OUR NEXT VISIT was to be in the Easter holidays. We planned to drive down on Easter Saturday and stay the whole week. We had a lousy journey down; there were several major traffic jams, and we arrived around three hours later than we intended, at around 9 p.m., when but then it was dark.

Prior to coming out, I'd emailed Serge a couple of times. I thought it would help him to understand how long we'd be there for. There was still some outstanding building work, mostly downstairs. In my email, which I'd sent two weeks before our trip out there, I said I assumed the house was habitable, but that if it wasn't, to let me know. I hadn't heard from Serge, but knowing he was a busy guy, I wasn't too worried.

We drove into the drive, parked the car, and entered the house. I turned on the lights. The house was an absolute mess. Building materials were scattered everywhere. The walls which had been knocked through had exposed, jagged brickwork. There was dust and dirt everywhere!

I walked upstairs. That was just as bad. The place was filthy, apart from the bedrooms, which thankfully had been sealed off. But the house was freezing cold. It was mid-April, and the outside temperature was quite low. I then discovered that the water couldn't be turned on. The stopcock had vanished. There was no obvious way of having any running water.

At that point, I lost it. I generally have a long fuse, and while I can occasionally get cross quite easily, it's more irritation. I think I've only lost my temper a few times in my life. I lost it that night, though! I was absolutely livid. I was also tired, hungry, and thirsty. I spent the next thirty minutes or so walking around the house, getting more and more angry, shouting and swearing really badly.

Patricia tentatively wondered if Serge might be contactable.

'What?' I replied in frustration and tiredness. 'On Easter Saturday. At 9.30 p.m. A builder answering his mobile? No way.'

Patricia gently persisted and said it might just be worth a try. I said I'd wait for five more minutes to calm down. Then this is what happened.

I called Serge's mobile number. It rang several times, and then a voice said, 'Oui?'

'Serge?' I asked. 'This is Nigel Wilson. We have arrived at our house here in Pellac, just half an hour ago. The place is an absolute mess (*un bordel*). What's going on? You knew we were coming out. Why didn't you tell me the place is uninhabitable?'

I could hear Serge breathing hard. 'You say you told me?' he replied. 'I don't recall you telephoning me.'

'No, Serge. I didn't call you. I sent you an email. In fact, I sent you two emails. Another one a week later, to ensure you knew exactly when we'd arrive.'

There was silence. Eventually I heard him say, 'Merde. Oof. I don't check my email very often.' More silence followed. Then he said, 'J'arrive. Vingt minutes.'

Sure enough, Serge arrived within twenty minutes. He was deeply embarrassed, and full of apologies. But he was a man of action. He quickly got the water turned on and helped me move the couple of radiators we had around the house to get some heating going. He held up his hand, turned to Patricia and apologised again, and said he'd be back in the morning. By that time, my anger had completely dissipated, and we shook hands. I found a bottle of wine, Patricia got some food on the go, and by eleven o'clock we were all in bed.

Sure enough, Serge was back at ten the next morning with a couple of massive builder's lights, another radiator, and also a huge hamper of food and wine, which he presented to Patricia. Furthermore, he managed to fire up the boiler and get the central heating going. The world was looking far rosier than it had twelve hours previously.

He explained the following day Easter Monday was a public holiday, but that he would be back with various builders on the Tuesday, and he'd have men on-site all week. He really had pulled out all the stops. As I said previously, this was a man who you would follow into battle with (not against!). And we genuinely appreciated all his sterling efforts.

Sure enough, the plumber and his accomplice arrived on the Tuesday, as did the plasterer and the electrician. By the end of the week, the house was looking much more habitable. Lots of decorating and cosmetic 'making-good' were required. Patricia and I decided to paint the newly created upstairs – which we imaginatively named the 'loft'. We'd brought a significant quantity of white emulsion paint with us; paint in the UK is substantially cheaper and of better quality than paint acquired in France. It didn't take us too long, and armed with rollers and extension poles, we had the upstairs loft rooms all completed by the end of the week.

Serge came back on the Friday to check progress and to confirm our satisfaction. Amusingly, he handed me his latest invoice, and then asked me how the economy was in the UK. 2009 was proving to be a tough year all round. My recruitment business bore this out. I hadn't received any enquiries since January, and after the vacancies during the first quarter had been filled, nothing more was coming through. We assumed Serge was perhaps checking, in a roundabout way, that I still had the means to pay his remaining bills!

All the contractors were great, except the electrician. I'm not criticising his work, but he came across as distinctly anti-English. He was difficult to communicate with. He'd give one-word answers, or simply shrug as if he couldn't be bothered to talk. The only favour he did us was when Chelsea were due to play Liverpool in the Champions League quarter final.

By then we'd moved the TV and lounge furniture upstairs into the loft, as the downstairs rooms still needed finishing off. I had difficulty hooking the TV up to the satellite dish, and in desperation, I'd bought a load of cable, which I'd run through our bedroom and into the main loft living area. When the electrician saw this, he took a ladder up to a small loft space and fiddled around with it. He then came down and cut the cable and pushed it through an electrical socket behind the TV. When I expressed my thanks, he looked at me as if I was an idiot!

Patricia was keen to have an additional wall socket in the kitchen, and we wanted to have this fitted before the end of the week. I called the electrician countless times on his mobile and left several messages on his home answering machine. Eventually, in frustration, I left another message, speaking loudly and slowly. I must have got under his skin, because he turned up the following day with a couple of his young apprentices.

We showed him what we wanted, which he delegated to his two lads while he cleared off. It was pretty clear the two young lads were quite scared of their boss – he was quite an intimidating figure to them. He was a weedy little man, but rather narcissistic. Maybe he'd had problems dealing with English people before, perhaps not getting paid. We put it down to experience, but we've had no reason or desire to call him back for further work.

We went back for half-term week, which was the last week in May. The Monday was a bank-holiday in the UK. We treated it the same, and were enjoying a sleep-in, when at eight am, there was a loud and repeated knocking at the front door. I went downstairs with a towel around my waist.

Outside stood a small man in his sixties. I greeted him and asked how I could help.

He introduced himself as the floor tiler. We were under the impression he was coming the following week, but he said this week would suit him better.

No concern for our feelings, obviously!

I let him in and led him into the dining room. He was going to tile the floor in there, and the newly built sunroom, which was essentially the former garage, and which had a small room behind it housing the boiler and various garden furniture and equipment.

While I made some coffee, I noticed he just stood in the dining room, looking at the walls and floor. He stayed like that for about twenty-five minutes.

Eventually curiosity got the better of me, and I asked him if there was a problem.

'No,' he replied and explained he was just acquainting himself with the room. I asked if he'd be there for two or three days. He pulled himself up to his full height and glared at me.

'I shall be here all this week and next week, Monsieur. I pride myself on the excellence of my work.'

That shut me up!

Serge came across that week to check and complete the snagging, and he handed over another invoice. There was little left to pay for now. Just the floor tiler and a few other miscellaneous items. We were almost there.

KITCHEN CAPERS AND WEIRD CAMPERS

2009

One of the remaining parts of the jigsaw concerned the kitchen. Originally, we had some grand ideas about creating one enormous kitchen and dining room. There were five rooms downstairs: the bathroom at the back of the kitchen, the kitchen itself, the dining/living room, the hallway, and our former bedroom. There was also the garage, which could only be entered from outside.

We turned the former bathroom into a utility room to house the washing machine and tumble dryer. It still contained the loo and also the wash basin. The kitchen was quite small, and we had the builders knock through the dividing wall into the lounge/living room, to create more 'openness' and light. This was the room we'd considered turning into a massive kitchen/diner, but given the decline in exchange rates, the building works ended up costing us approximately thirty to forty per cent more than we'd anticipated. We'd raided our savings, and some things had to go, such as the large kitchen.

Patricia and I had visited the *Grand Designs Show* in London in early May to get some ideas for the kitchen. We came across a company based in Essex who manufactured 'old-style' kitchens from reclaimed oak. They seem very flexible in terms of what they could supply. We gave them the measurements, and they drew up a plan for cupboards, a sink and drainer, and housing for a hob and oven. We also wanted a large unit with a worktop and cupboards on one side, which would act as the divider between the kitchen and the rest of the larger lounge /dining room.

We planned to make that into a dining room and have a separate lounge in our former bedroom. We also had a double doorway knocked into what was the garage from the new lounge. This would become what we call the 'sunroom', with sliding glass patio doors to the front, and a window on the far exterior wall. This would allow natural light to flood into the house, and we also had glass internal doors installed downstairs, so there was a long and clear line of vision right through the downstairs of the property.

We decided to order the kitchen units from the company in Essex. They seem friendly, knowledgeable, and good value. Patricia and I had planned a short trip back to France towards the end of June, and the kitchen company agreed to deliver them.

We arrived on Tuesday, 24 June. The weather was gorgeous – daily temperatures between thirty and thirty-five degrees. The kitchen company was delivering on the Thursday and in the afternoon, a van duly arrived, with two men – one in his late sixties and a younger chap. As they unloaded, I noticed the older man walked with a distinctive limp. It turned out they were father and son. His other son ran the kitchen company, which was operated from the family farm in Essex.

They brought in the first units, and really struggled. I went to give them a hand and called over to Maurice to see if he could also help. Between the four of us, we managed to get the wall units in, and then we brought in the granite worktop, which consisted of one long piece about four metres in length. Finally, we went to get the central unit in, which already had the worktop attached. This was incredibly heavy, almost dangerously so. We put it into position and looked at it.

Patricia raised her hand to her mouth. 'Oh my God,' she exclaimed. 'That's not right.'

The unit supplied had a cut-out for a sink, but it should have had a solid top. The father looked absolutely shattered. He checked the paperwork. They'd brought out the wrong unit. He made a phone call and verified the correct unit was still in England. They had no alternative but to take it back. We dragged and pushed and eventually lifted it into the van. Apologies were made. It was agreed they would drop it off sometime during early July.

Patricia and I spent the remaining days doing more decorating. On the Saturday, I painted the exterior walls surrounding the windows, which dramatically changed the appearance of the house. We then spent two very pleasant evenings eating well, drinking good wine, and watching Glastonbury on TV, and returned to the UK on the Monday.

Sure enough, the kitchen company confirmed delivery of the correct item would be made in mid-July. We knew how heavy it was going to be, so we asked Desmond if he and a couple of friends could just take delivery and slide the unit into the main hallway. We could then put it into position when we came out at the end of July.

The granite top needed to be installed on top of the wall units, and we had arranged that the plumber would do this once he'd fitted and plumbed in the new sink.

Patricia, Gemma, and I arrived on the last Sunday of July. We'd arranged to go camping at Le Soleil at Argélès for another fortnight, so we asked Desmond if he and his merry band of middle-aged men might be able to come and assist us in positioning the kitchen unit in its rightful place. Desmond said they would come after their weekly boules match on the Tuesday afternoon. Several Englishmen turned up, and between all of us, we managed to push, slide, and cajole this ridiculously heavy unit into position.

We noticed that our lovely next-door neighbour, Solange, was looking rather frail. Patricia felt she'd lost weight. We had a chat with her one morning. She admitted she was feeling exhausted, and she'd been suffering considerable abdominal pain. She was due to go for some tests over the next few days.

We drove off to Argélès early on the Wednesday morning and arrived mid-afternoon to put up the tent. We were used to it by now, and we had everything achieved within two hours. I'd sweated buckets installing all the bedroom sections and inflatable beds, sleeping bags and luggage etc. Patricia said she needed to go to the shop, and I asked her to see if she could find a few cold beers for me.

As I've previously noted, the French aren't great at 'cold beer' so I feared this might be a challenge. Around twenty minutes later,

Patricia returned with provisions, including two large cans of beer. I didn't hang around; I ripped the ring-pull off one can and downed it in one. That felt good. I did the same with the second can, and although I drank this more slowly, it was gone within a few minutes.

I felt strangely heady. Maybe it was the sun. I went into the tent to get my towel and wash bag for a shower and almost lost my footing.

'Are you OK?' enquired Patricia anxiously.

'I just feel a bit spaced out,' I replied.

On the way out, I picked up one of the cans. The beer was a Belgian ale – 8.7 per cent. The other was 9.3 per cent. No wonder I felt a bit woozy.

We spent the next few days chilling out. Patrik and his family had already been out for a week, and we spent a good couple of days catching up. His business had also suffered in the global financial crisis, and we compared notes (as you do) as we chatted on the beach.

My brother Hugh and his family then came out, which really livened things up. The first night they arrived, we got a takeaway, which we ate at their tent, which was less than ten metres away from ours. They'd brought us some 'gifts', which we opened up with great hilarity. There was a giant set of plastic boobs for Patricia, a Dutch dictionary for Gemma in case she got chatted up by any Dutch boys, and a medallion and a false hairy chest for me. We were all in hysterics. Goodness knows what their neighbours thought.

The following evening, Patrik and Johan (there again for his third year) stopped by for an early evening drink. We showed them our gifts, and when Johan put the false hairy chest on his bald head, we nearly died laughing. I still have a photograph somewhere.

It was good to be back on the beach and get away, but I found it hard to relax. It had been a very tough five months, and I was becoming increasingly worried about the future viability of my recruitment business. There was just nothing around. I agreed with Patricia that I'd turn my phone on during the morning and again early evening, so I didn't miss out on anything. We were still in the early stages of smartphones, so getting email through was always a struggle. There was no public Wi-Fi at the campsite apart from one tiny area near the reception. But as many other campers tried to hook up too, the speed was very frustratingly slow, and the signal dipped out regularly.

Patricia couldn't have been more supportive. She knew how concerned I was, and never once rushed me or chastised me for spending what were actually fruitless hours on calls. I started to relax about halfway through, and we spent some very enjoyable days together, mostly on the beach or around the pool.

We had our own routine; we'd get up around eight thirty, go to the shop for bread and... English newspapers! It sounds ridiculous now, but at that time, there weren't any digital newspapers. It cost us a fortune to order them in, but as Patricia said, it was part of our holiday. *The Times* for us and the *Daily Mail* for Gem. We'd then have a shower, make breakfast, and afterwards have another cup or two of coffee, reading the newspaper before washing up and tidying the tent.

We'd wander off to the beach around midday, which was when many French families were coming off the beach to go back to their tents for lunch. We'd spend about three hours on the beach, swimming in the sea, reading and listening to music. It was pure one hundred per cent pleasure. There was almost always a gentle breeze, which made the sun bearable. The sea was warm, and as we looked up to the right, we'd see the Collioure and the Pyrenees mountains. Pure bliss!

We'd leave the beach around 3 p.m. and go back for lunch. Gemma still talks fondly of those lunches – salads, paté, cheeses, and various breads with a couple of glasses of rosé, and Orangina for Gem. We'd have some great conversations, and Gemma often recalls she learnt so much about life as we all chatted together.

We'd head off for the swimming pool around 5 p.m., again when the French would mostly be coming back for showers and evening meal preparation. We'd stay at the pool for a couple of hours, and by the time we got back, the queues for the showers had subsided. Patricia would start to cook, and we'd have a glass of something to start the evening. This was the daily pattern throughout the holiday.

We went to Spain occasionally. We'd discovered a beautiful Spanish village – their version of Collioure – called Cadaqués. Whereas Collioure was renowned for Picasso, Cadaqués was famous for Salvador Dali. I remember one year we bought a Dali-inspired bowl, which we gave to our dog Fred. He still eats his meals out of this each day – cultured chap that he is!

We also went into Spain one afternoon with my brother Hugh and his wife Mindy and daughter Rhiain. My friend Jacques knew the area and recommended a restaurant in the first main town called La Jonquera.

'You must visit a resto called Bingo,' he instructed me.

It was the last restaurant heading out of the town going south. We stopped and did some shopping at La Jonquera – prices were keen for all sorts of things – food, alcohol, and even barbecue and paella sets. Later in the afternoon, we followed the main road through the town, and saw the restaurant Bingo on the left-hand side. We parked up outside. The place was enormous, and it already looked quite full. Jacques had advised us to get there early, as he said it was very popular.

We went in and found a table. It was a set-price meal, buffet-style, with lots of separate stations for salads, hors d'oeuvres, fish, meat, desserts, and cheese. The girls' eyes were almost out on stalks. We had a look around and started to make our choices for starters.

However, when we started to eat, we found the quality was actually quite poor. It wasn't badly cooked, it was just tasteless – in fact nasty, cheap food. We moved on to main courses, but none of what showed promise actually delivered. The restaurant obviously made its money from bulk catering for the masses – and they certainly showed up. By the time we left around eight o'clock, there were around sixty people queueing outside. We did have a laugh – a restaurant in Spain recommended by a Frenchman. It was a pretty awful experience!

We did have a much better experience a few days later. We all decided to go to a small village near to Argélès called Sorède. It wasn't far but nestled up in the Pyrenees.

When I worked at Camping Blois Fleurie back in 1975, we used to occasionally drive up to Sorède. It had a very Spanish feel to it. The village was mostly empty, but it had a small café/bar with a football table.

We used to play all evening, and when we ran out of money, we'd remove our T-shirts and stuff them into the goals. The owner used to shout at us and threaten to ban us. But we were good beer drinkers, and he couldn't afford to lose our custom. I remember one evening we all insisted on retaining the same glass, as you did in England at that time. You'd never be given a fresh, clean glass. You'd hang on to the same glass all evening. Sometimes, if you were buying a round, you could end up with someone else's glass, but that was all part of the spirit. The owner just couldn't get his head around it. Another night, Geoff took an old record player, which he ran off his car battery. We were joined by a few of the teenagers, who sat on the kerb, as we played various Grateful Dead LPs.

I hadn't been to Sorède since then, so we decided to go for a look around. When we arrived, we walked up to the main village square. At one end, some massive paella pans were in place, and cooks were already preparing food for what seemed like loads of people. Chairs had been laid out, and various people were wandering around during the early evening. We decided to find a restaurant and came across a decent-looking place just off the square.

As we tucked into our meal, the noise level picked up, and then we heard someone singing, almost karaoke style. When we finished our meal, we walked back into the square, and there was a Johnny Halliday tribute artist. He was in his fifties, with a billowing white shirt open to the navel. He was crooning into a microphone. Next to him was a sound box, which played the music for the guitars, keyboards, and drums. Behind him was a woman with a PC on a table. We walked behind to see what she was doing. She was broadcasting lyrics from the computer to a screen in front of the singer.

He was truly awful. Out of tune, no rhythm or presence. But the audience clearly loved him. In fairness, this was probably the main event of the year in the village. There must have been a few hundred people. As we stood there, I noticed a cable running across the road to an electrical supply. This was powering the computer. I nudged Hugh and asked him how fast he could run. He looked puzzled, and then I pointed out the plug.

'If we switch that off, he won't have any lyrics in front of him, which means he'll suddenly dry up. Shall we...?'

It was tempting, but there would have been an outcry, and we'd have been chased out of the village.

We had a further funny restaurant experience with Hugh and Mindy. Earlier in the holiday, we all went to Collioure one evening. We found a restaurant where we could sit outside and enjoy the busy atmosphere of this beautiful fishing village. We spent a good couple of hours there, enjoying our meal. When we were ready to leave, I called the waiter across and asked for the bill. Nothing arrived. Fifteen minutes later, I called him over again and asked once more for the bill. Again, nothing happened.

Eventually, I went to the bar and asked for the bill. I was told it would be brought to our table. Twenty minutes later, we were still sitting there. Hugh and I both went to the bar, and we waited and waited. We asked a few of the staff, but no one wanted to know. Admittedly, the place was heaving. But at that point, something snapped, and Hugh and I edged back to our table.

'Come on, we're going,' we said.

'Have you paid now?' asked Patricia and Mindy.

'Erm, not exactly,' said Hugh, but as we were standing there, other people who were waiting for a table had spotted us get up, and they came over to take the table.

We stood outside, and Patricia and Mindy weren't impressed. They thought we were setting a bad example to the girls. Eventually, Hugh and I returned and managed to pay the bill. We met everyone else outside and made plans to return to the campsite. We'd arrived by bus, but by that time, the last bus had gone. We'd have to get some taxis, which would be expensive. They were also in short supply. Eventually, a taxi turned up. We agreed that Patricia, Mindy and the girls would share a cab back, and Hugh asked the driver to return to collect us and take us back. Meanwhile, we'd find a bar somewhere, and agreed to meet the driver in the same place in about forty-five minutes.

We found a bar and watched some rugby on the TV. When the cab arrived, we got in and chatted to the driver on the journey back. It turned out he was a huge rugby fan. He asked where we were from in the UK. When Hugh told him he lived near Leicester, the driver couldn't believe it. He kept referring to it as 'Lycester.' Hugh explained he was a regular visitor to the Leicester Tigers stadium. The driver was totally overwhelmed. I think he thought Hugh was one of the players. When he dropped us off at the campsite, he refused to take any money. He said it was his honour to have someone from Lycester rugby in his taxi!

Hugh, Mindy, and Rhiain returned to the UK a few days before us. Being on our own, we had more times to observe our neighbours. There was a Welsh family behind us – mother and father and two teenage sons. One of the sons, Luke, was clearly out of favour. Every morning and evening, the father would ask him to do things, to which the boy would turn a blind eye. This resulted in the father getting cross, and he would chastise and verbally lay into his poor son. It was relentless. The family had a trailer, and one evening I heard another Brit ask him how much camping gear he could get into the trailer. The Welsh guy replied that they hired the tent from Eurocamp. The trailer contained a fridge, and was full of food they'd brought from home, such as fish fingers and sausages. He said he loathed foreign food!

Next door to the Welsh family was a young couple from Liverpool who had a baby with them. They played the strangest music every morning from around seven. I can't describe it other than to say it was weird. Unfortunately, the volume was quite loud, and after a few days, it became very irritating. One morning, I said I had the solution. Patricia and Gemma were keen to find out.

'Keith Emerson,' I replied.

'Who's he?' they asked.

I explained that when I was sixteen, a schoolfriend lent me an album by a group called The Nice, whose keyboard player was Keith Emerson, who subsequently formed Emerson, Lake, & Palmer

The Nice album I borrowed was called *Elegy*. One track was their version of the Leonard Bernstein classic 'America'. Halfway through, as the band improvised, came the sound of Keith Emerson's Moog Synthesiser. This was a keyboard that generated all sorts of weird and wonderful sounds. During the track 'America', there was a section which sounded as if he was kicking giant cans down the road.

I remembered that when I borrowed the album, I played it at home on my dad's precious Hi-Fi which comprised a very tasty Garrard deck. As I listened to the album in our lounge, Dad walked in horrified, and asked me what the hell I was doing to his Hi-Fi. I looked puzzled.

He said, 'That horrible noise... You've damaged the stylus.'

'No, Dad,' I calmly replied. 'That's not your stylus, that's music.' He stood there and shook his head in disbelief!

The following morning at around half eight, I'd had enough of the awful noise from the tent behind. I located The Nice on my iPod, got to the appropriate place in the track, plugged in the portable speaker, and turned up the volume. With two minutes the noise behind disappeared, never to reappear. Good old Keith Emerson. I've always had a soft spot for him!

After our holiday, we returned to the house for a few days and then drove back to the UK. We felt concern for our next-door neighbour Solange who was almost a shadow of her usual self.

In the absence of recruitment opportunities, I'd taken up the offer of some training work for some friends in Germany. This involved running a course in general management for some of the top young people working at a large multi-national company, who were being groomed as managers for the future. They were from all over Europe. It was fun and challenging, and I enjoyed the experience enormously.

WE WENT BACK with Mum in late September. The weather was still warm, but less hot than in July and August. We spent a few very enjoyable evenings eating and drinking together on our new balcony. There was one memorable situation that week; our friend Jacques came over on the Friday morning, and told me that on the Saturday evening, a play was going to be performed in a hall at a local village several kilometers away. It was in aid of a charity, and he urged us to join him and his wife. Patricia and Mum weren't overkeen to go, but I persuaded them it was part of supporting our local community. We arrived just before 7pm. There were around a hundred plus chairs, but only about thirty people there. The play started. It was a farce, and after about ten minutes I realized it was being performed in Patois, which is a French countryside dialect, that was widely spoken for many years until around 1950. This made the play difficult to understand. After an hour, there was a brief intermission. I went in search of drinks, but sadly no wine for Patricia and Mum, just small 25cl bottles of warm beer and soft drinks. Patricia was keen to leave, but once again I encouraged her to stay for the second half. Sadly, this went on for almost two hours, during which time, the temperature dropped. I passed my jacket to Patricia in an attempt to appease her fast-growing discomfort. Finally, at around 10pm, the performance came to an end, and we drove home. We entered the house. Patricia was not happy! 'That was one of the worst bloody evenings I've ever had' she loudly exclaimed. 'No wine, freezing cold, uncomfortable chairs, and I couldn't understand a word of that awful play'. She opened a bottle of wine, poured her and Mum a massive glass each, and stormed upstairs, only to discover I'd forgotten to record that evening's episode of 'Strictly'. Oh dear ...!

When we arrived in Pellac earlier in the week, we spoke to Maurice. He confirmed that Solange (who was his cousin) was unwell and in a care home at St Junien. We were very fond of Solange. I asked Maurice if we might be able to go and see her, and he encouraged us to do so. We drove there the following day and found the place, which was more a cottage hospital than a typical care facility and asked if we could see her. A nurse took us to her room. She was lying in bed. She looked tiny, bless her. She was astounded to see us, and very appreciative. But she was clearly unwell, and the words 'cancer of the pancreas' were mentioned. We said goodbye to her, and we both had a horrible feeling that it might be the last time we saw her. In fact, it was as she passed away in November. We still miss her. Patricia had taken a lovely photograph of her a few years earlier – with her proudly displaying a huge basket of ceps she'd foraged in the forest. We gave her son a copy of it and were really touched to discover they'd reproduced this image on the order of service for her funeral.

Other than that, we had a reasonable week, but there was still no work for me. I began to get really worried. Two weeks later, I received my first enquiry for several months from a Polish company. I managed to find them someone who they hired, and it reminded me how much I enjoyed what I did. Nevertheless, one completed assignment wasn't going to fund our lives. I needed more work.

Another assignment came in. I found a candidate who the client liked, but they couldn't decide whether to hire him. The candidate was out of work, and it all started looking pretty desperate. Towards the end of October, they made a tentative offer. By then, of course, the candidate had received another offer elsewhere. We went off to France for a week at the end of October, and I spent a very nervous few days while the candidate decided what to do. Eventually, on the Friday, he confirmed he'd accept the offer. You'll never know (Adam) how much I enjoyed my beer that night!

As we moved into the run-up towards the end of the year, business finally picked up, and enquiries came in from my existing and new clients. We drove out after Christmas to celebrate the New Year there with our friends Paul and Stephanie, and I really felt we'd turned the corner. The building work and renovations were all complete and paid for. Business had picked up, and I approached the New Year 2010 with real optimism. We had a great time there with our friends and drove all the way back to Calais through a snowstorm in early January.

ANDOUILLETTE AND FRENCH WI-FI

2010

During the first two months of twenty-ten, I was fully engaged on my recruitment business, but towards the end of February, we were keen to drive out to Pellac for a short break. We had a relaxing week, although one night we had a major storm. We knew the Wi-Fi was susceptible to going off during thunder and lightning. As the storm took hold, I dashed upstairs, and as I moved towards the router, a blue flash came out of the telephone socket. The result was no Wi-Fi. The router was completely dead.

The Internet was my lifeline to the business world. We had to resolve the situation. I called Orange the next day, and they advised me to go to the nearest shop in either Limoges or Brive, with the damaged router, and they would replace it free of charge. We decided to go to Brive for a change. We entered the Orange shop, and ten minutes later, we walked out with a replacement router.

I was so pleased, I decided to do something I'd been meaning to for a while. I'd often commented on how modern and classy French spectacle frames are. When we stopped at a supermarket on the way home, I noticed an optician opposite. I went to look at frames. I had my English prescription with me and asked if a pair could be made up to that prescription. I was told that not only was it possible, but that the turnaround was forty-eight hours, and that the glasses would be ready for collection on Tuesday. It also helped that the sales assistant was both attractive and charming. I always trust Patricia's judgement, and when the assistant endorsed her opinion, saying softly, 'These spectacles really suit you, Monsieur,' there was no going back!

The first thing I did when we returned to the house later that afternoon was to plug in the new router. It came with an instruction manual, which was based on a Windows PC. Patricia and I have been major Apple users since 2005, and I realised it was sadly going to take some time before I got online. I tried various things, but nothing worked. I called a helpline and was told no one was available until Monday.

I stewed throughout the weekend, and on Monday morning; I called the helpline again. I got through to someone on the English-speaking line who was totally and utterly useless. I might as well have spoken to someone in Swahili. In desperation, I called the French-speaking helpline, and to my joy and relief, I came across someone who understood Apple Macs. He talked me through it, and within ten minutes, we were back online.

On the Tuesday, I had a call from the opticians. My spectacles were ready to collect as promised. We popped down to collect them, and then drove back to the UK the following day.

THE SUMMER OF 2010 was an important milestone in Patricia's life – she set up her own catering business – Passionate Food. When we first met, she was working as a classroom assistant at the local comprehensive school. After assisting in a food technology lesson, the teacher (who was also the head of department), immediately saw the affinity Patricia had for the subject. She was encouraged to train as a Food Technology Teacher. As a degree was a necessary pre-requisite, she spent the next three years studying degree in her spare time. Less than a year after qualifying, Patricia contracted breast cancer. After much thought and reflection, she came to the decision that regrettably, the pressure of teaching at a vast comprehensive school was not going to be the best solution for her long-term health and recovery.

She maintained and developed her interest in food, and after establishing a chutney-making business, she channelled this further into a full-blown catering business, and in the course of doing so, she developed an excellent reputation.

As her business started to take off, she needed some planning time, in particular the conversion of our garage into a commercial kitchen to comply with health and safety regulations. So, we decided to spend a lazy couple of weeks at Pellac in June. This was also the time when we unknowingly embarked on an unbelievably expensive project for our kitchen in France.

For some time, Patricia felt that the kitchen needed brightening up, and she suggested we tile the back wall. We'd already searched for suitable tiles, and Patricia chose some small red, white, and blue tiles. As mentioned, DIY is not my thing, especially tiling. But an English friend who lived near us in France was looking for odd jobs, and we asked him to give us a quote. He came back with a price of €500, which we thought was a bit steep, but he explained it would probably take him all week. I had a petrol strimmer which I no longer used, but which I thought could be useful to our friend, so I offered this to him in part payment.

When we returned in July for our usual camping holiday in the south, we found the wall had indeed been tiled. Our friend called round a few days later, and explained the work had taken longer, and that he had to bring in an electrician to disconnect and move the electrical socket for the oven. As a result, he asked for another €200. He went to suggest that a shelf above the top line of tiles would finish off the wall nicely. Patricia agreed wholeheartedly. He said he'd find something suitable to match the oak kitchen units. When we got back from our trip, the shelf was up. It looked good, and our friend told us it would last for years as it was made from solid oak. As a consequence, the price was €100.

All in all, the cost of the tiles, plus the installation, plus the additional costs, and plus the figure for the shelf, amounted to around €1,000. Probably the most expensive wall in the village, if not the country!

We had a lovely, lazy, relaxing week again at Camping Le Soleil, washed in sunshine during the day, and in wine during the evenings.

Gem and I went for a couple of early evening runs on the beach. We also went back to Cadaqués, and drove further on around the coast to Roses, which is a very popular holiday resort for the French.

I was also keen to find El Bulli, which not only was a Michelin starred restaurant, but had won the acclaim as the best restaurant in the world. I wasn't intending to eat there, not at around €200 per head, but Patricia and I were interested to see what it looked like.

Following maps and the car satnav, we found our way down various tracks to eventually arrive at the restaurant – which was closed! There wasn't even a menu outside, just a small sign saying El Bulli. We wondered how on earth customers arrived there, given the difficult, uncomfortable cross-country drive we'd had. Then the penny dropped; the resto was on the coast and had a jetty. Presumably, most of their clientele arrived by boat.

We drove back to Soleil. It was a hot muggy day and wasn't helped by the fact my in-car air conditioning wasn't working correctly. Instead of pumping out cold air, it began to pipe warm air through the vents. It seemed as if the heating had infiltrated the air conditioning system. Within minutes, we were deeply uncomfortable. Sod's law – often when you most need something, it packs up. Like a TV breaking down five minutes before the end of a film. Or Wi-Fi failing when you need it most!

We drove back to Pellac and collected Fred from kennels. We called it his summer camp. They had been recommended to us. The kennels were run by a British couple in their 50s. The guy was a retired firefighter. It was his dream to open boarding kennels in the Dordogne.

The site was vast – around ten acres. Amazingly, the dogs all ran free, and the owner seemed to spend most of his time just walking around with the dogs. I queried this, asking if the dogs ever fought. He explained that the dogs generally found their level, like primary school children in the playground. They would find their circle of preferred friends. Sure enough, we saw this happen:

Fred looked a little uncomfortable at first, and quite apprehensive. A few dogs growled at him. One of the owner's massive Great Danes strolled up to Fred, sniffed him, and apparently indicated he should follow her. She walked into a pack of noisy dogs, with Fred in tow, and the message seemed to be this one's OK, and don't mess with him, otherwise I'll be on you'. When we went to collect Fred a week later, he almost didn't want to leave, and with a certain pride, he introduced us to some of his friends.

Lucy and Phil were flying out that day and we collected them from the airport before returning to a lunch Patricia had prepared earlier. The following day, we went out to lunch at a little local restaurant and sat outside, looking down the valley, eating our way through five courses.

We spent the rest of our time at our house simply enjoying warm days and long evenings sitting outside, both on our own and sometimes with friends. We also went to a local bar, where a jazz band would often play on a Friday night. One Friday night, we arrived to find a French rock band was setting up. They started to play at nine, and in all fairness they weren't bad. As is so often the case in the UK as well as in France, the musicians were mostly in their 40s, 50s, and 60s, accompanied with the customary long hair and beards, and skintight jeans.

A French family came to stay in one of the cottages near our house. Apparently, it belonged to a lady in the village who would let it out to relatives of her friends. Although they were only there for a week, they made their presence felt! The husband/father was a chap called Pierre, and his grandmother lived about one hundred metres away. He was a real live wire, singing along to his music, playing with his daughters who were aged five and seven. Fred thought it was great, as the little girls loved him and kept giving him things to eat.

The family was from Paris. Pierre and his father ran a kiosk opposite the Comédie Française. He explained that the Parisian kiosks are available on a lease. When the principal lease holder either retires or dies, the lease passes back to the authority. So I understood why Pierre was such a vibrant, outgoing guy given his job.

One morning, after chatting together, he said he was inviting a few people from our end of the village across for a drink. He asked us to bring chairs, as we'd be sitting outside in the road/track opposite his cottage. We wandered across with a couple of bottles of wine. After a couple of hours, his wife went inside. We could smell food being cooked. And then she reappeared with a large pan.

She handed around plates and served the food. I suddenly realised what it was – andouillette – which consists of chitterlings, seasoning, and tripe. It smells disgusting and tastes absolutely foul. I can eat most things, including snails and various shellfish, but andouillette makes me want to reach for the sick bag.

It was too late – she'd already put food on my plate. I glanced at Patricia and quietly said, 'I can't eat this.' But I really didn't have an alternative. It was my fault – I should have recognised the smell as it was being cooked and invented an excuse. I have one now – it's 'j'ai une allergie…'

We sat outside for another couple of hours – the wine helped to take away the taste of the andouillette and then I realised how cold it was. Incredibly, the temperature had dropped to ten degrees.

AFTER A BUSY and hectic month recruiting in September, I returned in October. I took Mum with me, and we spent a lovely week together, before Patricia came out the following weekend with Gem and Jo. Work was still very busy during that week, but I landed my biggest ever deal, and Mum and I celebrated with a beautiful bottle of Montbazillac wine.

We managed to get out and about, including a trip to Périgueux. On the Friday night, we went to dinner at Jacques and Marguerite's.

I had to get up early on the Saturday morning. I was catching the 6.30 train from Limoges to Paris, where I would meet Patricia and the girls. I'd volunteered to organise a lunch in Paris for former pupils from my old school who lived in France. Given the size of the country, many of them weren't able to make the trip just for lunch, but around twenty of us sat down to lunch, including the previous headmaster and his wife, who had recently moved to the Burgundy area.

Mum spent the day in the house, and during the evening, Jacques and Marguerite kindly brought across some supper for her.

I arrived in Paris and made my way to Gare du Nord to greet the girls off their Eurostar, and we went for a coffee before arriving at the restaurant. We all had a good lunch and made some new connections. We then caught an early evening train back to Limoges and got back home around eleven.

We spent a great week together. I was able to take some time out, and we met with various friends throughout the week for various meals and had a day trip to Limoges. We also went to the market at Brantôme, on a cold but beautifully sunny Friday morning.

We returned home at the end of the week, and although we didn't know it at the time, that was the last time we'd be in Pellac until August of the following year.

A Tragic Start but A Happier Ending at a Brittany Manor

2011

The year began with a short trip to Switzerland in early January, to meet with some of Patricia's long-lost and newly found relatives. Unfortunately, our trip was cut short as we received some devastating news. My brother Simon and his wife Julie owned a hotel up in Cumbria. Over the Christmas/New Year period, they'd developed that winter's epidemic – swine-flu. They both became ill, as the flu developed into pneumonia. I had a call from my mum two days into our trip to learn that Julie had tragically passed away during the night. As the day wore on, we learnt that Simon had been admitted to hospital. We flew back the following day, and I went straight up to Carlisle. Simon didn't recover, and twelve days later he too passed away. It was unbelievable, and very, very distressing.

A joint funeral was arranged for the last day in January, and virtually the entire village turned up at the church to pay their respects. Simon and Julie were popular and much-loved, and it was a very poignant and moving occasion to see the church packed out, with many additional mourners outside.

Life took a couple of months to get back on an even keel, and we decided to remain in the UK and to support my mother through this immensely difficult and sad time.

ODDLY ENOUGH, WE went back to Switzerland in May, this time with one of my cousins and his wife and another couple they were friends with. They used to go every year, and knowing what we'd gone through, and with our previous trip to Switzerland cut short, asked Patricia and I if we'd join them. We spent a very pleasant week walking in the Swiss Alps, which was both cathartic and healing.

As the year wore on, we held off going to Pellac until the summer. We went out at the beginning of August with Gemma, and after a couple of days, we drove down to Argélès for what would be (at the time of writing) the last time we camped at Le Soleil. I'm very much looking forward to going back someday with our grandchildren. We spent a quiet, relaxing week there, and came back to Pellac. Lucy and Phil flew out for a long weekend, and on the Saturday afternoon, we sat down and planned their wedding the following year. I have to say to their absolute credit, both Lucy and Phil stuck implicitly to the budgets we agreed, which culminated in a fabulous wedding the following July.

A day later, Patricia's eldest daughter Vicky and her then boyfriend Reef flew out to join us, and we all went to the Mechoui together. We had a great time and met some Irish people (who live in Holland) and who have since become good friends – Ruairi and Siobhan. As a result of a fairly large English (and Irish) contingent at the Mechoui, the beer ran out, and further supplies had to be quickly commandeered from various private sources!

During late August, Pierre and his family came back to the village for a week. We returned the compliment from the year before and invited them for drinks one evening, together with some other friends. Pierre's wife was somewhat haughty and cold, and when I asked her what she wanted to drink, she replied, 'Je ne bois que du champagne.' *I only drink champagne*. This took me by surprise – we only had red or white wine, so she chose to drink mineral water. I parked this memory for the future!

PATRICIA AND I returned with Mum at the end of September. We had become friends with an English guy – Perry, who had moved to Pellac a couple of years beforehand, and who had transformed a derelict stable barn into a magnificent house.

Before coming to Pellac, Perry had suffered a stroke, which badly affected his movement and also his speech. He was actually fluent in French, and could understand it perfectly, but could only communicate in his mother tongue of English, albeit in a very limited way.

Perry was quite a character; charming, persuasive, occasionally pushy, and a kind and generous host – a real one-off. He immersed himself in village life and became very popular among both French and English residents. That September, he celebrated his sixty-fifth birthday, and as a consequence he invited the entire village to his house for a party. The invitation was from 6 p.m. We sat on our balcony beforehand and watched the villagers make their way to his house before six.

We were amazed. The done thing in the UK is not to arrive at the start of a party, but generally, an hour or so after it starts. But not in France. A party for Brits is generally about the drink, and then the food. For the French, it's the opposite. Hence the reason they arrived on the dot, so they could make the most of the food.

We wandered across at about 7 p.m., and found the party in full swing, with a large amount of food already consumed. Mum was especially fascinated by the fact that when we introduced her to various French villagers, their first question was about her age. We realised that life expectancy in rural France was traditionally less perhaps than we would have thought. When it was discovered that Mum would be eighty that November, it was greeted with both surprise and respect.

One of my fondest memories of Perry's party was a jazz duo who played upstairs. The interior of his house was unusual – a large lounge opening onto his front terrace. At the back was a magnificent staircase which led to an open-plan upstairs, featuring two bedrooms which had no walls. This was Perry's style. It meant that sixty plus people could sit on the beds, chairs, and floor upstairs and all enjoy the music.

FOR CHRISTMAS THAT year, Patricia, me, Gemma, and Mum all went up to Simon and Julie's hotel in Brough, as much as anything to lend comfort and support to their twenty-one-year-old son Jamie who was running the business. My other brother Hugh and his family also joined us for an unusual festive period.

Patricia and I had been invited to spend New Year with some friends from Tenterden – Roger and Harriet – at their house in Brittany. They explained they'd already been invited to a New Year's dinner party with some friends, but they kindly offered their house up to us that evening so we could spend a quiet, relaxing evening in.

Well – that was the plan, until halfway into our journey, we had a call from Harriet, to say that one couple who were due at the dinner party had dipped out due to illness. The offer was that we could join them, but only if we wanted to. Although we hadn't brought any smart clothing, we agreed it might be fun. It certainly was.

The hosts were an English couple who were permanent residents in France who lived at a 'manoir'. We arrived late afternoon on New Year's Eve and were shown to our rooms. At 7 p.m. we went downstairs to start the party. The tradition was for each couple to prepare a course. Given there were twelve people present, that meant six courses. The hosts, Roger and Harriet, and us being the English contingent, and the other six guests were French.

We ate like lords. We began with a magnificent seafood course of crab, lobster, oysters, mussels, and crayfish. Although seafood is not Patricia's favourite, she was gently encouraged and tutored by the French couple responsible for this course, and she ended up surprising herself with how much she enjoyed it.

The whole meal was excellent – hors d'oeuvres, main course, desserts (including an enormous pavlova topped with a flaming candle, which Patricia had prepared), and cheese in addition to the seafood and the canopés which preceded the dinner.

All washed down with some superb wines. We ended up dancing to various Scottish reels until three am!

A New Boiler, A Log Burner, and a Weekend in Paris

2012

At the start of 2012, Patricia and I fancied a change, and so we decided to go to Germany during the early part of May and visit some of her relatives in the beautiful Black Forest.

In June, we went out to Pellac and enjoyed a lovely week in the sun. Patricia took me to a fantastic local restaurant to celebrate Father's Day, to which we've been several times since – L'Hostellerie St Jacques. We sat outside in the garden in the sun, and I was truly spoilt.

The big family event that year was Lucy and Phil's wedding on July 14 (Bastille Day in France). The wedding took place at Burnham-on-Crouch, and it poured with rain all day! Nevertheless, we all had a wonderful day, and a memorable evening too, as we danced at a brilliant disco at the venue – The Royal Corinthian Yacht Club. I believe the bar took record takings that night. My slight hangover the next day bore testament to that. But seriously, it was a thoroughly enjoyable occasion.

It was also the summer of the London Olympic Games. As a result, we delayed our annual summer trip until mid-August, and we spent a whole month out there. Gem came out for a few days, with her then boyfriend Eliot. We all relaxed – sunbathing, with gentle walks around our favourite lake, and eating well and healthily as always. On the way back from the airport, after taking Gem and Eliot to catch the plane back home, Patricia and I popped into Leroy Merlin. We had nothing specific in mind apart from Rawlplugs. But as we walked around the store, we noticed there was a price promotion on log burners.

We were tempted to browse and came across a lovely dark red log burner. We checked the measurements and were certain it would easily fit into our fireplace. We found an assistant, and said we'd like to buy it, and would want it delivered. This was slightly tricky, as an external delivery company had to be hired, and as is so often the case in France, something we took for granted for being simple in the UK became complicated in France.

First of all, the assistant couldn't get through to the company, then he eventually did get through, to be asked to call back later that afternoon. The assistant shrugged and apologised and said it would be easiest for me to call them when I got home. I started to visualise the problems doing this. I asked the assistant for his name and extension number. He gave me his word he would process the order, and post (not email) the paperwork through to the delivery company. He suggested I called them in a couple of days. We left the store, pleased with our purchase, but uneasy about organising the delivery.

We had already engaged our local boiler engineer Stephan to supply and fit a new boiler for the following week. I called him and asked if he could fit the log burner at the same time. He agreed and suggested we arranged delivery while he was at our house installing the boiler.

I duly called the delivery company a couple of days later and found, to my surprise and delight, that they were already in receipt of the order. I asked for a delivery the following week. They suggested the week after. I said that was too late; they then suggested this week, and I replied that this was too soon. Eventually, we settled on our preferred date.

The delivery company then made it very clear that delivery would be kerbside; in other words, they wouldn't carry the log burner into the house. If we wanted that option, the price for that would be an additional forty Euros. I said kerbside delivery would be fine – no way was I paying an extra forty Euros for them to carry this into the house. Stephan and at least one other of his team would be there, and I was sure we could manage this between us.

The delivery arrived on the allotted day. The driver spoke to our boiler engineer and said he'd drop the log burner on to the grass verge outside our house. Stephan suggested he reversed into our driveway. He might as well have asked the delivery man to drive to the UK. His request was met with an emphatic 'non!'

Stephan cunningly pointed out the driver would have to turn the van around, and by reversing into our drive, that would make things easier for him. The driver had the cheek to say he'd leave the log burner on the verge, and then reverse into our drive. Stephan stood his ground, leaving the driver no other option other than to follow his request. The driver's face was a picture. He was extremely irritated. Stephan and his two colleagues picked up the log burner with ease and carried it into the house. I couldn't resist cheering, and with a big smile on my face, gave the driver a thumbs-up, and called out, 'Allez, ciao.' He accelerated hard out of the drive, almost skidding into the gatepost as he left.

Stephan and his men did a great job installing both the boiler and log burner. Perry came over and gave the log burner his approval. He sat down in front of it, in his shorts, pretending to warm his hands.

'You'll be able to stay here the entire winter now,' he exclaimed. Perry couldn't understand why we never stayed longer than our usual two to four weeks. We always went through the same explanation that we had family at home, as well as businesses to run. But he never seemed to quite get it. I could appreciate where he was coming from. It must have been a lonely existence for him and having us nearby would have made his life more fun. He was a very kind man; he'd often pop across with a bottle of wine, or a large box of vegetables from his garden. We even arrived one summer to find a large wine box sitting on our front step, which was so thoughtful.

The following day, Patricia and I caught a train to Paris for the weekend. We'd decided the previous week that an early September weekend in Paris would be wonderful. Hopefully, fewer tourists would be around, and we could enjoy exploring the city in warm weather.

On the Friday morning, we took Fred to the kennels where he went the year before, and drove to Nexon, parked the car (for free) for the whole weekend, and caught the local train to Limoges, where we changed trains to catch the 'grand ligne' to Paris. We arrived in Paris at around 5 p.m. We'd booked an apartment in the Paris 17 arrondissement, but we had to go elsewhere first to get the keys. We finally got to our apartment around six-thirty. It was in a good, quiet neighbourhood, although the flat itself was fairly primitive. But we reminded ourselves it was just somewhere to sleep for two nights and went out to find a restaurant.

I always find that Friday evenings in France have a special atmosphere. Everything in our village quietens down after 6 p.m., and by 7 p.m. it's all very calm and tranquil. Although Paris was naturally different, the atmosphere in the restaurant was very chilled and laid back, with people coming out for dinner to celebrate the start of the weekend. We ate well and enjoyed a warm, balmy walk back to our apartment.

We got up fairly early the next morning and found a nice café for breakfast. We then walked across to the Arc de Triomphe, and then started to walk up the Champs-Élysées, stopping off to peer into various shop windows. We continued our walk across la Place de Concorde and meandered through the Jardin des Tuileries before crossing the Seine on the Pont Neuf. We were meeting some friends for lunch – a couple of guys who had been to my old school. Both of them lived in Paris, and one had suggested a restaurant on the left bank in the St Germain area, called Alcazar.

We had a splendid lunch. I chose tuna carpaccio to start with, prepared in a Japanese style. I remembered there were some accompaniments on the plate. As we got into conversation, I looked at my plate, and absent-mindedly noticed what I assumed was avocado purée, and placed the entire forkful into my mouth. Suddenly I couldn't speak. I could barely breathe. My eyes watered, and my nose began to run. I'd eaten a whole mouthful of wasabi.

The two friends hadn't noticed, but Patricia had. As we walked out of the restaurant around three hours later with full tummies and that warm feeling you get from an excellent couple of bottles of Médoc, she asked, 'Why did you eat all the wasabi at once? It must have been unbearably hot.'

When I explained what I thought it was, it was Patricia's turn to have wet eyes as she burst into laughter with tears running down her face. My earlier discomfort had now become hilarious to her!

We spent the rest of the afternoon and early evening just walking around central Paris. We found the Kiosque opposite the Académie Française where Pierre worked, although he wasn't there that day. We introduced ourselves to his father, who couldn't believe we had a house in Pellac – the tiny village where he was born and brought up.

We walked all the way to Boulevard Haussmann and went into a few of the large stores. We then wandered down towards the Elysée Palace, where we didn't see much apart from various miserable-looking guards. We carried on down the Rue du Faubourg Saint-Honoré, and as we digressed into some of the alleyways, the smells emanating from the perfume shops percolated into the street. Absolutely gorgeous. We finally and slowly walked back to our apartment, and after downloading The Times on to our laptops in a McDonald's en route, we opened a bottle of Muscat and sat on the balcony overlooking the street where we were staying.

We got up early again the next day. After breakfasting locally, we decided to deposit our luggage at the railway station we'd be departing from that evening. One of our friends the day before recommended that we avoid the Tube and catch the bus. Apparently, the buses had become popular with business community in Paris, and as a result had become a more upmarket – and unquestionably more pleasant – way to travel around Paris.

We dropped off our bags in the lockers at Gare d'Austerlitz and decided to take a stroll via the Sorbonne and Latin Quarter, then find a suitable restaurant in the St Germain district. We came across a busy welcome resto, with tables outside. We sat down and ordered côte-de-boeuf and a bottle of Côte-de-Rhone. Looking around, the plates were arriving extremely full, and as well as the portions being large, the food looked very good. In fact, it was way too much – a real meat-fest. Patricia struggled to eat hers. I persuaded her to join me in having a dessert, then feeling slightly too full, we decided to spend a relaxing afternoon back in the Jardin des Tuileries. We found some deckchairs and, surrounded by various families playing ballgames, we fell asleep.

I woke up around five fifteen. Patricia was already awake.

'What time's our train?' she asked. I looked at my watch.

'Ten minutes past six,' I replied. 'We should go.'

We walked fast, crossing the river at Pont Neuf. Patricia absolutely hates walking fast and being in a rush. She knows that I like to live in the fast lane, and that I see it as a challenge when I'm up against the clock. This time we really were, because we had to collect our luggage before boarding the train.

We got to the luggage office just before six and hunted around for change to open the lockers and retrieve our luggage. We ran out on to the main concourse and searched for the right platform. We also had to go through the French practice of getting our tickets 'stamped' before boarding the train. We made it with just two minutes to spare. Poor Patricia. She sat opposite me, on a crowded train, panting and perspiring. I tried to smile empathetically. I could see conversation wasn't going to be on the cards for the next hour!

We pulled into Limoges at around 9.45 p.m. and caught our connection to Nexon. We arrived home hot and exhausted and collapsed into bed around 11.30 p.m. But we had had a fabulous weekend, about which we still reminisce fondly.

The only other thing of note that happened before our return to the UK the following week is that I decided to move some furniture around. We'd bought some 'IKEA style' chairs from a similar shop called Altea. We thought it would make the loft area upstairs brighter and lighter if we positioned these chairs up there. This meant bringing the large two-seater sofa downstairs. But Patricia didn't think we'd manage it. She suggested I ask Maurice, our neighbour.

But I was certain that if I removed the cushions, I'd be able to get the sofa downstairs. What I hadn't reckoned with was the weight of the sofa. It was incredibly heavy and unwieldy. I managed to get it onto the stairs and started to bring it down one step at a time. However, when it came to the dogleg on the staircase, the sofa got stuck. I simple couldn't budge it. I also couldn't get past the sofa to the other end of it. I thought I could perhaps tip it up on to one end. But that wasn't possible.

I called Patricia. Together we tried to lift the sofa from the bottom, but we just couldn't do it. Rather meekly, I asked if she'd mind getting Maurice to come to help me. Maurice is a very private man. When Patricia asked him in her halting French if he could come over to our house, he mistook this for an invitation.

'Not today,' he replied. 'Perhaps later in the week.'

'Non, non,' said Patricia. 'C'est, Nigel. Urgent.'

Thinking I'd had a heart attack, Maurice followed Patricia into the house and saw me on the stairs under the sofa. I explained to him what I wanted to do, and his strength enabled us both to lift the sofa over the bannisters, and gently lower it on to the hallway floor. As I started to effusively thank Maurice, he looked at me curiously and asked why I wanted to bring the sofa downstairs.

I started to explain, then laughed, and said, 'C'est compliqué.'

Maurice gave me another curious look, shook his head, then shook my hand, and went back to his gardening.

We went back in November for a quick autumnal visit. We took Mum, and Lucy also flew out for a few days. She arrived at Bergerac airport, and after collecting her we popped into Bergerac for a snack and drink at a café opposite a statue of Cyrano de Bergerac. The town is pleasant and attractive with some interesting shops.

We had a relaxing few days, and on the Tuesday lunchtime we booked a table at a restaurant which had been strongly recommended to us by some French friends. At first, they were reluctant to disclose its whereabouts, and simply said their favourite restaurant was at Rochechouart, a small town about forty-five minutes away. They seemed concerned not to let the resto become overrun by tourists, but knowing we're foodies, they told us the details.

We arrived at Le Roc du Boeuf at midday. The restaurant is situated just outside the town, down a quiet country road, and opposite a river. We were welcomed by a charming lady, who we found out was one of the joint owners. The décor was beautiful. Old thick stone walls, flagstones on the floor, and a large open fire. The tables and chairs were attractively covered in various fabrics. There were lots of ornaments and table decorations consisting of feathers. The overall effect was an interior that was quite feminine in a masculine, rugged setting.

We were presented with the menus and selected a prix-fixe menu of around €30. Apéros and canapés were brought to the table before the starters, main course, and finally the desserts, all of which were ordered at the same time. The food was absolutely exquisite. I could write for ages about the wonderful spectrum of textures and tastes. Everything was perfectly cooked. It was all quite superb. The presentation of the various dishes and drinks was also gorgeous. The food was tastefully and imaginatively placed on a variety of dishes.

The crockery and glassware were beautiful; the cutlery was modern and stylish. The water jugs in particular caught our attention; simple earthenware jugs, without handles, making them look slim and unobtrusive, with a fishing float inside, so the serving staff could easily detect when the water levels were low, and would immediately replenish them.

The wine list was perfect, just a few choices from various French regions and very reasonably priced. We spent a magical few hours savouring not just a magnificent lunch but also a fabulous experience. As I paid the bill, I looked the owner in the eye, and said we'll certainly be back soon!

We spent New Year at Roger and Harriet's house in Brittany again. Not quite such a lavish occasion as the previous year, but very enjoyable once again.

EXPIRED PASSPORTS, AND MICE

2013

We returned the compliment in April 2013, when we went out for a week to our place, and Roger and Harriet came out and stayed for a few nights. We took them to Le Roc du Boeuf, and they too were fulsome in their praise.

We had a funny episode on the way back; as we sat in the car at Eurotunnel Calais, queueing for Passport Control, I did the usual thing of 'nothing to do so let's look through the passports', and discovered that in fact, both Patricia's and my passports had expired in March. I told Patricia.

'Oh my God, what are we going to do,' she asked, clearly alarmed.

'There's nothing we can do,' I replied calmly. 'We managed to get into France without having our passports properly checked. Had it been realised then that they were out of date, that would have really spoilt our holiday. In fact, we wouldn't have been able to enter France. But as we're on the way home, they'll just have to let us through. But don't say anything. Let's play dumb and see what happens.'

We eventually pulled up at the checkpoint. We handed our passports over. The woman looked at them and did the usual checks then came back to the window, and asked if we knew our passports were out of date?

I looked suitably shocked, and replied, 'No, no. Not at all'

'I'm amazed you were let into France when you arrived last week,' she said. 'You'll need to renew them as soon as you get back.'

And with that, she let us through. As we drove on to the shuttle train, Patricia remarked that Freddie was in fact the only legal traveller, as his passport was the only one valid!

IN MAY, PATRICIA and I went to Italy for ten days. We caught the Eurostar to Paris, had lunch, then caught an overnight sleeper train to Florence. A long but comfortable journey. This was more of a working holiday for Patricia, as she was providing the catering at an 'art retreat' at a fabulous Italian chateau in the Umbrian hills, to ten British delegates and a renowned professional artist. It was an interesting time, enjoyable but also unforgettable for several reasons, largely due to the strange people who owned the house and ran the retreat.

It was our first foray in Italy, and we loved it. We completed the trip with a twenty-four-hour visit to Rome.

We went to Pellac in late July for our summer holiday and were joined by Gem and Jo. Both of them were single girls at that time, and they got up to all kinds of harmless mischief during their stay.

One of the most memorable occurrences was the intrusion of a mouse in the house, which we spent a few nights trying to catch. I fondly recall visiting a DIY store, and as we searched for a mousetrap, Jo (who speaks no French) approached a sales assistant, and through a combination of noises and facial expressions managed to find the mouse traps before the rest of us. On the night we managed to catch the mouse, Patricia and I were lying in bed, about to fall asleep, when we heard a loud cheer from the girls' room. They'd heard the trap spring.

I went downstairs around eight the next morning to make a coffee. I noticed the trap had been sprung but held no mouse. As I walked towards the trap to pick it up, I narrowly avoided treading on the unfortunate mouse, which was no longer alive. It had managed to evade the trap as it pulled out the chocolate bait but must have received a blow to the body as the spring came down (or maybe heart failure due to the shock). Poor thing, but we certainly didn't want vermin in the house, especially when it's empty. Fortunately, we discovered the entry point in the wall by the kitchen sink pipe, which we immediately blocked up.

After the girls returned to the UK, we went to have lunch at our friends Bruce and Diana, who live about an hour away towards Brive. The weather was glorious, but then it suddenly turned in the evening, and we drove back through a massive thunderstorm, which lasted several hours, and lightning flashed repeatedly. I managed to take some amazing photographs.

WE GOT BACK to the UK in mid-August, and a few days later my mother was suddenly and shockingly diagnosed with cancer. She was very swiftly operated on, and thankfully she recovered strongly.

In late September, Patricia and I managed to grab a weekend in St Ives, Cornwall. We also discovered it was time to replace my car after some major repair work was deemed necessary.

At the end of October, we drove to Pellac in our new four-day-old car, and had a fairly quiet week, although I was very busy work wise and seemed to spend too much time on the laptop and phone. I was actually glad to get home so I could focus fully on my work, rather than feel pulled in two directions as I sometimes do when I'm in France. I have to say Patricia has always been brilliant. She's never once complained about the amount of time I need to spend working or take and make calls. The payoff is that I can get away to France often, even though I might spend rather too much time occupied in my business.

VASECTOMIES AND ICE-BUCKET CHALLENGES

2014

We find that winters in our village are less fun. While it's always good to spend time at our French house, winter days tend to be grey, cold, and very quiet, with few people out and about. We generally find it's more interesting and productive to remain in the UK between November and February. As a consequence, the next time we were in France was during March 2014 – when it was my birthday. The first night we were there we were kindly invited to dinner by our friends Jacques and Marguerite. They both had birthdays in February/March, as did Patricia, so it was a good occasion to celebrate together. Two other French couples were also present, both of whom we'd met before, so conversation flowed. We ate well and enjoyed some fine wines.

As we went to go, Jacques looked at both Patricia and I, and commented we both looked young for our age, and gave us a naughty wink as he said you can have a good lie-in on your birthday. The conversation then moved on, and Jacques looked hard at me, and asked if he was correct in thinking I'd had a vasectomy?

'Yes,' I replied. 'About thirteen years ago.'

The two other Frenchmen looked stupefied.

'Thirteen years ago,' remarked one of them. 'So that's it? No more sex.'

I laughed and suggested they ask Patricia.

'Vraiement?' said the other man. They seemed to think that once a man had a vasectomy, that was it. He'd have lost his manhood and his ability to 'rise to the occasion'. Patricia and I laughed and laughed.

After further discussion, it turned out that according to our friends, vasectomy was a rare thing in France. They expressed their concern regarding surgery in a delicate area. I grabbed a pen and paper and drew a very rough diagram to explain where and what the surgery entailed, and that it took less than thirty minutes.

'And after... you couldn't walk for several days?' splutter one of the men.

Patricia burst out laughing again. 'He walked out of the room and got into the car. I drove him home, and all he did was take it easy for the next twenty-four hours.'

'And you can... you know... still ...?' said Jacques.

'Bien sûr.' Patricia grinned. 'Demain matin.' *Of course – tomorrow morning!* And she winked naughtily at Jacques.

The women had remained silent during all of this. The penny dropped.

'If only I'd known...' said one of them.

'Yes,' said another, and looked at her husband.

'You should make an appointment with the doctor this week.'

'Mais non,' replied her husband. 'I'm too old.'

'I'll remind you of that,' said his wife with a sly look!

WHILE WE WERE out there, I telephoned our joiner Marc. Over the years, he'd done some sterling work for us; as well as the staircase, he'd replaced our gates, all the windows, built our balcony, and designed and installed a new front door. Our next project for him was a pergola.

On the last leg of the journey, during the final twenty km on our way to our house, we went past a company who specialised in building metal pergolas. A metal frame appealed to us in terms of durability and maintenance. We called in one afternoon to take a look. We got talking to one of the guys, who seemed to understand our requirements. We gave him an idea of size, and after disappearing to provide an estimate, he came back. The price was four thousand Euros. We looked at him in amazement.

'Four thousand Euros – are you sure?' I asked.

'Oui, Monsieur. But I can give you a special spring discount.'

He re-quoted us three thousand four hundred Euros. We looked at him in disbelief, thanked him, and walked outside and into the car. We were staggered. That would pay for a week's holiday in the Maldives!

The following day, I called Marc, and after exchanging the usual pleasantries, I asked him if he built pergolas. He said absolutely – that was his specialism. He came out the next day, measured up, and quoted us one thousand three hundred Euros. He also said he'd have it built by the end of the month. We gave him the order, and three weeks later, I received a text message with photos of our splendid new pergola.

We were keen to see the new pergola and went out for a short visit during the first week of June. We were delighted with Marc's work, and we spent several sunny days sitting outside under the pergola. We decided to plant some foliage which would eventually grow and provide a natural roof, which would act as some protection from the sun. But this would take a few years to develop. As an interim measure, we bought a cane trellis which we laid across the roof beams, which let the sun rays through, but also enabled us to sit outside without getting sunburnt.

The last night we were there, we woke in the early hours to hear Freddie being sick. This was quite unusual, although not unknown. I got up to let him outside while I cleaned up the floor. When we got up again at seven, I fed Fred, but he wasn't at all keen to eat. We needed to leave by nine-thirty to travel back to Calais. Freddie managed to jump up into the boot, where fortunately I had a couple of rear-window screens to shield him from the heat of the sun. The journey back was quiet; we stopped several times to give ourselves and Freddie a break. He refused any food and drank sparingly.

We arrived at Calais around 6.30 p.m., and I stopped at the pet terminal to go through the usual process of checking Freddie in and getting his passport details approved. He seemed a little brighter as he accompanied me into the office, but as we waited at the counter, he suddenly lost complete control of his bowels. It was as if the floodgates had opened, and diarrhoea just poured from the poor dog.

He pulled to get outside. At the same time, other people were coming in with their dogs. The floor was an absolute mess. I looked across the counter to the woman serving me.

'Mon Dieu, Mon Dieu,' she shrieked.

I patted my pocket for my mobile, so I could call Patricia to come and take Freddie back to the car, but unfortunately, I hadn't got the phone with me. I leant over the counter towards the semi-hysterical woman, and calmly asked if she had any tissues.

The woman was freaking out so much – you'd think a bomb had gone off – she couldn't speak properly. Eventually, she understood and virtually threw a large roll of toilet paper at me.

At this point, the other dog owners were staring, trying to restrain their dogs, some of whom had become overexcited at the smell. I managed to tie Fred's lead to a hook at the front of the counter, and I began to wipe the floor. Within seconds, I had piles of soggy toilet tissue that, in the absence of any bag, I had to place to one side. Eventually, I was able to clean up most of the mess.

During this time, one of the woman's colleagues came out and surveyed the situation.

'Ça pue, ça vraiment pue,' *that really, really stinks*, she said.

I asked her if there was a cleaner on-site who could help me.

'Yes,' she replied. 'But they won't touch that yet. You'll have to do a better job in cleaning up.'

Then, to make matters worse, another colleague walked around us, giving us a very wide berth. She averted her eyes and shouted to her other colleagues that she was just about to go off on her break and have something to eat, but the sight and smell made her want to vomit.

Finally, after about five minutes, a cleaner appeared. I apologised profusely, but he ignored me and proceeded to clean the floor. He found a plastic carrier bag, and handed it to me, so that I could pick up and collect all the heavily soiled toilet tissues.

Poor Freddie just stood, with his lead tied to the counter hook, and stared at me dolefully. He whined and looked utterly sad and unwell. I was frankly disgusted at the lack of support and sympathy. Fred can't have been the first dog to have been ill in the pet check-in office, yet the staff there treated both of us with derision. When I got back to the car, Patricia was shocked at what had happened to Freddie, and even more so at the attitude of the staff in the office.

I then went to clean myself up, and we gradually embarked on the final leg of our journey home.

Poor Freddie was sick for the next week. I took him to our local vets on three occasions. It seemed he had ingested something very toxic. We eventually suspected he'd found some meat one of our neighbours had thrown out for the cats, and in the heat, the bacteria on the meat had multiplied.

As the week wore on, we became increasingly concerned about his health. He was barely eating, and finally, we were asked to take him to a larger vets practice in Ashford and leave him there for twenty-four hours for his condition to be closely monitored. We then got a call to say he'd responded to treatment, and we could collect him. Whatever had caused the problem, the upshot was that his white blood cell count had massively diminished, which was of major concern to the vets.

But Freddie, bless him, is made of strong stuff. And as has generally been the case, that when he is – fortunately rarely – ill – he manages to shake it off. Being a mixed-breed dog has its advantages, as pedigree dogs do often seem more sensitive to illness. Within a few days, Fred was back to his normal self, eating hungrily, and enjoying his daily walks.

With some trepidation after Fred's illness, we returned to France at the end of the July. We watched him closely, and also explained to the neighbours what had happened, lest they should continue to throw meat out for the cats, although I don't think they took much notice (the neighbours that is – not the cats). We were going to spend an entire month at the house, which was the longest spell we'd ever been there. The first priority was to see if we could watch the Tour de France live, as it was passing Bergerac and Périgueux on the Saturday morning. In fact, it was a time trial between the two towns.

We decided to get there early and arrived near our chosen spot around 7.45 a.m. I'd highlighted an area near some woods about ten km into the time trial. We tentatively drove down some quiet country roads, trying to find our spot as we followed both a map and the satnav. I noticed a car some distance behind me, which seemed to be driving quite fast. He almost started to tailgate me. I slowed down and pulled to the left. The driver pulled alongside, wound down his window, and simply said, 'Tour de France?'

'Oui,' I replied.

'Follow me,' he instructed. 'And don't stop at the parking.'

He drove off swiftly. I managed to keep up. We approached an area where cars were parked, and a barrier. The guy in front drove around the barrier, and about one kilometre further down the road, he stopped and parked behind a line of cars. I pulled in behind him and got out.

'Voilà,' he said, smiled and walked off ahead. We were less than two hundred metres from the road for the time trial. We managed to find a space at the road edge and waited.

After about an hour, I began to wish we'd brought a flask of coffee. But in due course, the 'caravan' began to arrive. This is a long procession of team cars and race sponsors. They're there to drum up anticipation and excitement. They also throw out various freebies and goodies really intended for children. But when a baseball cap landed by my feet, it would have been rude not to have picked it up. Especially as the kids around us had all collected armfuls of the stuff.

It reminded me of the time the Tour came to the UK in 1994. Lucy, Vicky and Jo went to watch with their respective classes, and when I got home from work that night, Lucy proudly presented me with her Coca-Cola baseball cap, which she called her 'buvez' hat as it said 'buvez Coca-Cola'.

After another hour, the first cyclists started to filter through. They were at the tail-end of the Tour, so didn't create much excitement. But gradually, more of the well-known cyclists came through. Although the road was marshalled by Tour de France security and the odd Gendarme, this didn't stop many members of the crowd jumping into the road ahead of the cyclists, and then running alongside them, shouting and gesticulating.

We'd seen the Tour in the UK quite recently, when it passed through our hometown of Tenterden in July 2007 but seeing it in France was something else. The atmosphere was electric, and overall, it was much more fun. I vowed to do this again, maybe one of the cross-country stages.

THE FOLLOWING WEEK, all four of our daughters and their fellas came out for a long weekend – Lucy and Phil, Gemma and Justin, and Jo and James. At that time, Vicky was 'between' boyfriends. We ate superbly, the weather wasn't bad, and we had a lot of fun together. The girls all get on really well with each other, and when they're together, their men can barely get a word in edgeways. During their last evening with us, we set up the music in the front garden and had an impromptu disco and dance. A memorable feature of this was when Gemma presented me with a 'dish-dash' she'd bought for me in Kuwait, (a 'dish-dash' is like a long shirt, but which extends down to the feet, and is traditionally worn by men in the Middle East) which of course I immediately put on, much to the amusement of everyone.

It felt a bit flat after the girls went back to the UK. But we'd arranged to visit some very old friends of mine, Doug and Philippa, who I got to know when I lived near to Huntingdon. Doug is Lucy's godfather. We hadn't been in touch for several years, but he and Philippa were invited to Lucy's wedding in 2012, and since then, Doug and I had renewed our friendship and met a few times in London.

He and Philippa have a house not far from Riberac, and they invited us across to spend the night with them. They have a magnificent swimming pool, and their two teenage children were there with some of their friends. We had a great time and ended up staying an extra night.

My brother Hugh and his family were also in France in August with some friends. They'd all been staying in a gîte in the Dordogne, and we'd invited them to come over for the Mechoui on the fifteenth. Although there were eight of them in total (four adults and four teenage children), we said that we could put them all up for the night.

We'd already talked about the Mechoui with Hugh and Mindy, so they had some idea of what to expect. After a few drinks at the bar, we sat down to eat. The starters were served, and bottles of wine were opened. As usual, we all sat along trestle tables in a massive marquee. I was sitting opposite my niece Rhiain when all of a sudden, we heard a loud guttural noise, to which Rhiain responded with utter and sheer disgust.

She pointed behind me. I turned around to see one of the younger guys in the village, in his early twenties, who had clearly got carried away with the atmosphere, and who'd already had a skinful to drink. Upon finishing his hors d'oeuvres, he promptly threw up the lot, vomiting all over the table. The 'serveuses' who were mostly ladies of pensionable age simply grabbed the paper tablecloth, rolled it up, and disposed of it in a bin. The poor guy's mates dragged him outside. At least that's one advantage of paper tablecloths!

We had the usual 'fill your face' quantity of food and drink. We went back to our house later afternoon, and keen to keep the party going, Hugh, his friend Charles and I carried on drinking beer outside, and while I was deemed to be absolutely useless as a drinks waiter, Patricia amazingly prepared a supper for us all – paella I seem to remember.

The following day, both Hugh and Charles looked worse for wear. Their wives took control, got behind their respective wheels, and drove their families home. Charles's wife reversed straight out; Mindy – you won't thank me for this, but I have strong memories of you taking several attempts to reverse out of the drive. But Hugh would have taken far longer!

The summer of 2014 was the summer of the 'Ice-Bucket Challenge'. Patricia had enjoyed watching various videos of both celebrities and friends doing their own challenge. Patricia then suggested we did our own. We'd take it in turn, with the other one filming. My challenge was first. We agreed it would be best to stand on the balcony, so we could set the video rolling in the bedroom, while one person poured the ice-cold water on the other.

I stood there, waiting for the inevitable. It was unbelievably cold. I shrieked with the shock – so much so that our neighbour

Maurice came running to the property; he thought I'd fallen off the balcony. His relief was palpable when he saw me still standing there. We went downstairs and explained to him what we were doing. He was utterly bemused. He clearly thought we were completely mad. This was a man who didn't even know what social media was about, so he had no idea what crazy people around the world were doing. We warned him I was going to 'do' Patricia. He watched outside from below the balcony, and he certainly saw the funny side of it.

We didn't return to until after Christmas. During the autumn we went to Germany, to the Black Forest, and took Mum with us, where we spent a lovely week.

We had planned New Year in Pellac with two sets of friends – Paul and Stephanie, and Irving and Serena. Patricia and I arrived on December 28, and a couple of days later, as we were preparing for the others, I took a call from Irving to say that Serena wasn't at all well, and sadly, they would have to pull out. Paul and Stephanie flew out on the thirtieth as planned, and we had our usual riotous New Year celebrations together, which necessitated me taking an embarrassing quantity of empty bottles to the bottle bank in the village a few days later.

YOGA, CYCLING, AND ENGLISH FIZZ

2015

In the early part of 2015, I had a couple of trips abroad. The first was a long weekend at Rio de Janeiro in March, thanks to Gem working for British Airways. As I boarded the plane, I was lucky enough to be offered to fly business class, which I also enjoyed on the way back. In early April, we had a long weekend in Madrid with our friends Bruce and Diana.

We were really looking forward to being back in France and drove out to our house in late April. Irving and Serena also drove out for a few days, accompanied by their dog, Russell. It was around this time that we started to think of selling our house.

To put this into perspective, Patricia and I had watched a programme in March which featured British people buying properties in Europe. It was all pretty standard stuff and what you'd expect from programmes like this. What struck us was the episode in Germany. We were staggered at how reasonably priced the property was there. At the end of the programme, Patricia looked at me, and simply asked if I was thinking what she was thinking. As is so often the case, our minds were focused on identical thoughts. We embarked on a long discussion, the nub of which was that after ten fun years in France, why not sell the French property and buy one in Germany?

We became very enthusiastic, to the extent that before the arrival of Irving and Serena, we visited a local estate agent and asked them to place the house on the market. This also triggered something else in me. I felt we were missing out; in that every summer we went back to our place. I was finding it hard to separate my work from my holiday time. It was becoming a cause of deep frustration. I started to drive the sale hard, although Patricia wasn't quite so enthusiastic about selling.

Patricia and I went back for ten days in June. I was busy, the weather was glorious, and I was getting moody and grumpy, which is quite unlike me. On the Friday afternoon, at the end of our first week, Patricia came upstairs, where I was working on the laptop.

'Don't you fancy joining me outside for a glass of wine?' she asked.

'Not yet,' I replied. Patricia stood there staring at me.

'What the fuck is wrong with you?' she demanded.

'What do you mean?' I said surprised.

'It's you,' said Patricia. 'You're so bloody miserable. Come and join me outside and tell me what's going on in your head.'

I tidied up and went downstairs to join Patricia outside. The sun was shining as we sat under the pergola. She poured me a glass of wine. 'What's up?' she asked.

I sighed deeply. I didn't really know, but I just started talking from the heart. I explained that it kept going through my head that

I'd be sixty the following year. This had started several thoughts running. How much longer did I want to carry on working? Did I really want to be running my recruitment business for the next five plus years? Although the business was successful, and I enjoyed it and made a decent living, I wanted something else. I elaborated that unlike Patricia I'm not someone who has hobbies, and that apart from playing my guitar and watching Chelsea play football, I hadn't anything that would meaningfully fill my time. I wasn't quite ready to retire – I wanted to keep earning for the next few years before drawing on my pension. I was at a real crossroads. Coupled with my desire to sell the house, I really wasn't enjoying my week there.

Patricia sat back and thought. She started a dialogue, which went like this:

'Have you ever thought of doing anything with your yoga?'

'No. Why?'

'Maybe that's something you could explore further?'

'Such as?'

'I don't know. Teach yoga, perhaps?'

'Me? Become a yoga teacher? How do I do that?'

'I don't know. Find somewhere to train I suppose.'

'Where?'

'Google it.'

'Then what?'

'Set up a yoga business.'

'How?'

'You tell me! You're good at business.'

'Where from?'

'Home?'

'Home?'

'Build a studio.'

'How?'

'Use some of our savings?'

I sat back and reflected. There was a lot of sense in what Patricia was suggesting. I'd started practicing yoga a couple of years ago. The year before, we'd joined an expensive gym at a local hotel. We'd each taken out a twelve-month membership. After that, we compared notes. Neither of us really felt any benefit, and the cost of membership was considerable. I wanted to do something to keep in shape, so I joined a yoga class at our local leisure centre. Although that particular class didn't work for me, it provoked something in me. I began to practise online, then joined another local class. I also started doing hot yoga in London. I really enjoyed yoga and was feeling the benefits.

Although we have a conservatory at our home in Tenterden, which we'd built shortly after buying the house, Patricia had regularly commented she'd love another on the side of the house.

I often use the example of a coin being dropped into a slot machine and trickling down through various bends. That was my mind during our conversation. The coin (penny!) was slowly dropping. I stood up.

'I need to think. I'm going for a bike ride. I want to let this percolate through my mind.'

Patricia nodded wisely. 'How long do you think you'll be?' she asked.

'Just a couple of hours.'

'I'll have dinner waiting for you for when you get back.' Patricia really is an absolute darling.

I got on my bike and headed off on a familiar ride. I began to think and pedal hard. It was a challenging route. When I got back, I was tired in both mind and body, but I felt a whole lot better.

Over the next few days, I began googling yoga teacher training courses. Once I've got a plan, I want to crack on with it. After reviewing several courses, I applied for a twelve-month teacher training course at YogaLondon, which would start in September and finish in July 2016.

I then sat back and enjoyed the rest of our holiday. Thanks to Patricia, I had a plan for the foreseeable future and beyond.

By the time we got back to England, I'd arranged for quotes to build a yoga studio. I was offered a place on the teacher training course. It was all systems go.

I was still keen to sell the house, though. We'd planned our summer holiday out there, and frankly I really wanted to be elsewhere. Nowhere in particular, just anywhere apart from there. I hadn't fallen out of love with France. But I wanted something else. It wasn't helped by looking at pictures from one of my friends on Facebook from his holiday in Croatia.

I brought my bike with me on the roof of the car. I'd started cycling the previous autumn and had invested in a decent road bike.

I came to love cycling in France; the roads around us are generally quiet, and the French are much more tolerant to cyclists than they are in the UK. In fact, they seem to really have a respect for cyclists.

I got chatting to the son of our former next-door neighbour Solange, whose name is Clément. He's a very keen cyclist. He lives near Limoges and belongs to a cycling club. They go out a couple of times a week throughout all seasons. Clément came over to his mother's house once or twice a week, to tend to the garden and keep an eye on the place.

Interestingly, unlike the British, French people don't appear to be in any rush to sell former family homes once their parents have passed away. The houses mostly remain empty other than for occasional holiday breaks for various family members. This is perhaps the reason there are so many empty houses in France, especially in rural areas. Our village is a prime example; more and more houses have become empty since we've had our house there. I wouldn't be at all surprised if in twenty years' time the entire village becomes uninhabited, which would be sad. I don't think French inheritance law helps; once the remaining parent is deceased, the family home, as in the UK, is shared among the surviving siblings. In the UK, the house is inevitably sold, and the proceeds divided up within the family.

But in rural France, an inherited property often seems to be the cause of dispute, with some family members keen to sell, and others not willing to do so, for deeply personal and sentimental reasons. As a result, the houses remain empty and unsold for years, until perhaps someone from the next generation decides to do something about it. Another consequence is that part of the property is sold, with adjoining land remaining unsold. This is perhaps why houses are put up for sale, but with a garden across the road or elsewhere. It can be very confusing! Equally, I've spoken to French people who are mystified as to why the Brits are so keen to sell the family home and dispose of its assets following the death of the last survivor living there. This in turn explains why furniture shops are much less evident in France than in the UK. Furniture is often passed down the generations, which is why so many houses have such old furniture. In contrast, it seems that many younger people will buy their furniture from IKEA, or similar shops such as Altea.

Clément is several years older than me, but he's thin and wiry, and a very experienced cyclist. When I told him I'd brought my bike with me, he immediately suggested we went on a ride together. We agreed a date, and duly set off. Within minutes, he was leaving me far behind. I thought I was reasonably fit, but this was nothing in comparison to Clément. We completed a 50 km ride, and at the finish, I could barely walk!

Vicky came out for a few days with a girlfriend of hers – Evie. The two girls livened things up; Vicky is outgoing and sporty, and before long we had walks and bike rides planned.

When we arrived at the start of our holiday, we were shocked to see our neighbour, Maurice. He'd had treatment for prostate cancer the year before, which seemed to be working. But when we saw him in July, he looked tired, and completely lacking in energy, which was very unlike him.

One evening, a bat flew through our open lounge window. The girls shrieked – it really freaked them out. Fortunately, we managed to coax the bat out after a few minutes. That was also the summer we were plagued by wasps. Every time we sat outside; the wasps were there. It was much worse when we were eating.

Eventually, I'd had enough. I visited the Mairie and was given the number of a local wasp/bee catcher. The following evening, a chap in his seventies turned up. I showed him where the wasps were coming from him. He took a close look and agreed there was a nest of wasps just off the balcony. He got changed into his protective gear, took a ladder and his tools to the site, and started to pour smoke/poison into the nest. He advised us to remain inside and close all the windows.

Although he said he'd been a wasp/bee catcher all his life, he was quite apprehensive. He went back after half an hour, and then said he'd need to repeat the exercise as there were still lots of wasps. After another thirty minutes or so, he went to his car, got changed, and came into the house. 'That will be ninety Euros please, Monsieur.'

'Well done,' I said as I counted out the money. 'So all the wasps are gone?'

'Ah, Monsieur. Yes. I think there were about 80,000 in the nest. But they weren't wasps, Monsieur. They were bees.'

I was gobsmacked. 'You said they were wasps,' I said accusingly.

'Yes, I thought so. But when I went back just now, I discovered they were bees. Anyway – pouf – they are gone now. Ça y'est. There it is.'

We were genuinely shocked. Although we're not knowledgeable, the bee catcher should have been. When we discovered that he'd exterminated around 80,000 bees, we were quite horrified. Normally, catchers should know the difference, and arrange for the bees' nest to be collected by a beekeeper. But it was too late.

THE GIRLS FLEW back to England the following day. When we got back from the airport, Freddie trotted off to see Maurice, but his door was shut, which was unusual. The following morning, Perry came round.

'I have some sad news,' he said gravely. 'Maurice is dead.'

We were horrified. How did this happen? Perry explained that Maurice had been taken to hospital the day before, which was why his front door was shut. It was difficult to understand, but it appeared that Maurice might have contracted a lung infection. His immune system had been seriously compromised by the treatment he'd been having for cancer. Whatever it was, he hadn't been able to fight it off. At the age of just sixty-seven, our quiet, friendly neighbour had passed away. We couldn't believe it. Maurice was always active. He had looked in great shape ever since we had known him.

The funeral was arranged for two days later. We agreed we would go. On the Friday, the day of the funeral, the weather changed. The wind got up; it poured heavily with rain, and the temperature dropped to below fifteen degrees. A crowd of people stood outside the church, many of whom we recognised from the village. We filtered into the church and stood at the back. A group of men remained outside. We later learnt that they were Communists; they wouldn't come into the church, but they turned up outside to offer their respects.

As we went into the church, we noticed a large photograph of Maurice on the altar. He was sitting with our dog, Freddie. It was a photograph Patricia had taken a couple of years earlier, which she'd given to Maurice as he was very fond of our dog. To see that picture was a shock which hit us both quite hard.

Although we didn't really know Maurice terribly well, it was one of the saddest funerals I'd ever attended. Towards the end, everyone queued up to shake hands with his family – two brothers and a sister. I'd met one of the brothers before a few times. As I went to shake his hand, he pulled me towards him and embraced me. 'Merci' he said. I was very deeply moved. When the funeral finished, I took Patricia's hand, and we walked home. We got inside and I poured a couple of large whiskies. We drank to Maurice.

Before we returned to the UK, we caught up with Pierre and his family who were down from Paris for a week and invited them over for a drink. I'd remembered the previous occasion the year before. In anticipation, I'd brought out a bottle of Chapel Down fizz from our local vineyard in Tenterden. It's extremely good so I thought I'd put it to the test.

I asked Pierre's wife, who was as haughty and cold as she was before. I told her I remembered she only drank champagne and made a point of opening the bottle in front of her, hiding the label towards me. I poured her a glass of Chapel Down.

'What do you think?' I asked.

'Oui,' she said, shrugging. 'C'est frais.' *It's chilled.*

'Is it to your taste?' I asked.

'Ah oui,' she replied. A lady of few words.

'Très bien,' I said. 'Champagne from England.' And I showed her the bottle – Chapel Down fizz from our hometown Tenterden. Her face was a picture. She tried to look disgusted, haughty, and cool all at once. Gotcha! She must have enjoyed it though: she polished off the entire bottle!

A GRANDDAUGHTER, AND NEW YEAR FUN

2016

Twenty-sixteen was a busy year. My yoga teacher training course was a key priority. We managed to snatch a wonderful long weekend away in Mallorca with our friends Bruce and Diana. Then in June, Patricia and I had our first summer holiday away from Pellac for several years. We went to Croatia, inspired by my friend the year before. I'd contacted him about his holiday, and following his recommendation, we stayed in the same village at the same apartment. We had a wonderful twelve days there, and the only bad memory we have of that holiday is that towards the end, the result of the Brexit referendum came through. We were utterly staggered and depressed.

When we went out to France in late July, I was feeling pretty refreshed. I'd also just qualified as a registered yoga teacher. Patricia had become very uncomfortable about selling the house; it had become a big part of her life. And we both loved France. So, after much soul-searching and discussion, we took the house off the market. It was the right decision, and this would be borne out big-time a couple of years later.

All the girls came out again, and fresh from qualifying, I practiced my teaching experience with family yoga sessions each morning. The weather was fantastic. Lucy was heavily pregnant. We all ate and drank like lords (as usual!)

Patricia and I went to the Black Forest in early October. Then at the end of October, Lucy gave birth to our first grandchild – Sophie.

At the end of 2016, we finally managed to celebrate New Year in France with both sets of our friends Paul and Stephanie and Irving and Serena. We had some very late nights, which once again resulted in several visits to the local bottle bank. We also managed to squeeze in lunch at our favourite restaurant Le Roc du Boeuf, which everyone thought was quite magnificent.

A Very Expensive Tank of Fuel

2017

We adore spring, especially late spring in the Limousin. The countryside looks fresh and green. All the trees are in full bloom, and we couldn't wait to go out for Easter. The weather was warm, and we got out and about a bit, including visiting the chateau at Montbazillac, and also a wander around Bergerac. My yoga classes in the UK were going well. A few people said they'd also like to practice at home too, so I spent some of my time recording some of the key sequences and classes. I really enjoyed practicing yoga at Pellac. The atmosphere and the vibe felt so right up in the loft. It was a perfect place for it.

We went out for lunch to Le Roc du Boeuf on the Saturday. After a typically excellent lunch, we decided to stop off at the lake and walk Fred. Afterwards, we drove into St Mathieu, and I noticed two police cars in the village centre. There was very little traffic, and as I drove towards where they were parked, a Gendarme put up his hand and stopped us. He walked round to my window and simply said he wanted to breathalyse me. No reason, no questions. He just produced a kit and asked me to blow.

As a rule, I tend not to drink when I'm driving, although in rural France, I occasionally have a glass of wine with a large lunch. I felt fine, but as I blew into the breathalyser kit, I felt as if I was on trial, and almost guilty. I blew carefully and tentatively.

'Plus fort,' said the Gendarme. *Blow harder.*

I complied. He held the tester up. Everything was fine.

'Merci' he said. 'You can go.'

WE HAD A rather stressful situation on the return journey back to the UK. I'd ordered some wine from Majestic at Calais, and we needed to be there by seven pm latest to collect. Our aim was to arrive slightly earlier. We left Pellac around 10 a.m. and decided to take a different route back, that our friend Irving had recommended. This entailed driving up the A10 to Tours, and then heading up to Le Mans, and picking up the autoroute there heading north via Rouen. Irving was convinced this was quicker than our usual route of picking up the A20 at Limoges, and take the motorways going north, and travelling to Calais via Chartres and Rouen.

I instinctively drove off to go via Piégut, and it wasn't until I got there that I realised it was market day and traffic through the town was closed. We lost about twenty minutes finding alternative routes on small country roads. As we got close to the A10, I was keen to refuel cheaply at a supermarket. A large Intermarché came into view. I followed the signs to the filling station, which was unusually empty.

I got out of the car, pulled open the filler cap, and then inserted my credit card into the pump as it was self-service. When my card was approved, I received a message on the pump to say I could add fuel up to the value of seven hundred Euros. I was a bit surprised; normally the limit was one hundred Euros. I grabbed the filling lead, but when I tried to insert this into the opening of my fuel tank, it wouldn't fit. It took me a good minute to figure out why: I'd mistakenly gone to the filling station for lorries.

I jumped back in the car, and as I drove out, I noticed an alternative petrol station for cars. Once again, I got out of the car. When I put my card into the machine, it was refused. I was a bit shocked, but took out another card, filled up my vehicle, and drove off.

About a mile down the road, something was bugging my mind. I couldn't understand why my credit card had been refused. I decided to call John Lewis Partnership card services. When I got through, I explained the situation. After checking my details, I was informed the reason why the card had been turned down is that a payment for seven hundred Euros of fuel had just been taken. I couldn't believe it.

'What?' I almost shouted. I explained the circumstances. The person I spoke to couldn't understand why payment had been taken. She suggested that perhaps someone had driven behind me, and that although my car couldn't be filled from the pump, as the payment had been cleared, they'd filled up at my expense!

I was gobsmacked. It seemed as if I'd just lost around six hundred and fifty pounds. I was told the matter would be passed on to their security department, and that someone would be in touch.

After ending the call, I came to the conclusion that the best thing to do would be to go back to the store and talk to someone in management. It took over ten minutes to get back. I parked, and entered the store, and went to the customer services desk. I waited for a few minutes, and when someone appeared, I explained my predicament.

They couldn't quite get their head around this. Eventually, they spoke to someone senior, who advised that there was no way anyone could have driven in after me and profited from my mistake. They suggested I spoke to my credit card company. That was it. The outcome of this story was that when we got back, I contacted the credit card company. It transpired that when fuelling from unmanned pumps, a sum of money is provisionally reserved on the account, until the actual transaction goes through. I subsequently learned that transactions of this nature carried out abroad can take a few days to go through.

We drove off. By this time, we were about an hour behind schedule. As the journey continued, I realised we'd be pushed to get to Majestic before they closed. I called the store and explained I'd probably be half an hour late. Was there any chance someone could wait for me? The answer was a definitive 'No'. I had to be there by seven at the latest, or no wine.

We rolled into their car park at 6.55 p.m. Just in time to collect the wine. It had been a rather crazy dash. And, Irving, your recommended route wasn't quicker!

SUMMER IN PROVENCE, AND MONEY LAUNDERING

2017

As in 2016, we planned an alternative summer holiday. Our friends Bruce and Diana had a flat in Provence, about twenty minutes from Avignon. They'd often offered to let us use it, and that summer we took them up on their offer. We'd never been to Provence – it was a long-held desire of mine to go there.

We decided to catch the train. We could actually catch a direct train with Eurostar from Ashford International (just fifteen miles away from Tenterden) to Avignon. We had a fabulous journey down; after arriving at Ashford and grabbing a quick coffee and croissant, we got on the train. Once we entered France, the train increased its speed, and we literally shot through the French countryside.

The scenery was gorgeous – and the early June sunshine enhanced the setting. We sat back; I listened to music and read. Patricia looked out of the window as she crocheted. We duly arrived at Avignon on time at two pm – a journey of just over six hours. We collected our hire car and drove to the apartment where Bruce and Diana were waiting. They showed us around, then we walked into the village for a drink. Afterwards, we drove to the nearest town –

Saint Rémy de Provence. This was a beautiful place; Vincent van Gogh spent his later life here painting. He was attracted by the light, which was quite stunning.

We found a restaurant, and enjoyed a meal together, before Bruce and Diana embarked on their eventual journey back to the UK. Bruce's business is supplying and delivering British furniture largely to the ex-pat community and second-home owners in France. We came across him when we first bought the property. We discovered how difficult it was to find and buy reasonable furniture in France. It seemed that furniture was either passed down from one generation to the next, or people, especially younger folk, would get their furniture from IKEA. We wanted neither. After some searching online, Patricia came across Bruce's company. The rest is history. He and Diana have become good, close friends.

Their apartment was great; compact, but with everything in place. The garden was lovely and housed a decent sized swimming pool. The weather was hot. We spent the first day touring around some of the villages mentioned by Peter Mayle in his books about Provence. Although we were too early for the lavender, the tranquil scenery was gorgeous.

On the Saturday, we drove to Arles for the weekly market. This was amazing; the market was huge, a vast array of stalls selling mostly food, but also clothing, textiles, and crockery and glassware.

The atmosphere was electric – a real genuine bustle. It was busy, with a cacophony of different smells of meat, cheese, fish, fruit, vegetables, and salads. We spent a good two to three hours there until we finally succumbed to our hunger and found a restaurant on the edge of the market.

We went to Avignon a couple of days later, and while we were there, we learnt that our friend Perry, who lived fifty metres from our house in Pellac had become ill and had been admitted to hospital. Sadly, he didn't recover. This was really quite upsetting. He'd become an integral part of our lives in France. We would greatly miss him.

We spent the rest of our time touring around Provence. We thought that Avignon is a beautiful town. Nîmes was a disappointment – less vibrant and somewhat scruffy. We travelled west to Uzès and caught the end of the market before securing a table in a resto just off the marketplace. We also went south to the coast. I was keen to visit Cassis, which I'd read much about.

This was when I learnt a valuable lesson. If you're going on holiday and intend to drive various distances, then don't go for a small, cheap car. I'd hired a Fiat 500, which had a primitive air conditioning system, and also very poor acceleration. It would have been fine as a city car, or for exploring locally. But once we joined the motorway heading south, I quickly realised the limitations of the car. The power from the engine was quite puny. It seemed to take ages to get up to speed. We felt very intimated by large lorries bearing down on us. Overall, it felt uncomfortable and not at all enjoyable. We were glad to get to Cassis and leave the car for several hours.

The weather was superb – at least thirty degrees. The other key learning point of this holiday was to invest in a couple of insulated flasks, which would keep our drinks cold. Given our recent travels further abroad in the past few years, they've become an absolute godsend.

Cassis is very pretty. There were lots of touristy restaurants on the main front. When we explored the backstreets, we came across several interesting shops, including some perfumeries selling the delightful Eau de Cassis.

We went back to Saint Rémy a couple of times. There was a good choice of shops and restaurants, and the vibe was gently sophisticated. We also checked out the wondrous Pont-du-Gard, where a photograph of my yoga pose in front of this amazing creation was published in a yoga magazine a few months later.

On our penultimate day, we decided to visit Orange. Other than the magnificent Roman theatre, we found the rest of the town somewhat underwhelming. We decided to take the scenic route back and agreed to stop off at Châteauneuf-du-Pape. We turned off at a sign indicating the village and came to a car park. There was a low barrier, and it wasn't obvious the car park was open or in use. We decided to 'act French' and drove under the barrier and parked the car.

We followed a pathway towards the old village wall and descended into the village. We walked past a building indicating it was a wine cellar. It was open for tours, although visitors could walk-through the cellars providing they didn't get in the way of the tours.

As we walked around, we came across a small tour party. We stopped to listen to the guide, who was talking in English. The tour was a small coach party of various nationalities – European, US, Australia. The coach driver saw us stop and eyed us suspiciously.

We stood there for several minutes, and suddenly the guide picked up some bottles, which he proceeded to open. Glasses were passed around the visitors, and suddenly a lady in front of us turned around and passed each of us a glass. It would have been rude to refuse! We just hoped the coach driver wouldn't grass us up, but fortunately he started to slip away.

We stayed there for the rest of the talk and tasted some very excellent wines. At the end, the guide explained all the wine we tasted was for sale. He joked that unlike the British, good wine shouldn't be drunk with pizza, and that Americans equally shouldn't waste good wine to accompany hamburgers. Instead, he recommended that all one would need to really enjoy a top wine was good quality bread and some decent cheese.

We decided to take him at his word. We bought two bottles of Châteauneuf-du-Pape (one for us and one for our daughter Vicky – this was her favourite wine, and it would be a lovely way for her to celebrate her thirtieth birthday that year). At thirty Euros a bottle, it wasn't cheap, but we felt we had redeemed ourselves for busting into the tour. We stopped off on the way back to buy some good local bread, and armed with a couple of fine cheeses, we spent a very pleasant final evening over this superb combination of simple food and excellent wine.

After joining up with Bruce and Diana again at Glastonbury (one of the top ten experiences in my life so far – a real shame Patricia wasn't with me, but she'd already committed to catering for a large party), we drove out to Pellac in August. The following day, we went over to Bruce and Diana's for a long lunch followed by an overnight stay. Before heading back, we went to the Dordogne market town of Montignac.

Now is the time to declare that Patricia and I are ardent Europeans and Remainers – as are Bruce and Diana. We voted Remain in the 2016 referendum and were absolutely gutted when the result was to leave the EU. I say gutted – I was both very angry and deeply upset for several months afterwards. I'm feeling these emotions again as I write.

I've been passionate about being part of Europe since I was sixteen – that's forty-four years ago to the year we had the 2016 EU Referendum. As a boy, I'd been fortunate to have had holidays in France, Germany, and Spain. I learnt a lot about other cultures, and more importantly to understand and respect how people in these countries lived their lives.

When I was at school in the early 1970s, studying French and German at A level, the dream and possibility of being able to travel, and even work and live in Europe, was a very attractive proposition. I was especially smitten by Germany; I'd seen the way the country had risen up and developed after the Second World War, and the capacity and willingness of the Germans to work hard (and play hard) to make the most of their lives had a major impact on me. I

331

strongly admired the German desire and ability to manufacture high-quality consumer goods. I also liked German girls, who combined beauty with brains (at least the ones I'd met), and often thought I'd like to marry a German girl. By pure chance, with Patricia being half-German, I've pretty much managed to achieve that!

THE FOLLOWING PARAGRAPHS were written in *The Guardian* by Ed Vulliamy in 2020. It encapsulates perfectly my thoughts: -

I didn't want to be a tourist; I wanted to be a European. A true 'cosmopolitan', as envisaged by Diogenes, who coined the term. For me, to be European is existential. It's about who and what we are. It defines a way of being, sans frontières, a state of curiosity about the way other people live and a burning need to partake in it, speak their tongues and understand not just their cultures but their quotidian modus vivendi: beliefs, music, football, food, firewater, and wine.

Millions of people whizz, work, and abide across a continent not without its problems, but without internal seams. And remember they're the grand- and great-grandchildren of those who endured slaughter in the First World War. Children and grandchildren of a Europe ravaged by Holocaust and the Second World War. Children of the cold war and Berlin Wall. Have the Italians, Dutch, French, Romanians, Latvians, and Portuguese lost their identity to this process? No, they're just part of it. Nor did the British, and we were part of that too, but now we're not. I was all my adult life, and now I'm not. In 2008, I submitted an article to the Observer on the slipstream of England's failure to qualify for the 2008 Euros (played in Austria and Switzerland), arguing that this was a metaphor for what Europe would look like without Britain – calmer actually, without England's awful fans.

Fair Europa, fare thee well – and thou shalt, without us. I'll still savour your ways, your beauty, and your tribulations – but as a visitor, not a citizen.

I loved working in Europe, which I did originally in 1975, and then extensively from 1994 to 1997. I love European lifestyle and culture. While I would say I was born in the UK, I took genuine pride in being a European citizen. The EU isn't perfect – but what is? Being in a union with other nearby countries, with their own languages, cultures, and identities is, to me, something that's to be optimised and appreciated.

I always felt that if we wanted to effect change, we needed to be in the EU, not outside. I very much hoped that future UK governments would negotiate successfully, not so much as to improve the UK's position, but more importantly to improve the overall structure and purpose of the EU, so that it had a more meaningful and productive effect on the lives of all EU citizens. In summary, we were part of something so much greater than what the UK can ever offer on its own. We should be looking forward, not trying to turn the clock backwards.

After we parked our car in Montignac, we walked down to the riverside, and as we gazed across the river, we encountered a Dutch family. We got chatting, and their question to us, which was becoming understandably but horribly familiar, was, 'What have you British done?' We explained we weren't part of this decision.

The Dutch showed their regret too, and as we parted, the husband called out, 'Well, whatever happens, we'll still love you.' My eyes smarted with tears. I literally couldn't speak as the emotions rose to the surface. It still gets me.

As our holiday continued into August, Lucy and Phil and little Sophie flew out, along with Vicky and her new boyfriend Tom (who she married in 2020). Gemma and Justin came out the following day. We went on walks and bike rides and some kayaking and sat outside in the sun. We all missed Perry. There was some added poignancy as earlier in the year, he'd told Patricia and me that he wanted to host dinner for all of us one evening. He would provide the food, which he wanted Patricia to cook. The girls were all fond of Perry.

WHILE THE FAMILY were with us, we discovered a leak coming through our dining room ceiling. To be honest, I'd been aware of some water stains on the ceiling for some time. Patricia blamed me for splashing too much in the bath. But this looked more serious.

After some close inspection by Justin and Tom, they informed me there was a leak emanating from the corner bath. There was a 'seat' in the centre of the bath edge, but this hadn't been propped up by anything below. As a consequence, every time someone sat on the edge, this pushed the bath down, breaking through the sealant, enabling water to pass through the gap. Fortunately, with these two practical guys in the house, they made good the situation and the necessary repairs.

The following week, we went supermarket shopping. It was a Friday afternoon, around 3 p.m., and as we approached the crossroads about two miles out of the village, I spied a stationary police car. I guessed what was coming. I was stopped. The police must have a penchant for stopping British cars. The Gendarme didn't even say, 'Bonjour'. He just passed me the breathalyser kit. I hadn't had a drop of alcohol for almost twenty-four hours. I grabbed the bag and blew really hard into it. So hard the police officer looked at me in amazement. He held the kit up to the light. One hundred per cent clear. He just grunted and walked away. Utterly charmless.

A quote sprang to mind, made by John Major in the late 1980s. He'd just been appointed Foreign Secretary, and John Prescott had made some very disparaging remarks about his ability to do the job. As he was interviewed on the *Today* programme, the presenter asked him what he thought of John Prescott's remarks. 'John Prescott is a man of great charm, well hidden,' replied Major. A wonderful quote which I've never forgotten.

After the family went back, we remarked on the fact that no one had made use of the Wi-Fi. Roaming in Europe was now free, and 3 g/4 g was sufficient for everyone's needs. On reflection, we decided that having the broadband was an expensive and unnecessary resource – the cost was around thirty-six Euros per month.

I decided to cancel the contract with Orange. I was told there would be a cancellation fee of fifty Euros, which I found pretty

335

staggering. I was also instructed to return the router to a local Orange shop, otherwise there would be an additional charge of fifty Euros. So one morning, we drove into Limoges, and eventually found the shopping centre where the shop was located. We walked into the shop. I provided my details and handed over the router. I was then asked where the leads and plugs were. To be honest, I hadn't thought them necessary. But the shop stood firm. They needed those back, too.

I asked to speak to the manager, who of course wasn't there! A more senior assistant joined the conversation. I offered to post the cables and plug, but that wasn't good enough. They had to accompany the router. I explained I lived an hour away, so to come back to the shop with the missing bits would at least a two-hour round trip.

The guy smiled, but he wouldn't budge. I deliberately became angry, as I could see charm wasn't working. I believe I even stamped my foot to forcibly make my point.

'OK,' I finally said in total exasperation. 'What would you do in my position?'

The guy looked at me, and then suggested that I could also return the router to my local Intermarché supermarket, which was only ten minutes away.

'Why didn't you tell me that before?' I demanded.

'You didn't ask me, Monsieur,' came the reply. I was tempted to throw the router on the floor, but this would have been a pointless, expensive gesture. Back home we went. Intransigence or what!

I had one more ridiculous and unbelievable experience that holiday. Over the years, we had accumulated a large number of coins, or shrapnel, as we call it. We obtained the appropriate packets for the coins so we could put the correct denominations in the right cases. While we were in St Mathieu, I decided to take all these coins to the bank and deposit them into our account.

There was an old man in front of me who seemed quite confused and distressed. Listening to the conversation between him and the bank clerk, it appeared that in order to do his banking, he would have to use a tablet. The poor bloke had probably never seen a computer in his life, let alone a tablet. The clerk was trying to explain to the man how to use the tablet – which buttons to press, and when. The final straw came when the chap was asked to sign the screen on the tablet. He kept asking for a pen but was told to use his finger. It took ages for him to understand how to do this.

As he walked out, he muttered angrily about how difficult modern life was and how banks had changed.

I addressed the clerk and presented my coins. He asked for my paying-in book, which I gave him. He then told me he couldn't accept the coins. I asked why not and was told that due to money laundering reasons, coins were no longer accepted by banks.

'But I thought that was what banks are for?' I retorted. The clerk shrugged. This was crazy. I only had about thirty Euros of coins – hardly major money laundering.

'Then what am I supposed to do with these coins?' I asked.

'Spend them in a shop, Monsieur. You could try the tobacconist next door.'

I couldn't believe what a mad situation this was. An old chap wanted to do his banking in person, but as it's all online, he had to go to the bank and use a tablet, which was totally foreign to him. Yet when I wanted to pay in some coins – actual, hard money, I was told that banks in France don't do this anymore.

I went next door and asked the man running the tobacconists if he would give me some notes in exchange for the coins.

'Only for the denominations of two Euros, one Euro, fifty cents, and twenty cents.' I was told.

'What about the remaining coins?' I asked.

'You could try the bakers,' he replied.

I went to the bakers and asked if they would like the smaller denominations of ten, five, two, and one cent coins. There was about five Euros worth.

'I'll accept these in payment for bread and cakes,' said the lady.

So I walked out with a couple of loaves and two cakes!

We returned to England and spent the next few months working hard in our respective businesses. At the beginning of December, Patricia was commissioned to provide a dinner for around fourteen people who had rented a large house in a nearby village. When she arrived, she found out that most of them were French and were spending the weekend in Kent.

She spoke to some of them in French, and when asked how come she spoke French, she replied that we have a house in France.

One chap called Erik was full of personality. He asked Patricia where exactly our house was. She told him it was in the Limousin. He asked her to be specific. She laughed and said it was a small village about forty-five minutes south of Limoges. He asked her to name it. When she said Pellac, he literally couldn't believe it.

It turned out that he ran a business not far away, designing and manufacturing metal pergolas.

'Not just outside Chalus?' said Patricia.

'Yes,' replied Erik. 'You know it?'

Patricia explained that a few years earlier, we went there to enquire about a metal pergola, but that we were put off by the cost.

'You must have another pergola,' stated Erik. 'This time, I'll give you a special discount.'

Patricia laughed and carried on serving the dinner. As the evening wore on, and Erik drank more wine. After each successive course, he would call out 'forty per cent discount,' followed by 'fifty per cent discount'. His final offer was 'seventy per cent discount'. Patricia grinned and told him if she poured him more wine, maybe we'd get it for free!

At the end of the evening, he insisted that we visit him. We're yet to do so, but who knows …

We had been running our 'Learn Real French' group for twelve years, but as our holiday drew to a close, Patricia and I realised it had run its course and that it was probably time to call a halt. I was already teaching yoga two evenings a week, and we really wanted to reduce our commitment to a third evening. We held a final Christmas party in December, where we invited former and existing members, and we had a great evening together with speeches and laughter.

Some of the group members were very witty, and they responded vigorously to my closing speech, as I gently and light-heartedly made fun of some of them. Many of us are still in touch, and one day we'll get round to having a one-off reunion.

A MAJOR LEAK, THEN YOGA IN FRANCE

2018

Patricia and I spent New Year in France on our own. It was very quiet. We went for regular walks with Fred, and that was about it. But it gave us a chance to plan; I'll explain. A few months before, some of my Yogis had mentioned yoga retreats, and I was asked if I'd thought of running a retreat. I mentioned this to Patricia. She thought this was a great idea. We agreed to 'park' this until our New Year break.

We certainly had the space. We worked out that if we cleared the upstairs loft of furniture, there would be enough space to accommodate nine or ten people to practice yoga. That was the easy part. The next question was where would they stay? And how could we cater for them? We'd got to know a French couple in the village who'd bought a house from some former English people who had gone back to the UK. They had extensively renovated the property, and they'd set up a bed-and-breakfast. We got in touch and went across – it was only a three-minute walk away – and talked through our plans for a retreat. They showed us the rooms, and gave us a provisional quote, based on our needs.

We needed additional back-up, so we approached a Dutch couple who run a much larger accommodation complex just outside the village. They gave us a tour and indicated what they had available.

Patricia figured out that she'd be able to provide the catering for breakfast and dinner. After all – that's what she does – she's a caterer – and she has an excellent reputation for providing top quality food, expertly prepared. Her planning skills are also second to none, and her experience catering for the Art retreat in Umbria a few years before had really boosted her confidence and credentials.

With this in mind, we talked and talked about how we might make this work. We already had a very large table, which we'd bought from some Dutch friends. It would comfortably seat twelve people. We would need to transport a fair amount of stuff from the UK before the retreat, such as a fridge-freezer, another sofa, more crockery, and glassware, plus yoga mats and blocks, and also dried food and kitchen appliances. But it was all possible. We thought we'd run a retreat in May, and if there was sufficient interest, possibly another in September.

We returned to the UK in early January, and I advertised the retreats among my Yogis. To our astonishment – and delight – both retreats became fully booked within a few weeks.

In mid-February, Patricia and I went to South Africa, ostensibly to celebrate her sixtieth birthday, but also as part of our plan to travel more. When we got back, I arranged for all the various stuff to be transported to France. I was planning to fly out ahead of the delivery.

However, two days before, the delivery company called. They wanted to deliver everything four days earlier. Although this could have been inconvenient, especially as I'd booked my flights, I realised this could work. I called our friend Desmond, who had keys to our house, and he kindly agreed to accept the delivery on our behalf.

The delivery was due on the Saturday morning. At 10 a.m., I received a call from Desmond. As a true Yorkshireman, he got straight to the point:

'Good news and bad news. The delivery has arrived. Everything has been taken into the house. No problems. Now for the bad news – you've got a leak.'

I waited. 'How bad?' I asked.

'Well, your dining room is an absolute mess. Water has come through the ceiling. It might need replacing. I think there's been a problem in the bathroom.' Desmond had already called out a plumber, who had turned the water off, and inspected the cause of the flood. He'd agreed for the plumber to come back early the following week to do the repair work.

I explained to Desmond I was already flying out a few days later, and that I'd meet him at the house when I arrived. He was right – the dining room was a complete mess. The cause of the problem was due to pipes that had frozen during a cold spell in February. When the pipes thawed, the rush of water had literally blown off one of the bathroom taps. Our mistake was that while we always turned the water off, we hadn't left the taps open. When the water flowed, there was nowhere for it to go. The pressure built up, forced the tap off, and the water had leaked all over the bathroom floor, across on to the wooden floor in the loft area, and down through the dining room ceiling.

I spent the afternoon mopping up and clearing up. The room badly needed airing. The plumber arrived early that evening and repaired the tap. He looked at the ceiling and explained that many ceilings in properties of similar age were constructed of terra cotta, and the damage was therefore mostly cosmetic. It would require redecorating. I'd already contacted the insurance company, and they were sending out someone the following week to meet Desmond on-site and confirm the necessary repair work.

I'd taken various photographs, although I held off sending these to Patricia. She was already concerned the retreat would be in doubt. But I was confident we'd be ok. Indeed, as Desmond said in his inimitable style, 'Your guests won't be looking up at the bloody ceiling, they'll be looking down at their food.'

Bang on – absolutely!

Desmond also sensibly suggested I left the window open, because that would accelerate the drying process, and with the shutters closed, no one would know the windows behind were open.

I returned to the UK. The retreat was only a few weeks away. I heard from the insurance company. They'd agreed to the repair. However, getting a decorator in time for the retreat wasn't going to happen. The ceiling still needed more time to dry, and time was too tight.

In May, ahead of the retreat, Patricia and I drove out to France. The car was packed with food. I was also taking my road bike out again, but this time I was going to leave it at the house. Although I'd previously driven through France with the bike on the roof, for the first time I forgot it was there. As we drove through the autoroute péage, I went under the barrier. Clunk.

'Shit,' I exclaimed. I'd forgotten about the bike. I stopped and jumped out of the car. Fortunately, there wasn't any damage to the bike or the car, but it certainly gave me a shock.

We arrived at the house. Patricia inspected the damage for the first time. She was visibly shocked. She looked at the photographs again and realised much of the clearing up had already been done. But we still had some work ahead of us.

The following day, we did our first major shop. Patricia knows how much I detest supermarket shopping. She tried hard to get through this very long task as efficiently and quickly as possible and had produced a MOAS (mother of all spreadsheets) of all the items required in their respective categories. At the same time, I pulled on my 'patience' hat, and between us, we got it cracked within one afternoon. The car was packed full of food and drink. We spent the next couple of days preparing the house ahead of the Yogis coming out. We'd already warned them that there had been a flood.

Our accountant Chris came out first, having driven out the day before. When I showed him the ceiling, he was not at all put off, and congratulated us for getting the room sorted out so quickly.

The Yogis flew out the following day. Chris and I collected them from the airport in our respective cars. We drove back, dropped them off at their B&B, and shortly they arrived for pre-dinner drinks, and we then sat down to dinner.

The schedule was to start the day with yoga at eight am. We encouraged everyone to arrive fifteen minutes earlier so they could have a mug of tea or coffee before starting. The yoga continued for ninety minutes, after which we all sat down to a large breakfast – more of a brunch, really. That left everyone with the rest of the day free until yoga started again at five thirty pm. After another ninety-minute session, we'd come downstairs and fell into a lovely routine of a gin & tonic before sitting down to dinner half an hour later. Around 10.30 p.m. the Yogis would go back to their respective B&Bs.

We had planned various outings; we drove to Brantôme for the Friday morning market, we did a couple of lake walks, and we visited a massive porcelain shop just outside Limoges. On the Saturday morning after breakfast, everyone sat in the lounge to watch the royal wedding (Harry and Meghan) on TV. Both tissues and fizz were passed round as we watched the occasion.

The mealtimes were wonderful. Patricia excelled herself and produced some stunning and delicious food. Wine was on tap, and conversation flowed with lots of fun and laughter. On the Saturday evening, we invited our friends Desmond and Cassie over. Cassie is also a yogi and has taught for years. I invited her to take the evening class, and then she and Desmond stayed to dinner, and regaled us with some of their hilarious stories.

We went to the Roc du Boeuf for lunch on the Sunday. It was a warm, sunny day. The atmosphere inside was welcoming, cosy, and gently formal, with everyone dressing up smartly for the occasion.

The time flew by. The retreat went really well. Everyone simply loved practicing yoga in the loft. I was asked (and have been asked several times since) if we had designed the loft for yoga. We hadn't of course; at the time of the renovations, I wasn't even doing yoga. But people were right. The loft was perfect for yoga. Plenty of space, with natural light filtering through the skylight windows, and with the large beams and vaulted ceiling, the atmosphere was absolutely perfect. I also did something I'd vowed I'd never do in my classes. We chanted: it just felt the right thing to do. I'm not particularly spiritual, but everyone felt a certain warmth spreading as the sound of our chanting resonated magnificently in the loft space.

We spent a couple of days relaxing. Running the retreat was great fun and also pretty exhausting. We reviewed what we'd done and came up with alternative ideas to make things easier and better for future retreats. We drove home on the Thursday, and we looked forward to our combined birthday treat on the Friday; our daughter Lucy had bought tickets for us and herself to see my favourite rock band – The Rolling Stones – play at the London stadium. What a wonderful way to finish off the week.

Patricia and I went back in August for a shortish holiday. We spent two lovely lazy weeks there. I was gradually working less and less in my recruitment business. I was finally able to take time off. We sat in the sun, met friends, and we totally chilled out. I'd also started to get what Patricia calls my 'Pellac mojo' back. I could see a very good reason for wanting to go out there more – yoga retreats – and I was also able to let go and relax.

We came back to the UK. We had some family occasions planned, including a weekend in Leicestershire where we all celebrated our niece Rhiain's twenty-first birthday with a large party.

The following week was the next yoga retreat. We needed a couple of days before the next party of Yogis came out. The September weather (as is so often the case) was gorgeous, and even warmer than May. The retreat – or yoga holiday as it was more appropriately renamed – followed a similar format as before, but with different people, there was a different dynamic, which made it just as enjoyable and memorable for different reasons.

After the retreat had finished, we went over to see Desmond and Cassie one evening. Their garden looked beautiful. Desmond mentioned he'd found an English chap, who had a digger, and that he'd had him round to dig out his hedge. I asked him why he'd done that. Desmond replied it was unnecessary and that it blocked the sun. He suggested we considered our hedges; we had high hedges around most of the perimeter surrounding the garden.

On the way back, Patricia started the germ of an idea. Over the years, we'd spent a fortune employing a gardener to come several times a year to keep the hedges neat and trimmed. Each year the price went up. The last time (two years earlier) was the final straw. Almost nine hundred Euros for a year's maintenance. I told the gardener we wouldn't require his hedge-trimming services and asked him to simply cut the grass. He was obviously offended, because we never saw him again! Patricia's only regret was that he was good 'eye candy'.

Over the next two years, I'd managed to keep the grass down with a 'makeshift' strimmer. But the hedges were looking a real mess. The following day, I emailed the English chap with the digger, whose name was Josh. He called me back that evening and suggested he came over to take a look.

He's a very pleasant chap, and we got on well. By then, Patricia and I were considering what we'd previously thought unthinkable: to remove the hedges entirely. We talked to Josh. He agreed it was certainly possible. I asked the obvious questions: how long it would take, how much would it cost, and when could he start. He explained it was difficult to give us a meaningful answer, as he really couldn't tell how long it might take, given the height and depth of the hedges. He suggested he came back a couple of days later, and spend three days cutting back, to give him and us an indication of what the timeframe and cost would be. He also agreed to remove the debris, which again would impact on his cutting time.

After three days, Josh had made significant progress. On that basis, he estimated a further five to six days, and quoted us a price. We agreed but given we wouldn't be back until the end of December, we told him to simply schedule the work in as and when he could. This would work well for all parties.

On our final night, we caught up with our friends Jacques and Marguerite. We hadn't seen much of them, as they too had been away. We all went out for dinner at a local restaurant and spent a lovely evening together. I was very fond of Jacques – we had a lot in common – and their company was always enjoyable and fun.

We were delighted to be back in time for the birth of our second grandchild (and first grandson) – Finley – son to Vicky and her fiancé, Tom.

We returned just after Christmas. Vicky, Tom, and Finley were driving out for a short break over New Year. The weather was cold and sunny. On New Year's Day, Vicky, Tom, and I went out for a forty-kilometre bike ride. They are both quite sporty, although this was the first major exercise Vicky had undertaken since giving birth to Finley three months earlier. She was also breast-feeding. Despite the cold and sheer physical effort required, she made it, although around the halfway mark, I don't think she was thanking Tom and me for suggesting it!

On January second, we decided to venture out and find a restaurant for a light lunch somewhere. We drove to several places, including the local town, Nontron. There wasn't a single resto open. We explained to Vicky and Tom that this is rural France, although we too were surprised that everything was closed. We ended up having a coffee and cognac in the local branch of Super-U. To our amusement, tables had been laid out with cutlery and glassware ready for lunch. You certainly wouldn't see that in Sainsburys!

Vicky, Tom, and Finley left on January third, just as we received a delivery of furniture from IKEA. We had decided we needed some decent dining room chairs. We had ordered ten chairs from IKEA, which after some initial hassle, were due to be delivered on the third. The hassle was due to the fact that in rural France, many of the roads don't have names, and certainly no house numbers. Our address was simply Le Bourg – which was the same for at least a dozen other houses. As online delivery started to take off in France, this prompted a lot of local action, culminating with us now having a proper road name and house number. Meanwhile, the only way I was going to get IKEA to deliver was to send them a photograph of our location on Google Maps.

Our flat-pack chairs were delivered by the local post van. We were expecting a large van, even a lorry. But our local post lady rocked up, rang the bell, and proceeded to unload several large and heavy parcels from her van!

The next task was disposing of all the cardboard packaging. We'd be returning to the UK in a few days, and we didn't want to leave this task until the next time. I also had various other items, including an ancient and very heavy sofa bed which we inherited with the house. It had come to the end of its useful life. Tom and I had spent a good hour breaking it up; I could imagine being turned away from the local dump if I offloaded a sofa comprising wood, metal, and fabric upholstery.

I checked the opening times of our local dump. It stated it was open on Thursday between 2 p.m. and 5 p.m. In France, at least in our area, we also need to carry a credit-sized card, confirming where we live. There's a limit on how many times a year we can visit – I think it's fifteen – and our card is marked each time accordingly.

We drove to the dump, to be greeted by locked gates and a handwritten sign saying it was closed that afternoon. I was not amused! The car was stacked to the gunnels with stuff to dispose of. I looked for alternative dumps on my iPhone and saw the nearest dump was at Rochechouart around twelve kilometres away. It took some finding, but we arrived twenty minutes before it was due to close.

I drove in and up the ramp. The site operative was typically bossy and awkward. He asked to see what I had. The metal frame for the sofa bed was extremely heavy, and I asked him if he could give me a hand. He reluctantly agreed, helped me drag it out of the car, and following his guidance we ceremoniously threw it over the side of the appropriate skip. As I started pulling the rest of the stuff out of the car, he asked to see my card.

'Ah non non non.' He thrust the card in front of my face and told me I was not entitled to use this dump, as I didn't live in the local commune. I explained that our local dump was shut. He shrugged and said it wasn't his problem. He turned his back on me.

'Well, what am I supposed to do now then,' I asked testily.

He turned back round, and simply said, 'Carry on, Monsieur. It's too late, you've already started. Just don't come back here again!'

THE LOSS OF A DEAR FRENCH FRIEND

2019

During this short period in France over the New Year, I came to make a major decision about my recruitment business. I'd been thinking for some months that running a recruitment business and teaching yoga weren't really compatible. I'd had too many situations over the past two years when I was getting ready to teach a yoga class, when I'd received an important call or email regarding a recruitment matter that needed urgent attention. Not the best state of mind to be in when teaching yoga.

I'd already decided that the main basis of my working future was going to be involved in yoga and not recruitment. I was preparing to gradually let my recruitment business go – the baby and child I'd nurtured over the past twenty-odd years.

Matters came to a head during the last few days we were there. During that first week in January. I received a call from my biggest and most valuable client. To be honest, I'd been on the point of calling him before Christmas, to let him know about my intentions. But somehow, I just wasn't quite ready to do that.

I answered the phone. We exchanged the usual pleasantries, and then my client excitedly told me he had four key vacancies he wanted me to fill. While he started to run through what these were, I knew it was time to have that conversation.

I listened attentively, and then explained that after much soul-searching, it was time for me to gradually remove myself from day-to-day recruitment. On that basis, it would be wrong of me to accept the vacancies and not be fully committed to them. It would therefore be in my client's best interests if he found another recruiter to work with. He told me that he appreciated my honesty. He knew I was also running my yoga business, and he'd guessed that at some point, that would be the direction I'd be turning. I added that I was still available and keen to be involved in one-off senior appointments, but I was pulling away from what I called 'bread and butter' recruitment.

After I finished the call, I went downstairs to tell Patricia. I could tell by looking into her eyes that I'd made the right decision. And it felt right. Not with sadness nor with regret, but with the feelings of relief, contentment, conviction, even warmth that comes after making a major decision.

WE RECEIVED SOME sad news in late March.

During the first two weeks of March, Patricia and I went on a long-planned holiday to Sri Lanka and the Maldives. The day before we left, I received a text message from my friend Jacques. He had developed lung cancer. He asked me not to call, as he found speaking difficult. He was due to have an operation in mid-March and asked me to contact him through his partner Marguerite.

The first week after we got back from holiday, I was teaching yoga on the Friday morning. During Savasana at the end of the class, when everyone was lying quietly on their mats, a text came through on my watch. It was from Jacques' eldest daughter. It simply said that his cancer had quickly worsened, and that he'd passed away during the night. I was so shocked and upset.

After the class, I told Patricia. We messaged his daughter back. There wasn't much more information. Basically, he had developed a cold in early January, which turned into a cough. Thinking he had bronchitis, he asked his doctor for antibiotics. But when the cough got worse, he went back to the doctor, to discover that it wasn't bronchitis, but cancer of the lungs. He was just sixty-five and had been a non-smoker for many years. This was such a sad loss of a good friend.

IN MAY 2019, we held our third Yoga-in-France Holiday. This year, the Yogis were flying out on the Saturday. The weather was cool and damp. The garden, however, was looking really good. Josh the digger-man had completed the removal of all the hedges we no longer wanted, and the whole area felt much more open. We could actually see other parts of the village, rather than being hemmed in by high hedges. Josh had also removed several of the lower branches of a huge fir tree in our garden. This too opened the garden up, with more light (as well as forming a great den area for grandchildren).

There were a number of weeds that had grown on the driveway, due no doubt to the rain and the warmth of the spring. I decided to invest in a small strimmer from a local DIY superstore. When I got home, I set about tidying up the driveway, and had pretty much completed the work when I hit a hidden rock. The strimmer stopped working. On examination, I appeared that the plastic housing for the trimming wire had cracked and fallen off.

I returned the machine to the DIY store the following day. I explained that for seventy Euros I expected more. The young guy I spoke to said he'd see if he could order a replacement part and asked me to call him a couple of days later. I wasn't entirely happy, but there seemed to be no other way around this. I called him two days later as requested and was told he was ill. I asked if anyone else was dealing with his work, and was informed another sales assistant was dealing with enquiries, but she was off that day. I could see I was going nowhere fast.

I called again the following week and managed to speak to the original guy. He told me that now his colleague was dealing with the matter, I should speak to her. But guess what – she was on holiday for the next week. I was not impressed. We were going back to the UK in three days' time. I'd have to wait until the summer.

THE YOGA RETREAT went well. The weather gradually improved, and we all had a fun time together. The Roc du Boeuf had changed hands; the sisters had, (we understood), decided they'd had enough of running a restaurant, and wanted a change. On that basis, we decided to change the venue for the Yogis, and instead went to the Hostellerie St Jacques, where we had a splendid Sunday lunch.

After the Yogis returned to the UK, we decided to try out Le Roc de Boeuf under the owners and went with our friends Desmond and Cassie for lunch. It confirmed we'd made the right decision in not bringing the Yogis there. The food, service, and ambiance weren't a patch on the restaurant run by the former owners. We didn't go back and heard the following year that the restaurant had closed permanently.

We returned in early August. Bruce and Diana came over for a couple of days, and we spent many pleasant hours chatting outside in the sun under the pergola with its new 'sail' roof, which certainly made sitting outside more bearable in 30+ degrees.

We also caught up with our Irish friends Ruairi and Siobhan. They live in Holland, and own two houses in France. One is in a village nearby. It sleeps up to fourteen people and is used for holiday rentals. They also bought a property some years ago in the village. They had started to renovate it, and in 2019, kick-started the work again.

The two of them are great fun. They share good family values, and it's great to spend time together over some food, wine/beer and some interesting, fun conversation. We always have a really good laugh when we get together. Although their house is less than a five-minute walk, we went straight back to their house after returning from the restaurant we'd eaten at. After several more drinks, I left the car there. I did 'the walk of shame' the next morning to retrieve the car so we could get some bread for breakfast!

Talking of bread, we noticed a new initiative in some of the local villages; a bread machine. This is normally placed near the baker's shop and is in use only when the shop is closed. You can buy a baguette for one Euro. Only in France!

ONE OF THE tasks I had remaining from May was to resolve the matter of my broken strimmer. I drove to Nontron and went into the store with the useless machine. I spoke to an assistant and explained the problem. She consulted with various members of staff and managed to find the one who was dealing with the matter. I went through the process of describing what had happened, and that I'd had to return to the UK meanwhile. The sales assistant listened carefully, then took the machine and disappeared.

I waited for five minutes, then ten minutes, and after almost fifteen minutes had passed, she returned. She asked me to tell her once again what had happened. Then she looked me hard in the eye and said she would treat this as an 'exceptional' case, and only on this one occasion, she'd replace the machine with a new one. I played along, and thanked her profusely, then accompanied her to the display, took possession of a new strimmer, and promptly left the store before there was a change of mind. I could almost read the invisible sign stating, 'do not come back here again'. French customer service once again raising its charmless head.

OUR STAY IN August was just for two weeks, as we returned in September for the second Yoga-in-France Holiday. Meanwhile, I was invited to be in the audience for *BBC Question Time*, which was an interesting experience, particularly as Brexit was hotting up under the newly elected Johnson as prime minister.

The weather that September was absolutely glorious, with daytime temperatures around the twenty-five degrees mark. As well as enjoying some great meals at home (and of course the yoga), we went back to the Hostellerie St Jacques for Sunday lunch. All ten of us sat around a large table on the terrace outside, surrounded by various trees and plants. The setting was idyllic, and the food as always was superb.

After the Yogis left, we spent a few days relaxing and clearing up. I also had an interesting conversation with my friend and former client Martin, whose company I helped to facilitate the sale back in 2007. Martin had previously owned a house in France which he'd sold around ten years ago. He and his wife had recently bought another house in south-west France, which was considerable in size. Martin called me to ask how the yoga retreat had gone, then introduced the idea of holding a yoga retreat at his property, which could sleep a dozen people. He suggested that I could teach yoga, and Patricia could do the catering. This was a very attractive proposition; it wouldn't conflict with our own retreats, as Martin and his wife have access to a broad range of potential attendees/yogis who they would invite. I confirmed that we'd certainly be very keen to join them in this exciting venture.

We completed our packing and house cleaning with care. We were going directly to the Black Forest for four days. We weren't planning to come back to Pellac at the year end, so we needed to prepare the house for winter.

We decided to stay overnight halfway to the Black Forest. I found somewhere on Airbnb, and we arrived there around 7 p.m. It was a strange place, almost a farm building, just outside the village. We were told that the owners wouldn't be there, but we found the key in the allotted place. The accommodation was a little spartan and grubby, but it was only for one night. And it had Internet, which enabled us to download the latest IOS operating system to our iPhones.

We walked down into the village for something to eat. It was a small, quiet village, but with a bank and several shops. The next day, I offered to walk down to the bakers to get some bread for breakfast. Patricia also wanted me to buy some bakers' flour, but as I didn't have enough cash, and they wouldn't accept a card, I offered to walk back into the village after breakfast and go to the bank first.

I walked in, got my cash card out, and tried to withdraw some funds. But the machine wouldn't work. I tried again, and assuming the machine was out of action, I went to the next machine and stood behind an old lady. She too was having problems getting cash out. She must have been on her third or fourth attempt, when another, younger woman walked in. She called out to us all and asked if anyone had parked a car outside. The old lady in front of me grunted and nodded as she continued to withdraw some money. The other woman went up to her and exclaimed that her car was blocking the flow of traffic through the village centre.

It appeared that the old lady couldn't find a car parking space, so she'd left her car in the middle of the road and walked into the bank. Meanwhile, it was chaos outside, with people shouting and cars hooting. But the old lady was having none of it. She wanted her money, and she wasn't moving until she got it.

She called out to the sole assistant in the bank that she was having problems. The assistant went up to the machine and impatiently pressed various buttons. It was at this point that I mentioned I too had problems withdrawing cash. 'Mais non,' said the assistant. To prove her point, she went behind the counter, and came back with her own card, and proceeded to withdraw some cash. 'Voilà' she said. She must have cleared a blockage in the system, as suddenly, the old lady retrieved the cash she wanted, and slowly ambled out of the bank among a cacophony of noise outside. I then inserted my card and thankfully got some cash out.

We enjoyed a lovely time in the Black Forest with our friends Bruce and Diana and returned to the UK for the autumn and winter. Little did any of us know what was on the horizon!

MEANWHILE, EARLIER THAT year, I'd started to prepare for the sale of my recruitment business. A guy who I'd previously placed some years ago got in touch.

Long story short, and after various conversations, he came to work with me on the basis he would head up the recruitment side of things and buy the business from me in twelve months' time.

I was really pleased; I didn't want the business or the reputation to dwindle. I was excited to help keep everything bubbling until its eventual acquisition the following year.

Covid, Then a Glorious French September

2020

Twenty-twenty started fairly quietly, although we became increasingly aware of a nasty virus that seemed to be spreading around the world. We had intended to go out to our place in early March for a week and saw no reason to change our plans. When we arrived, we already noticed a distinct change in behaviour. The French were no longer greeting each other in their customary way by shaking hands or kissing. Supermarkets had started to run short of essentials such as hand sanitiser and toilet rolls.

We went for lunch to a restaurant recommended by friends, which was about forty minutes away. The restaurant was full and lively. Life still seemed quite normal. As the week continued, we watched the British news closely. It appeared the Coronavirus situation was rapidly getting worse. It also seemed that France was moving faster, and on the Friday, we had it confirmed that from midnight on Sunday night, France would be entering a national lockdown. Fortunately, our Eurotunnel crossing was already booked for Sunday evening ahead of this.

I spent part of our final day working out how I might teach yoga online via Zoom. Then on the Sunday morning, we locked up the house and drove back to Calais. As we entered the last stretch between Rouen and Calais, the motorway became noticeably quieter. By the time we arrived at Calais at around seven pm, there seemed to be very little traffic. We checked in and caught our train back to the UK.

The UK entered its own lockdown just over a week later. As the year continued, we weren't sure when we'd be able to go back. We managed to get across to Calais in July on a day's crossing to buy some wine, as our stocks were seriously depleted. We went to our usual wine merchant just outside Calais and stocked up. We didn't hang around; everyone was wearing face masks and socially distancing, and frankly it didn't feel comfortable. On a positive note, July 2020 was highly memorable, in that our new grand-daughter – Hope – was born, a daughter to Jo and James. Later that year, our family expanded further, with the birth of Archie – a son to Lucy and Phil and a brother to Sophie.

As the summer rolled on, things seemed to be easing in both the UK and most of Europe. We decided to take our chance, and we drove out to the house at the end of August. We decided to make the most of it and stayed for three and a half weeks. We had a very quiet time; we barely saw anyone, and apart from a daily dog walk around our favourite lake and the odd trip to the supermarket, we barely ventured out. But this suited us fine. There had been very few outbreaks of Covid in the entire region where we live. We felt safer than we did in the UK. We stayed at home and spent lots of time outside enjoying the sun and the high temperatures, which exceeded thirty degrees on several days. I have many happy memories of some lovely tranquil days, sitting in the garden, listening to music, reading, and sipping chilled wine. The only people we saw were Desmond and Cassie, and also Josh who came over for dinner one evening with his wife Pippa and their teenage daughter.

I'd decided to renew the Internet connection in the house. We had had it for several years, but it was expensive, and when the family came out a few years ago, I noticed that none of them asked for the password. They were all happy with 3G/4G which was now free when roaming.

But I wanted to continue to teach yoga via Zoom while we were in France. As I searched for suitable Internet providers, I came across a website for a Paris-based company written in English. It was for ex-pats and second-home owners. They promised to find the most competitive package for your needs. I called them in July and told them what I wanted. They came up with a heavily discounted off/package for twelve months, at a monthly price of twenty Euros, which I thought was very reasonable, certainly in comparison to what we had before. Again, the package and terms were complicated, but it was cheap, and also included two free SIM cards which I thought might be worth having. A router was dispatched to us, which a friend kindly took into the house.

I'd also decided to get another TV set; I could take the TV in the lounge upstairs to use for yoga, and I looked for a larger screen TV, which would provide a better experience during our Yoga Holidays, should any of the Yogis want to watch TV. Originally, I thought of buying a TV in the UK and taking it out, but I realised it wouldn't fit in the car with everything else. I looked at websites for local retailers, and also Amazon, but the choice was poor, and even Amazon wasn't great. I suddenly had the brainwave of looking at Fnac. I knew they had stores reasonably locally. Sure enough, I found the TV make and model I wanted, at a reasonable price. I bought the TV online and arranged for it to be delivered to a local branch of Fnac.

On the allotted collection date, I thought, *hmm… buying a TV in France, online, collecting from store – what could possibly go wrong*? We arrived at Fnac, which was a tiny branch in a small retail complex at St Yrieix. I walked in and tentatively said I'd come to collect a TV.

'Ah yes, Monsieur Wilson, your TV is right here,' said the assistant.

And there it was, behind the counter. Another assistant offered to bring it out to my car and helped me load it into the car. I got home, unpacked the TV, connected it to the satellite dish, and also the Internet. Hey presto – everything worked!

We went out for lunch just twice, to local restaurants. One was up for sale, and it was obvious the owners had already given up; the standard of food and customer service was pretty poor. This particular restaurant provides tables outside in the summer. The view down the valley is beautiful, and on a warm, sunny day we looked forward to this.

When we arrived, we waited outside. The owner came out and asked if we wanted to eat inside or outside. I replied outside at the rear as usual. 'The tables outside are here, Monsieur,' she said briskly.

'OK,' I replied. 'But we'd rather eat in the garden.'

She ignored me and repeated that tables outside were at the front. I looked surprised and gently asked about tables at the rear. She gave me a steely smile and repeated once again that if we wanted to eat outside, it would be right here by the car park. We sat down. I was pretty cheesed off. First, we'd been looking forward to sitting in the rear garden with the view. Second, I resented her patronising attitude. I had suspicions that as we weren't regulars, and also English, we weren't permitted to eat in the garden. But as other people arrived, they too had to sit out the front by the car park. However, a little charm wouldn't have hurt!

But the other restaurant was fabulous – excellent food, and sparkling service. We can't wait to go back again.

THE DAY BEFORE we left, we did a major clean up. We then locked up the house, not knowing when we'd back, but certainly not again in 2020.

At the time of writing, both the UK and France (and indeed most of Europe) are in lockdown. It seems unlikely that travel abroad will be possible until at least the summer, and maybe not until even later in the year.

Then, of course, we have Brexit. The UK has now formally left the EU. We're not yet sure how we'll be affected, although we understand it will be much more complicated to bring our dog Freddie with us when we next go out. We've also heard that we won't be allowed to take meat and dairy products from one country to the other. No longer will we be able to take and eat our own sandwiches en route. It also means that Patricia's opportunity to prepare meals in the UK in advance of the Yoga Holidays won't be possible. Everything will have to be procured in France when we get there. This means we'll have to go out even earlier ahead of Yogis coming out to enable meals to be prepared in advance. This is of course providing that we'll be able to hold our Yoga Holidays again. It certainly looks unlikely this year.

We also will be limited on the amount of wine we'll be able to bring back to the UK. A figure of 18 litres a head is being bandied about. We're not sure how the reciprocal health and medical arrangements will change. Our EHIC cards will apparently be replaced by a new GHIC card, which is supposed to operate in a similar manner.

Taking our dog Freddie is now much more complicated. Previously, we could take him with us to France at the drop of a hat. Now however, we have to notify our vet around two weeks before travelling, so that they can complete a nine-page form, which we then need to go and sign (and pay for!), and we have to do this each time we take our dog abroad.

We will have to carry a Green Card for car insurance purposes, and this will have to be renewed each time we go out. We will be limited on the amount of time we spend in France – a maximum of ninety days in every one hundred and eighty days. But given we're generally not in France for more than sixty days a year, that shouldn't affect us.

There is one ray of sunshine. GB cars will no longer be subject to speeding fines, as the arrangement between the French authorities and DVLA ceased at midnight on 31st December 2020. The speeding fines have been the bane of our trips to France during the past few years. They never existed before, but a joint arrangement between the two governments in 2017 enabled both countries to issue speeding fines to foreign drivers.

Since 2018, I think I've received a speeding fine every time we've either driven out or back – sometimes both. The difficulty is that speed limits can suddenly change, and unless corrective action is taken immediately, it's generally too late. Also, the tolerance level is completely different in France. You can be caught going just 1 km over the limit. As each fine is around forty-five Euros, our trips to France and back have been quite expensive. I finally managed to crack the system in September. I installed Waze on my Apple CarPlay, which very conveniently buzzed each time I exceed the limit (it would instantly recognise any change in the speed limit and notify me). It also provided warning of speed cameras. I believe apps or devices like this are illegal in France but knowing I could easily exit the app if stopped, I was prepared to take the risk. Suffice it to say, we didn't get one speeding fine for the September trip.

So we are waiting to see what happens next. Having to cope with both Covid and Brexit at the same time is both depressing and challenging. Has Brexit crushed our dream? We certainly hope not. But it's patently clear that things won't be the same again, certainly not in our lifetime. We remain positive. We are keeping our fingers crossed. We really are missing our house in France.

THE PROCESS OF writing this book has enabled me to reflect, consider, and confirm the key elements of what I both like (or rather love) and dislike about France – after all, life isn't perfect!

Although the 'dislike' list is almost equally long, on balance, the 'love' list is both practically and emotionally far stronger. These are the real things that pull me to France, and the pull towards is much more intense than the push away

The list of 'exasperations' largely consists of things that are different but also which cause both amusement and occasionally bemusement.

What I Love About France

- The scenery, the countryside, the gorgeous landscape
- The seasons – four distinctly different seasons and climates
- The gentle pace of life in rural France, especially long, warm Friday evenings, when everything seems to slow down in advance of the weekend
- The wonderful feeling, especially at the start of a trip, that you really are abroad. So many things feel really quite different
- Sparsely populated areas within rural France
- The acceptance and friendliness by the people we encounter
- Good wine at affordable prices
- The wonderful sense of anticipation in a good restaurant, particularly at lunchtime
- Duck breasts – always much bigger and so much tastier than in the UK
- French bakeries – a large selection of good bread, pastries, and cakes
- Cycling in France – fewer cars by far, and much greater tolerance from other road users
- French roads – well built, and very few potholes
- Uncrowded French motorways
- Le Tour de France

- The enthusiasm to celebrate local occasions, such as the mushroom season, the chestnut season, summer steak & frites nights, Mechoui, etc. In fact, any reason for a local get together
- French markets – the choice and range of products, and above all, the atmosphere
- Hot chocolate – especially in Café Paul
- Humour – French humour is often funny and expressive, and when extended, the French love reciprocation

What I Dislike About France

- Customer service – at times, it rarely seems to exist, and if it does, it's done with obvious displeasure and indifference
- French supermarkets, which tend to be poorly merchandised; obvious food categories are often split up
- Supermarket checkouts – the propensity to hurl the goods down the conveyor belt to the packing area. This is especially bad if the store is about to close for lunch
- Shops opening and closing times; to arrive at a supermarket around lunchtime to find that it's closed and not due to re-open until 2.30/3.00 p.m. is unbelievably annoying
- Car parks (where do I start!); ridiculously small entrance and exit points, tiny parking bays, which means car doors are regularly smashed into neighbouring cars; lack of obvious directions for entrance and exit. This applies to supermarkets, petrol stations, and most of all motorway service stations
- The police – officious, threatening, over-serious, no sense of humour
- Internet and mobile phone contracts – complicated, incomprehensible, and expensive, and virtually impossible to cancel
- Intransigence – the French can be renowned for this, which can be very tiresome
- Rubbish disposal – we generally find that if we're at our house less than a fortnight, we miss the refuse collection. Yet

frustratingly, there is nowhere to dispose of rubbish. Public bins are small, with signs stating no household refuse. We reckon each time our bin is emptied it costs €50, as the annual charge is €150, and we only seem to catch it three times a year

- French banks – which operate in a way that's about twenty years behind the UK. Their intolerance if you accidentally go overdrawn, even by €1, and then you're 'fined' normally about €8 for each transgression

- Payment options – unlike the UK, cash is still often the only way to pay, especially in small shops and bars. The use of cheques for payment seems so old-fashioned, and the waiting time in supermarket queues for this to happen seems interminable. Apple Pay almost never works

- French TV – which in general is quite appalling

What I Find Exasperating but can Tolerate Most of the Time

- The universal custom of kissing people unknown to me 2, 3, or 4 times on the cheek. It mostly applied to females, but occasionally males too. I don't always find this pleasurable, mostly for hygienic reasons (Covid may have put a stop to all this)

- The incessant talking: it seems the French will talk forever. This can be irritating if you're waiting in an often-long supermarket queue, and the checkout assistant and customer are exchanging interminable pleasantries, including 'la bise' (kissing). Often, as I drive, I come across a car in front, going incredibly slowly. The two people in the front of the car being engaged in deep conversation without any apparent awareness of what's happening around them

- French pharmacies: it seems there is a culture of excessive medication, which is borne out of personal experiences and stories from friends. This means that if there are more than a couple of other people in the shop, you're in for a long wait while all the prescribed medication is counted out

- Typically, small measures of beer. However, this is gradually improving, as some bars now offer ½ litre measures

- Adults behaving like teenagers. Excessive flirtatious behaviour, which is often used to hide or get round a problem. I find this very irritating, when shop assistants (usually) or restaurant staff use this approach, and treat me like a teenage boy, thinking that a smile and a wink, and a hand on my arm will make the problem go away, when actually I want a replacement/refund/problem resolved

- Haughtiness – strangers approaching to tell you that you can't park here, enter there, walk with your dog off the lead, put your rubbish there

- Invitations for apéros – does this mean simply for drinks, or is food/supper included? Despite gently enquiring, we never seem to know!

On balance, I wouldn't keep going back, let alone own a property in France, if there wasn't a strong love for the country and its people.

And as in any relationship, it's the love that is the foundation and bedrock of that relationship.

After all these years, that love remains viscerally and deeply powerful.